Oinyel

e an earle eyen gels the name
phone number 66803, Fin
cull. love

Michael.

om Gorman handed me
what it was like: a long,
to your Dublin Book of Irish
r who would do anything to
romanybody else with two arms,
ING FOR YOU...William

b you itel you too
a piece of editing, for love
otes, do something about

Love by on both

Bill

Bill.

This was intended to be two,
t moment I decided to give te
another chance. I'll have a go at
w.

eeping the well free but for Tuesday,
w at 3 when we go to see a half.
'Oedipus' and later from
w, we should be free
is 5. East 57th Stree

No. 2
t at

Date Stamp
10 IV
62

No. of Words
ERN UNION 21=

PLACE DUBLIN2

BACK COME

34 Court Flats,
Wilton Place, Dublin

Dear Bill,
        I came into Harriet the
other night, wailing 'I want
Bill Maxwell', and she said 'Y
mean you think you've done som
good.'
        I didn't mean that at all,
but an hour with that hard pe
of yours making notes would l
me with a very nice opening
chapter for the new volume, s
if you find yourself inspire
please scribble as the notio
comes to you.
        Harriet got a note from
Elizabeth, saying that afte
it might be better if I did
meet her young man, but two
later he blew in on a part
priests and set us all by
ears.   We were trying to f
our grounds of difference
Betty's young man attacke
insisting on attending Pr
funerals, the six priests
on him and rent him.
        Poor child!
                Love to Emmy,
                        Michael

ALSO BY FRANK O'CONNOR

Stories

COLLECTED STORIES 1981
A SET OF VARIATIONS 1969
COLLECTION THREE 1969
COLLECTION TWO 1964
DOMESTIC RELATIONS 1957
STORIES BY FRANK O'CONNOR 1956
MORE STORIES 1954
THE STORIES OF FRANK O'CONNOR 1952
TRAVELLER'S SAMPLES 1951
THE COMMON CHORD 1948
CRAB APPLE JELLY 1944
BONES OF CONTENTION 1936
GUESTS OF THE NATION 1931

Novels

DUTCH INTERIOR 1940
THE SAINT AND MARY KATE 1932

Criticism

A SHORT HISTORY OF IRISH LITERATURE:
A BACKWARD LOOK 1967
THE LONELY VOICE: A STUDY OF THE SHORT STORY 1962
SHAKESPEARE'S PROGRESS 1960
THE MIRROR IN THE ROADWAY: A STUDY OF
THE MODERN NOVEL 1956

Autobiography

MY FATHER'S SON 1969
AN ONLY CHILD 1961

Poetry

THE LITTLE MONASTERIES 1963
KINGS, LORDS, & COMMONS 1959
THREE OLD BROTHERS & OTHER POEMS 1936

Biography

THE BIG FELLOW 1937

ALSO BY WILLIAM MAXWELL

ALL THE DAYS AND NIGHTS   1994
BILLIE DYER AND OTHER STORIES   1992
THE OUTERMOST DREAM   1989
SO LONG, SEE YOU TOMORROW   1980
OVER BY THE RIVER AND OTHER STORIES   1977
ANCESTORS   1971
THE OLD MAN AT THE RAILROAD CROSSING
AND OTHER TALES   1966
THE CHÂTEAU   1961
STORIES (with Jean Stafford, John Cheever, and Daniel Fuchs)   1956
TIME WILL DARKEN IT   1948
THE FOLDED LEAF   1945
THEY CAME LIKE SWALLOWS   1937
BRIGHT CENTER OF HEAVEN   1934

Children's Books

MRS. DONALD'S DOG BUN AND HIS HOME
AWAY FROM HOME   1995
THE HEAVENLY TENANTS   1946

~

ALSO BY MICHAEL STEINMAN

A FRANK O'CONNOR READER   1994
FRANK O'CONNOR AT WORK   1990
YEATS'S HEROIC FIGURES: WILDE, PARNELL,
SWIFT, CASEMENT   1983

THE HAPPINESS OF
GETTING IT DOWN RIGHT

THE HAPPINESS OF
GETTING IT DOWN RIGHT

~

LETTERS OF
FRANK O'CONNOR AND
WILLIAM MAXWELL
1945 ~ 1966

EDITED BY MICHAEL STEINMAN

ALFRED A. KNOPF   NEW YORK   1996

THIS IS A BORZOI BOOK
PUBLISHED BY ALFRED A. KNOPF, INC.

Library of Congress Cataloging-in-Publication Data
O'Connor, Frank, 1903–1966.
The happiness of getting it down right : letters of Frank O'Connor
and William Maxwell, 1945–1966 / edited by Michael Steinman.
p.   cm.
Includes bibliographical references (p.   ).
ISBN 0-679-44659-1
1. O'Connor, Frank, 1903–1966—Correspondence.   2. Authors,
Irish—20th century—Correspondence.   3. Maxwell, William, [date]—
Correspondence.   4. Periodical editors—United States—
Correspondence.   5. New Yorker (New York, N.Y. : 1925)
I. Maxwell, William, [date].   II. Steinman, Michael (Michael A.)
PR6029.D58Z49   1996
823'.912—dc20   [B]   95-42769   CIP

Manufactured in the United States of America
First Edition

Writing was what mattered to [Frank O'Connor]. The fascination of it. The difficulties. The happiness of getting it down right.

WILLIAM MAXWELL, 1969

As an adviser Bill is out on his own because he doesn't give you his own reaction and try to impose it on you, but guides you into the reaction that comes most naturally to yourself—like a good teacher who does not say "Imitate me" but "This I think is what you are trying to say."

FRANK O'CONNOR, 1963

The personal correspondence of writers feeds on left-over energy. There is also the element of lavishness, of enjoying the fact that they are throwing away one of their better efforts, for the chances of any given letter's surviving are fifty-fifty, at most. And there is the element of confidence—of the relaxed backhand stroke that can place the ball anywhere in the court that it pleases the writer to have it go.

WILLIAM MAXWELL, 1982

CONTENTS

INTRODUCTION

As a fiction editor at *The New Yorker* for forty years, William Maxwell worked closely with many famous writers. His correspondence with Frank O'Connor (born Michael O'Donovan), however, reveals an extraordinary friendship and editorial partnership. Although Maxwell said, "The older I got the less I touched, and Michael came in somewhere about two-thirds of the way along," O'Connor was eager to have such a writer read his work, and reciprocated by reading Maxwell's fiction with loving attention. Perhaps because O'Connor was often ill in his last years, Maxwell was the more faithful correspondent: "With me, letter writing was a little like keeping a journal," he told me. "I don't think Michael actually enjoyed writing letters. He had too many more serious things on his mind."

Although their correspondence began in 1945, the two men did not meet until 1952, when O'Connor came to America for the first time. In part, he chose to leave Ireland because his conservative audience was enraged by his outspoken criticism of "the emptiness and horror of Irish life." Making vindictiveness official, the Censorship Board regularly banned much of his work as "in its general tendency indecent" and bureaucratic obstacles were created that made his earning a living as a writer nearly impossible. Ireland still seemed an ideal place in which to write, yet ". . . in a country ruled by fools and blackguards a writer must fight and think and waste his time in useless efforts to create an atmosphere in which he can exist and work," O'Connor wrote in 1943. In 1947, he told John Kelleher, then a young Celtic scholar, "Of course I'd jump at a temporary job in Harvard, being of a flighty disposition with a mass of theories inside me which I'd love to work off on someone." Four years later, Kelleher arranged for him to teach at Harvard in the summer; Richard Ellmann "persuaded him to warm up at Northwestern . . . [and] he was prevailed upon to return the following spring."

Thomas Flanagan, who met O'Connor in 1961, remarked that "The American connection was always very important to him, and that's understandable. I remember once thinking in my own case how much at ease I feel in Ireland; in many ways I feel more at ease in Ireland than I do in my own country. Then it occurred to me that I've never been dependent on the Irish for my livelihood. That would make me very uneasy, I'd suspect. And I think that is one thing that the American literary connection meant to Michael. It meant that he would be a writer with an income and a reputation that wasn't dependent on the jealousies of the Dublin circles." Yet the "American connection" was personal as well as economic. If O'Connor came to America to escape provincialism, there he found dear friends.

The letters that form this book were preserved by Harriet O'Donovan Sheehy, O'Connor's wife, and William and Emily Maxwell. Maxwell has retained his correspondence with authors rather than let the letters remain in *The New Yorker*'s files, but the letters have remained private.

When, in 1983, I began to study O'Connor's unpublished work, I knew of this friendship only through Maxwell's memorial essay, "Frank O'Connor and *The New Yorker*," which I have included at the end of this book. At that time, only a tantalizing dozen of O'Connor's letters—to his friend Sean Hendrick—had been published. I remember vividly, while searching through Harriet Sheehy's files in Annapolis for drafts of stories, finding two letters from Maxwell to O'Connor and being electrified as I read them. In one, Maxwell described his daughters' delight at the Hansel-and-Gretel house his wife had created. The letter was a prose miniature in its own way as satisfying as Maxwell's story "Over by the River." The other letter, more formal, dealt with the editorial queries that O'Connor's "The Mass Island" had generated at *The New Yorker.* It was equally fascinating, a glimpse behind a story we know only as a completed creation. Even at its most businesslike, it was affectionate and humorous. When I interviewed Maxwell that year, asking him about his role as O'Connor's editor, his love for his friend shone through all that he said. After I had finished writing *Frank O'Connor at Work,* I did not let Harriet rest until she made the correspondence available; sure that the two letters I had found by chance were typical, I wanted to know more. Since O'Connor had been poorly served by an unsympathetic biography and Maxwell had not had to endure one, I hoped the correspondence would reveal more of the two men and their families as well as offering new insights about their writing, and I was not disappointed.

A reader who might be puzzled by Maxwell's early reference to O'Connor as "Michael" should know that this, too, is evidence of their closeness. "Frank O'Connor" existed only as a pseudonym he adopted in the late 1920s so that he could publish freely. As his daughter Liadain wrote, ". . . there was the public man, Frank O'Connor, and the private man, Michael O'Donovan. (I was always glad that he had a pen name. When he was in the middle of a controversy it was handy as a child to hide behind the O'Donovan name. After his death, it was also helpful. People sometimes would say to me 'Oh, yes, Frank and I were great friends,' and I would have my doubts. But if somebody said 'I knew Michael well when he was . . .' then there was a good possibility that he really did know him well, and I would listen with great interest.)" For consistency, I have referred to him as "Frank O'Connor" and his wife as "Harriet O'Connor" (although she was then Harriet Rich O'Donovan) throughout. She was called "Hallie," and their daughter "Hallie-Óg," or Young Hallie. The Maxwells, whether William, Willie, or Bill; Emmy, Em, or Emmie; Katie, and Brookie, pose no ambiguities.

In my annotations, I have imagined a reader familiar with Salinger and Updike but not Casement, someone who might not recall why Dag Hammarskjöld was referred to in 1961. Because I hope a reader will follow the letters in sequence, I have avoided cross-references.

Assigning appropriate dates to letters was sometimes difficult, for O'Connor and Maxwell wrote spontaneously for a friend's eyes rather than for future publication. However, an undated letter might contain information (an address or reference to a story's imminent publication) that shows it was from early 1959, not late 1963. Occasionally, Maxwell or O'Connor's first editor, Gus Lobrano, noted when a letter was received on its first page, a date separated from its writing by only a few days.

Since the correspondence is primarily made up of typewritten and handwritten letters, I have noted only the exceptions (a postcard, cable, or telegram). The few doubtful readings are indicated by a question mark. I think the relaxed nature of friendly correspondence should not be over-zealously tidied out of existence, so I have not tried to make all that seemed casual, such as idiosyncratic misspellings and typos, formally correct. Obviously, a few letters are missing, but the majority survive. At the request of the surviving participants, I have omitted a few statements which would pain others. These deletions, in total less than a hundred words, are indicated by [. . .].

I am particularly indebted to Harriet Sheehy, and William and Emily Maxwell, for enduring my questions, going back in their memories of forty and fifty years ago. While making inquiries of others who were involved with the O'Connors and the Maxwells, I found no one who had encountered them with anything less than delight; thus, I was always received with a kindness that reflected the fondness they inspired in others. I am especially grateful to Elizabeth Cullinan and Roger Angell for their diligence. Dorothy Lobrano Guth generously made available previously unknown 1948–54 letters from O'Connor to her late father, Gus Lobrano. Ruth Limmer and John Lancaster helped to obtain O'Connor's 1962 letter to Louise Bogan and offered valuable commentary. Anthony Bailey, William Cole, Don Congdon, Liadain O'Donovan Cook, Brendan Gill, David Hanlin, Michael Jasperson, William A. Koshland, Katharine Maxwell, J. F. Powers, and Ruth Sherry provided facts, insights, and texts only they could have.

I am also greatly obliged to librarians and archivists for materials they generously provided: Marilyn Rosenthal (Nassau Community College), Mimi Bowling (New York Public Library), Kathryn Talalay (American Academy of Arts and Letters), John E. Ingram (University of Florida), Kathleen Ferris (Center for Southwest Research, University of New Mexico), and Christopher G. Petter (University of Victoria). My colleagues in the English Department at Nassau Community College offered heartening encouragement, as did John L. Fell and Nancy Mullen. I have benefited greatly from the guidance of my editor, Judith Jones, and am grateful to my agent, Sarah Chalfant. For her enthusiasm and support, I am indebted to my wife, Carol.

All Frank O'Connor materials are reprinted through the kind permission of Harriet O'Donovan Sheehy. All William Maxwell and Emily Maxwell materials are reprinted through their gracious permission. All the letters, needless to say, come from the private collections of the participants. O'Connor's March 31, 1962, letter to Louise Bogan is from the Louise Bogan Papers (Box III, Folder 2), Special Collections Department, Amherst College Library, and is reprinted by permission of John Lancaster, Curator of Special Collections, Amherst College. The epigraph "As an adviser . . ." is reprinted through the courtesy of the Center for Southwest Research, University of New Mexico. The Katharine S. White and Roger Angell letters are reprinted by permission of Roger Angell. Letters from Gustave S. Lobrano to O'Connor are reprinted by permission of his daughter, Dorothy Lobrano Guth. Excerpts from Don Congdon's letters are reprinted with his permission. I thank Penguin USA for permission to reprint excerpts from *Writers at Work: The Paris Review Interviews* (First Series and Seventh Series).

THE HAPPINESS OF
GETTING IT DOWN RIGHT

1945 ~ 1951

Although the correspondence of Frank O'Connor and William Maxwell began even before *The New Yorker* published the first story O'Connor submitted, "News for the Church," in September 1945, only four letters from this period survive, two of them from his first fiction editor, Gustave S. Lobrano. O'Connor may not have saved every letter that documented his relations with the magazine, but he valued *The New Yorker* and they reciprocated by publishing ten more stories during these years: "The Rivals" (better known as "Judas"), "Christmas Morning," "The Babes in the Wood," "My Da," "The Drunkard," "Darcy in the Land of Youth," "The Man of the House," "The Idealist," "Masculine Principle," and "The Pretender."

FRANK O'CONNOR TO WILLIAM MAXWELL, JULY 1945:

57 Strand Road
Sandymount
Dublin

Dear Mr Maxwell,
    No, of course, there never was a Mrs Leary, and she never was in America or went on the booze or even had a son. The same is true for all stories of mine.*

Yours sincerely
FRANK O'CONNOR

(3)

———

* In Maxwell's letter, which no longer exists, he had asked O'Connor if characters in "My Da" were modelled on living individuals who could sue the magazine for libel.

WILLIAM MAXWELL TO FRANK O'CONNOR,
JUNE 13, 1947:

June 13, 1947

Dear Mr. O'Connor,

We're troubled by your deleting, on the author's proof, the clause at the end: "and left us all far behind him." which seems to us to add considerably to the poignancy of the story.* If you want it out, we will of course abide by your decision, but occasionally a writer's vision of his own work, after a lapse of time, can be over-strict, and we wonder if, in this, you aren't doing some slight damage to the story.

Cordially yours,
WILLIAM MAXWELL

Mr. Frank O'Connor
57, Strand Road
Sandymount, Dublin
Eire

———

* O'Connor took Maxwell's advice about the closing line of "My Da": "Stevie had at last become the man his father was and left us all far behind him."

GUS LOBRANO TO FRANK O'CONNOR,
MARCH 12, 1948:

March 12, 1948

Dear Mr. O'Connor:

Herewith the author's proof of "The Drunkard." We all enjoyed the story immensely, and we're grateful to you for it.

I think that, in general, the editing and queries are fairly restrained, sensible, and self-explanatory. But if there are spots where you feel that none of these adjectives applies, I hope you'll point them out and indicate the wording you prefer.

We'd appreciate your making it clear at the outset that this story takes place in Ireland, and it occurs to us that a good place to plant the locale is in the third paragraph. You could quite easily do it by naming the newspaper—the Dublin Times, the County Cork Tribune, or some such.

As soon as it seems likely that your patience might withstand another assault, I'll send along the proof of "Darcy in the Land of Youth."

Sincerely,

G. S. LOBRANO

Mr. Frank O'Connor
57, Strand Road
Sandymount, Dublin
Eire

GUS LOBRANO TO FRANK O'CONNOR,
OCTOBER 29, 1948:

October 29, 1948

Dear Mr. O'Connor:

Here's the author's proof of DARCY IN THE LAND OF YOUTH. I hope you'll feel that the editing has been reasonably restrained and sensitive. If you find any of it questionable, please say so and why. And, by the way, the allusion in the title seems to us pretty obscure; would you consider suggesting an alternative title?

A couple of notes: (1) On Galley 1 — This "took to her" seems to us very likely to be misleading. Reader is very likely to think his attachment is for Fanny and be surprised when it turns out that it's for Janet. (2) On Galley 1 — The phrase "has got quite steady" here seems to us to mean the reverse of what an American reader must think it means. She seems to have got quite unsteady in our usage, for she seems to be playing around with a lot of men.

We all hope to see some more full-scale stories from you soon. The pieces we've had recently seem to us to have been particularly local and sketches rather than stories. And I'd like to express our gratitude again for the fine stories we've had from you during the past couple of years.*

Sincerely,

G. S. LOBRANO

Mr. Frank O'Connor
57, Strand Road
Sandymount
Dublin, EIRE

———

* O'Connor did not revise the story as Lobrano advised in time for its January 15 publication, but Lobrano's suggestions contributed a great deal to the beautifully expansive version of "Darcy in the Land of Youth" in *More Stories*.

1952

In 1952, O'Connor was already a well-known author with an astounding publishing history—twenty-two books in twenty-one years. Yet, to summon up the writer and scholar who arrived in America in March, we must rely on the recollection of those who saw him plain. Eric Solomon, then a student in the Irish-literature class at Harvard, found him memorable: "O'Connor let us know from the start that he was to be a unique lecturer: 'Let me make one thing clear immediately,' he intoned in a deeper voice than he would later use: 'I'm three words starting with the letter A that no Irishman admits to: I'm anonymous—my name is Michael O'Donovan, not Frank O'Connor—I'm an agnostic, and I'm an adulterer.' All this in Emerson Hall!"

Another member of the Irish-literature class—whose ties to O'Connor would transcend the classroom—was Harriet Rich, who had read "The Saint" in *Mademoiselle* and was charmed by its lighthearted approach to Catholicism. Her humorous outspokenness, much like O'Connor's, caught his attention, and they spent much of the summer together. She wrote of her first encounter: "A casual, part-time student, I'd decided to take his course because of a story of his which treated with humor and urbanity problems I had never realized could be taken that way—not the best of academic reasons. It was summer and he wore a rumpled seersucker suit (which I later discovered he thought a variety of American tweed), a thick, fuzzy, blue and orange tweed tie, and a look both frightened and delighted—as though he didn't quite know what 'a simple Irishman' (as he often called himself) was doing at Harvard. With one pair of horn-rimmed glasses in his hand and another pushed up on his forehead he was describing people called 'P Celts' who seemed to be importantly different from people called 'C Celts.' I wondered briefly what this could have to do with the course I'd enrolled in for Anglo-Irish literature and which sort of a Celt Joyce would turn out to be. . . ."

O'Connor initially approached teaching warily. Before he left Ireland, he told an *Irish Times* reporter, "Frankly, the prospect of teaching anybody anything terrifies me. I've never even been to school." However, he was more confident about teaching writing: "If you cannot make a fool a Shakespeare, at least you can prevent a Shakespeare from making a fool of himself." Yet he often felt overwhelmed by unfamiliar academic responsibilities, preparing for lectures and reading students' stories, which left him little time for his own writing.

When the session was over, O'Connor attended the Bread Loaf Writers' Conference, where he met Robert Frost. He told a young Michael Longley, ". . . I can remember the two of us fighting like cats over the way Yeats read his poetry. I was all for it and Frost violently against. He wrote some bawdy poems which have never been published of course. There was a marvelously blasphemous one about the Blessed Virgin. Frost was disgusted that so many young poets were being converted—Auden an Anglican, Allen Tate a Roman Catholic. 'They haven't the courage of their sins,' he used to say. Yes, he was a very great poet."

The Stories of Frank O'Connor, his first retrospective collection, was published on August 18; Horace Reynolds, in *The New York Times Book Review,* called it "a new landmark in Anglo-Irish fiction." (I have included in this section a short self-portrait published in the *New York Herald-Tribune Book Review* on October 12.) In September, O'Connor returned to England, where his beloved mother, Minnie O'Donovan, died at eighty-seven on November 10.

In 1952, *The New Yorker* published "Crossroads" (retitled "First Love" in *The Stories of Frank O'Connor*), "Masculine Protest," "A Sense of Responsibility," "A Torrent Damned," and "Unapproved Route." They rejected "The Saint," "Anchors," and "Adventure," which were published in *Mademoiselle, Harper's Bazaar,* and *Atlantic Monthly,* respectively.

FRANK O'CONNOR TO GUS LOBRANO,
LATE MARCH OR EARLY APRIL 1952:

Dept. of English
North Western University
Evanston, Ill.

Dear Mr. Lobrano,

This is merely to give you my address until the first week in June in case you want me for anything. At the same time I hope I get away before that and that we can really have the meal and chat I've promised myself.

I still haven't settled down and doubt exceedingly that the Almighty ever had any intention of permitting me to teach.

Yours sincerely
FRANK O'CONNOR

GUS LOBRANO TO FRANK O'CONNOR, MAY 21, 1952:

Dear Mr. O'Connor:

Please forgive me if this should, more properly, be addressed to *Professor* O'Connor. I've thought about you a good deal out there, and I hope the experience has been generally pleasant.

I've just recently returned from eight days in the Adirondacks (a soul restoration project), and still feel slightly resentful of being back in civilization. There were, though, some compensations for being back—among them the re-reading of "Masculine Protest," proof of which I'm sending along with this note. The marginal queries are mainly concerned with punctuation, and where your opinion is strongly at variance with ours I hope you'll abide by your own. We'd like to have the proof back at your earliest convenience, because the story is scheduled for a near issue.

Hope you'll be along this way soon.

Sincerely,
GUS LOBRANO

Mr. Frank O'Connor
English Department
Northwestern University
Evanston, Illinois

FRANK O'CONNOR TO GUS LOBRANO, MAY 22, 1952:

Dept. of English
Northwestern University
Evanston, Ill.

22. 5. '52

Dear Mr. Lobrano,

I am naturally deeply hurt at not being addressed as 'professor.' 'Full Professor' itself would not be amiss. However as they've invited me back next year you'll have further opportunities.

Listen, I shall be deserting my professorship with indecent haste the week after next and hope to get to New York on Tuesday 3rd with good luck and a bit of wangling—now don't ask me what wangling is. I shall be doing a broadcast on Wednesday afternoon but would it be possible for us to have that meal another day—Tuesday or Thursday, say? If I don't hear I'll give you a ring when I arrive.

Yours sincerely,
FRANK O'CONNOR

Met another N.Y. writer acting as my opposite number in Chicago University, Peter Taylor. Really, I think you've been unfair to this city!

FRANK O'CONNOR TO GUS LOBRANO,
AFTER JULY I, 1952:

Q 21, Lowell House,
Cambridge 38, Mass.

Dear Mr. Lobrano,

Alas, here I only rank as Instructor. Like the man who was King only for a day I was Professor only for a month and now I am stripped of my dignities. I enclose the story.* I'm glad you liked 'A Torrent Damned.'

The other two stories I have now revised and you'll be getting them from Matson within the next few days. I still like them both though I see that one may be unsuitable for reasons that don't have to do with the story.

There's a Collected Stories waiting here for you, but either you'll have to come to Cambridge or wait till I get down to New York. My versatility has never extended to making up a parcel. I hope you'll like the book.

Ever,
FOC

———

* "Here" was Harvard. The story may have been "The Little Mother." O'Connor's literary agency, A. D. Peters, was represented in America by the Harold Matson Agency, and Don Congdon acted as his American agent.

GUS LOBRANO TO FRANK O'CONNOR,
AUGUST 15, 1952:

August 15, 1952

Dear Mr. O'Connor:

Here's the author's proof of "A Torrent Damned," and I'll be grateful if you'll give it fairly prompt attention. (Now *I* sound like a professor!) The only bit of real tampering I did was to make a cut of the passage in the story referring to the priests and particularly to one referred to as "Ring." This passage seemed to me, and to others here to be a bit hazy and, possibly, to require a good deal of explaining for American readers. This business about the priests not liking Tom is kind of sprung on the reader as a surprise at this point, and you wonder why they didn't like him (he was, apparently, doing all he could to conciliate them— took to going to Mass, Communion, etc.). And also you wonder about this Ring, who pops up pretty abruptly as a character in the story. But if this cut disturbs you seriously, I hope you'll say so.

Will you please return the proof to William Maxwell? I shall be away for the next two or three weeks, and he will be sitting in for me here. And he and I hope that you'll call to see him if you come into town during my absence. I had hoped to introduce you to each other, but I'm sure you'll both get along very nicely without that formality.

I had very much hoped to be there to see you, but my vacation plans have been shifted about, owing to various disrupting and confusing elements (mostly personal), and it seems now that I won't be in town between now and the 8th of September. I hope to God that you won't have sailed for home by then, because I should be terribly disappointed not to see you before you go back. But if I *should* miss you, let me say now what a great pleasure it was to meet you, and how heartening it is to me and to the other editors here to see your stories coming in.

Sincerely,
GUS LOBRANO

WILLIAM MAXWELL TO FRANK O'CONNOR,
AFTER AUGUST 15, 1952:

Dear Mr. O'Connor:

In Mr. Lobrano's absence—he's up north, on his vacation—
I'm plaguing you with one last query on "A Torrent Damned." It
seemed to us that in order to make it really clear what poor Mrs.
Dorgan wore at the three kinds of funerals the sentence ought to
be recast. What about the suggestion on the attached galley?
Would that do it?

Also, if you should be coming through New York, as Mr. Lobrano thought that you might, and if there is time, I hope that
you will call me. It would be an immense pleasure to me to meet
you.

Sincerely,
WILLIAM MAXWELL

Mr. Frank O'Connor
Q 21
Lowell House
Cambridge 38
Mass.

FRANK O'CONNOR TO WILLIAM MAXWELL,
AFTER AUGUST 15, 1952:

c/o Professor J. V. Kelleher
116 Westminster Drive,
Westwood, Mass.

Dear Mr. Maxwell,

This will do fine. I expect to sail on the Mauretania on the 4th
and to spend a couple of days in New York before that. I shall certainly look you up. Would it be possible provisionally to say you

might keep Wednesday free for lunch if you haven't got another engagement. Anyhow I shall ring you up the moment I arrive.

Yours sincerely,

FRANK O'CONNOR

FRANK O'CONNOR TO WILLIAM MAXWELL,
BEFORE SEPTEMBER 3, 1952:

Mr Maxwell

The proofs are incomplete but don't trouble yourself. You have full permission to make what changes are necessary.

I enjoyed our lunch and look forward to seeing you again.

FOC.

———

To complete the likeness of O'Connor at this time, here is his self-portrait, published in the New York *Herald-Tribune* in October under the heading "Some Important Fall Authors Speak for Themselves":

Most of my life has been lived in Dublin, with the one main object of proving to my fellow countrymen that I can't be intimidated. I spend a lot of my time cycling. I've cycled most of Ireland, a good part of England and quite a bit of France. I'm interested in architecture, and cycling is the best way I know of seeing architecture. It's wonderful how good an old town in Burgundy can look when you arrive there exhausted after a day's cycling, and my memory is packed with cathedrals seen for the first time in the dusk or after nightfall. My only complaint against America is that it doesn't have cycling tracks. There's so much in New England that I'd prefer to see from a bicycle, all those beautiful towns and churches.

I had always wanted to write poetry, but I realized very early on that I didn't have much talent that way. Story telling is a compensation; the nearest thing one can get to the quality of a pure lyric poem. It doesn't deal with problems; it doesn't have any solutions to offer; it just states the human condition. I am endlessly happy, writing stories, and editors who must deal with me as a story-teller find me angelic. I live in hope that somebody can improve a line I write. On the other hand, editors who have to deal with me as a man of letters usually find me diabolical. It's not that I don't work hard; it's not that I don't try to stick to date-lines and do the job as well as it can be done; it is merely that story-telling will keep cropping up, and then, everything has to be abandoned in pursuit of the will-o'-the wisp.

For the last six months I've been teaching in America. Seeing that I never had any education myself, I enjoy teaching. It brings out all the parent in me, and all parents try to give their children the things they themselves have most felt the lack of. And American students are magnificent; those that I've met at any rate. They are responsive and they're not afraid of the toughest assignments. But teaching is a temptation as well as being hard work; particularly teaching story-telling. After a time I find myself more concerned with whether some student is really going to bring off a big job of writing than with my own work.

At home I work in the mornings; sometimes in the evenings as well. I like my afternoons free for walking or cycling. In Dublin I prefer walking into the city and looking at the bookshops and talking to the people I meet. That's how I pick up most of my stories. I prefer to write about Ireland and Irish people merely because I know to a syllable how everything in Ireland can be said; but that doesn't mean that the stories themselves were inspired by events in Ireland. Many of them should really have English backgrounds; a few should even have American ones. Only language and circumstance are local and national; all the rest is, or should be, part of the human condition, and as true for America and England as it is for Ireland. The nicest compliment I have ever received was from a student while the authorities of the university were considering the important question of whether I was a resident or non-resident alien. "Mr. O'Connor, I find it hard to think of you as an alien at all."

1953

At Northwestern, O'Connor taught a course in the modern novel; his lectures, much revised, became *The Mirror in the Roadway*. A young Sylvia Plath yearned to be accepted into his Harvard writing seminar; when her story was rejected, she attempted suicide.

In December, O'Connor married Harriet Rich; she described his proposal forty years later: "... I got a short typed letter— probably one of the most unromantic letters anybody ever got in their life: ('*H, At last I feel morally and legally free to ask you to marry me. If you want to I'd be delighted. I don't know what I can promise you. Love, M.*')." Their marriage continued until his death in 1966.

Although O'Connor's first-reading agreement with *The New Yorker* was renewed consistently from 1945 to 1964, they weighed each story on its own merits. In fact, some of his finest stories were rejected as "not for them" and published elsewhere. In 1953, they took "Vanity" but rejected "The Little Mother" (published in *Harper's Bazaar*), "A Romantic" and "The Old Faith" (both published in *More Stories*), and "The Sissy" (published first in *Mademoiselle* and then as "The Genius" in *Domestic Relations*).

FRANK O'CONNOR TO GUS LOBRANO, APRIL 3, 1953:

Dept. of English,
Northwestern University,
Evanston, Illinois.

April 3, 1953

Dear Gus,
    Here are the old stories that I wished you to look at from the new book. 'Lonely Rock' is my favourite and I think it's among my half dozen best. 'A Romantic' is the story I talked to you about originally, which appeared in the 'Evening News' of London (the paper which pirated Gill's Profile) in what I have no hesitation in describing as a mangled parody. 'The Old Faith' is another story about the Bishop of Moyle, and though it has been re-written many times and largely changed, it is substantially as to theme the story which appeared in the London 'Argosy.' Putting myself in your position, I should decide that 'The Old Faith' had already been published and put myself in a dilemma. I should decide that 'A Romantic' had never appeared at all. In every sense, 'Lonely Rock' hasn't been published.
    You have my permission to send them all back to me without writing a polite letter about them. Don Congdon knows what I am doing and approves. The fact is, as you have probably already gathered, that I don't look on the paper as a market, but rather as I once looked on the Abbey Theatre, as a place where I belong. I dislike the thought of good work of mine appearing anywhere else, on the principle of the old man I once knew of, who referring to his two wives used to say 'I'd sooner a kick from Maggie than a kiss from Kate.' Consider yourself as Maggie.
    This place is rather tiresome this year, and the only talent I've found is in the University of Chicago. One of my old students says they have now begun to read me; they concluded I am 'in the money' and must protect themselves against me. Ah, your beautiful America! I shall never understand it.

Sincerely.
FRANK O'CONNOR

GUS LOBRANO TO FRANK O'CONNOR,
MAY 1, 1953:

May 1, 1953

Dear Frank:

I'm sorry to have been so long in giving you an answer on your stories, and acknowledging your generous letter.* The fact is, I've been feeling very seedy for several weeks, and, finally, last week ended up in the hospital for a couple of days of stomach x-rays. The trouble turned out to be relatively minor (the old hypertension cliché), and now, as a result of diet and sedative pills I'm feeling very much better and looking forward to a comparatively long life (last week I was giving myself, dolefully but heroically, anything from nine days to nine months).

My feeling about LONELY ROCK is that it's a fine idea and, in general, nicely done. I suspect, however, that the story is a bit hurried, particularly in reference to Sylvia, after Margaret and the baby leave the house—the business about her "seeking for support in the world outside" and "the bubble in which she lived was broken" seems somewhat insufficiently prepared for, somewhat hurried or arbitrary. And I should add, on a minor note, that the reference to "when the alert went", on p. 11, was somewhat bewildering for a while; there was no real indication before that that the story was taking place in war-time England. And since it was taking place in war-time England, why weren't these fellows in the army? Perhaps you'll feel that these several criticisms aren't well taken. If so, please return the story as is, and we'll consider it. Otherwise I'll hope to see it again after you've worked over it a bit.

As for A ROMANTIC, which I've also read, and am also returning, seems to me that you've had to explain too much of it, particularly towards the end. I suspect it's one of those that you'll do over, and I hope you'll let me see it again.

I think of you often out here, and hope you aren't getting too lonesome. It will be fine to see you here again, and I look forward to having you out at my house. Tomorrow I leave for the woods for a week, in the hope of composing my spirit and my stomach, and

I'll hope to have some news from you when I get back. Oh, and when I get back I'll write you about the other piece, THE OLD FAITH, which I haven't yet had a chance to read.

Yrs,

GUS

Mr. Frank O'Connor
Department of English
Northwestern University
Evanston
Illinois

Enc. LONELY ROCK
A ROMANTIC

———

* On February 2, Congdon had written O'Connor that *The New Yorker* had turned down a revised version of "The Little Mother." Lobrano may have been the unidentified speaker: "I'm very sorry, indeed, to have to report that the vote still holds against this piece. We feel that there are some improvements in this over the earlier version, but we can't help suspecting that Mr. O'Connor hasn't yet got this story completely under control. It still seems somehow contrived and to be, at times, mired down in too many words. But many thanks for giving us a chance to reconsider the piece."

"The Little Mother" gave O'Connor great difficulty through a decade of revision—seventeen versions exist, unpublished and published.

FRANK O'CONNOR TO GUS LOBRANO,
JUNE 1, 1953:

719 Noyes Street
Evanston, Ill.

June 1st.

Dear Gus,

I shivered like a guilty thing at a letter from Don Congdon, accusing me of having ignored a letter from you.* The fact is, as Don probably told you, that I haven't had time even to write a letter much less to think of revising a story. Term here ends on the 3rd, and after my examinations, I shall have a week to go through the story before I leave for Boston, where I hope to be an ex-professor for a whole month, work, and drop down to New York to see my friends. Then, all hell breaks loose. The short story class had a preliminary enrollment of about 60, and an assistant has had to be appointed, and I hear that for the novel course the enrollment is over 300! Definitely, no more teaching for me! It isn't even as if I liked it.

I'm sorry for your gastric trouble. I've suffered from it all my life, and it's as fertile in disguises as a Hollywood detective. Last time with me, it pretended to be cirrhosis, and I was kept off drink for three months.

WHY don't you do Frank Lloyd Wright in a Profile? I went up to Taliesin yesterday to see him, and he's too good to be true.

Ever,

FRANK

------

* Congdon to O'Connor, May 29, concerning "Lost Fatherlands," "Lonely Rock," "The Cissie," "The Face of Evil," and future teaching obligations: "My God, Harvard is beginning to sound like a living Hell already! Maybe having that many students though, will be a good thing; in that way, you could avoid letting a small number of a class chew you up as badly as they apparently did last year."

GUS LOBRANO TO FRANK O'CONNOR,
JUNE 15, 1953:

June 15, 1953

Dear Frank:

Here's the author's proof of "Vanity," and we'll be grateful if you'll deal with it at your convenience and return it to us.

It's good to know that you're back in the east, and I look forward to seeing you shortly.

Yrs,
GUS

Mr. Frank O'Connor
4 Trowbridge Place
Cambridge, Mass.

1954

Because *The Stories of Frank O'Connor* had been a critical and financial success, his publisher, Alfred A. Knopf, urged him to compile another collection, which became *More Stories by Frank O'Connor* (published in October). The new book did not please him: he was dissatisfied with the extravagance of earlier stories and believed he had not had enough time to revise them. In June, Harriet and he went to Cambridge, where he was to teach the summer at Harvard, again offering courses on the novel and an advanced writing seminar. In September, they moved to Hicks Street in Brooklyn, where he wrote "The Teacher's Mass" and "Orphans," and worked on *The Mirror in the Roadway* (completed at the end of 1955).

The New Yorker bought "The Face of Evil," "Lost Fatherlands," and "Francis" in 1954 (published as "Pity" in *Domestic Relations*); they rejected "The Wreath" (*Atlantic Monthly*) and "Don Juan's Apprentice" (*Harper's Bazaar*).

"Kate" (Katharine Farrington), William and Emily Maxwell's first child, was born on December 19.

WILLIAM MAXWELL TO FRANK O'CONNOR,
FEBRUARY 24, 1954:

February 24, 1954

Dear O'Connor:

My friend Robert McNamara from Evanston turned up last
week, and I found that you had been extremely kind to *him,* but
that *he* hadn't managed to arrange for you to find a place to walk
there.* Next time I'll come with you and see to it myself.

I can't remember any more the circumstances that led to my
editing this story instead of Gus Lobrano—perhaps he was about
to take off for a vacation.† Anyway, it's one of my favorites, and I
hope that among us we haven't succeeded in damaging it. That
isn't, of course, ever our intention. But perfection has a way of
turning and biting the hand that strokes it. A few of the queries
turned out to be a little too elaborate to explain on the margins of
the proof, so here goes.

(1) This "dummy insert" is to correct the fact that you neglect
to tell where the story takes place until the last paragraph of the
story, and for a good part of the way, because it appears in the New
Yorker, with your name at the end of the story, the reader is likely
to think that he is reading about America. I don't think much of
the insert, and hope you'll replace it with something more charac-
teristic.

(2) Lobrano suggests that you might possibly want to do
something here, and again on galley 3, about these two *it*s that
have no grammatical antecedent. It is a very tentative suggestion,
in any case, because the story, though easier to follow with the
change toward greater explicitness, is not really obscure without
it—the reader grasps what the "it" is by the end of the sentence,
and there is also the question of how the boy would think of it in
his mind—whether "it" isn't just the way he would think of it,
avoiding as much as possible the word saint? I feel sure you will
know what it should be, and as I say, it is up to you.

(3) Another dummy insert, because there has been no indication, apart from "sulking with Mother" several paragraphs above,

that he has been talking to his mother; it was the voice he was talking to.

(4) Lobrano wonders if it wouldn't help to mention this note-book earlier.

(5) Mr. Ross was a great admirer of H. W. Fowler, and a great many of his ideas have found a permanent place in the New Yorker style book, including the following:

> "The two kinds of relative clause, to one of which *that* & to the other of which *which* is appropriate, are the defining and the non-defining; & if writers would agree to regard *that* as the defining relative pronoun, & *which* as the non-defining, there would be much gain both in lucidity & in style. Some there are who follow this principle now; but it would be idle to pretend that it is the practice either of most or of the best writers."

There are several more of these queries, in this set of galleys. You don't of course have to agree with Fowler's suggestion, if it offends your ear.

(6) Lobrano doubts if it is clear what's never right. Do you care to be more explicit? For example, "It's never right to spy on people."

(7) Lobrano wonders how he knew Charlie had picked it up.

(8) I couldn't decide, when I edited the manuscript, whether the word "being" had been left out, on the manuscript, so I left it as you had left it, intending to ask you now. Lobrano, reading the story in galleys, also wondered if a word was missing. The proof-reader, more excitable, has a whole long note on this passage, which I have left on, for you to take seriously or not, as you please. Over here, "being with a girl" can mean—according to the con-text—sleeping with a girl or merely having a date with her. Am-plification would help, in any case.

I've left on a good many of the proofreader's suggestions, but, as always, you are to follow them only if they seem an improve-ment. Not knowing Irish speech, we can't really judge. It wouldn't be an improvement, needless to say, in this story, if it is toward grammatical correctness but away from what the boy would say and think.

Last week end we went out to our house in the country, to see a man about digging a deeper well, and the first daffodil points were foolishly above the ground. In town it is very springlike, and deceptive. The kind of weather that leads young men (or did me) to fall in love with girls they don't marry.

Yours, affectionately,
W.M.

Mr. Frank O'Connor
Primrose Hill
Nash, Bletchley
Bucks
England

Enc.

———

* Maxwell's friend was not the Secretary of Defense (1961–68).
† "The Face of Evil."

FRANK O'CONNOR TO WILLIAM MAXWELL,
MARCH 5, 1954:

Primrose Hill.
Nash, Bletchley.
Bucks, England.

March 5th 1954

Dear Maxwell,

I accept all the admonitions, which, by this time, you must be tired of giving out. As usual on all the minor things which you pick out for correction, you and Lobrano are right. You are in immediate relation to the audience. Lobrano is also right about that infernal notebook; not so much, I think, about its being mentioned earlier as about giving it proper significance. I was shocked on re-reading the scene on the wall between the two boys and couldn't resist the tendency to rewrite it; you don't have to use it unless you think, as I now do, that it strengthens the whole story. Of course, I don't mean 'sleeping with a girl.' I mean that the excitement of communication between good and evil has for the boy the same sort of magic that communication with somebody of a different sex will later have for him, as though it were an extension of his whole personality.

Will you please pass on my thanks to whatever angel in the house thought of sending me whiskey for Christmas? This is a Tudor house, full of Tudor draughts; I have a young American wife accustomed to central heating, and whiskey is sometimes my only refuge. I wish I had you here now to argue poetry with for a couple of hours. I have a feeling that we shan't be here long, and that I must move nearer Oxford and John Betjeman and Blackwell's bookstore if I'm to avoid writing a novel about Sin.

Ever,

FO'C.

WILLIAM MAXWELL TO FRANK O'CONNOR,
MARCH 10, 1954:

March 10, 1954

Dear O'Connor:

They aren't admonitions, as I'm sure you know, but the illusions of perfectionators, and individually we would probably get tired and quit worrying about this kind of thing, since the story stands or falls elsewhere, but we keep each other at it.

With "after with a girl" changed to "later with a girl" (Lobrano's idea) the passage in question became clear and everybody is happy. We are using the insert, and feel that the use you made of the notebook was a stroke of well why not say genius.

I wish you were here to watch the McCarthy trauma. It is so interesting to see how a failure of courage, or intelligence, or more likely both, in the very highest places has provoked courageous action in all sorts of lower ones. Stevenson, Ed Murrow, the Senator from Vermont, etc. Two weeks ago I was wondering whether to emigrate to England, France, or Ireland.

Lobrano says to tell you that we have only one more story of yours to run, and that we would very much like to have more.

Ever,
W.M.

Mr. Frank O'Connor
Primrose Hill
Nash, Bletchley
Bucks
England

GUS LOBRANO TO FRANK O'CONNOR,
MARCH 26, 1954:

Friday, March 26.

Dear Frank:

Be grateful if you'll give your attention to this proof, and return it to us as soon as you can. And, incidentally, I hope none of the queries will be too shocking or distressing.

I hear that you'll be coming over here sometime soon, and that's good news. I suppose there's no chance of your leaving now that April's you know where, but I shall look forward to seeing you shortly thereafter.

Yrs,
GUS LOBRANO

FRANK O'CONNOR TO GUS LOBRANO, APRIL 5, 1954:

Primrose Hill,
Nash,
Bletchley,
Bucks.
Tel. Whaddon 216

Dear Gus,
    No shocks in this at all. Now, I must settle down and write a few GOOD stories. I shall be back at latest some time in June, and as I shall have my family with me, I intend to spread myself instead of chasing back home in a hurry. We've just had my wife's relatives to stay, but the lack of steam-heating cleared them out in no time. I like steam-heating and I like no steam-heating, so I get the best of both worlds.

Yours,
FOC.

WILLIAM MAXWELL TO FRANK O'CONNOR,
AFTER SEPTEMBER 13, 1954:

Dear Mr. O'Connor:
    Partly because I thought Mrs. O'Connor would enjoy it and partly because I always feel selfish when I am the only one to hear what you are saying I have asked Brendan Gill to join us on Wednesday. I think you will both like him.*

Yours,
W.M.

———

* Brendan Gill remembered, "I was grateful to Bill M. for having brought me together with Harriet and Frank. He was, of course, wonderful to talk with, and readers of his letters must imagine the superb voice—dark, full-timbred, passionate—that matched them."

1955

O'Connor's health troubled him early in the year, culminating in an angina attack in March. His reaction was characteristically creative: he and Harriet travelled to Ireland in June, and he wrote "Expectation of Life" to tease her. It examines the marriage of an older man and his young wife, who worries lovingly about his health; against all predictions, she dies first.

When the O'Connors returned to America in September, they took a house in Annapolis, where Harriet had grown up and her family still lived. Harriet recalled, "In retrospect, this was not a good idea. While charming, Annapolis is even more of a small town than Cork, and Michael felt stifled and longed for the anonymity of New York. However, it was from Annapolitans that he got the themes for three stories: 'The Man of the World' from my cousin, 'Music When Soft Voices Die' from my memories of my first job, and 'The Impossible Marriage' from a friend of my mother's."

"The Teacher's Mass," "Fish for Friday," "A Bachelor's Story," and "Expectation of Life" all appeared in *The New Yorker;* they turned down "Orpheus in Exile," "The Paragon" (*Esquire*), and "Orphans" (*Mademoiselle*). "The Paragon" and "Orphans," although rejected, exemplify *The New Yorker*'s editors' efforts to help an author reshape a story to an imagined ideal.

FRANK O'CONNOR TO WILLIAM MAXWELL,
LATE 1954 OR EARLY 1955:

136 Hicks Street
Brooklyn 1, N.Y.
UL 8-8983

Dear Bill,

(If I may.) As I don't want you to think those half dozen stories I spoke about are all in my head, I am sending two of them
through Don Congdon. I hope to send the others in a week or so.
At the same time, I'm not entirely satisfied with them, and I can
only hope that by the time Gus and you have had a crack at them
I may have finally settled my own problems.

We enjoyed enormously the lunch with you and Brendan Gill,
and we hope you'll both come here. Can't you get a baby sitter
some evening and come here for a real talk-session?

Yours,
FRANK

WILLIAM MAXWELL TO FRANK O'CONNOR,
FEBRUARY 1955:

Dear Frank:

If they were all in your head, they'd still be as good as if they
were on paper. But it is good news that you feel you can start two
of them in our direction. It may ease your feelings to know that
the daffodils are up a good two inches, on the south side of the
house. When Kate is a little older, we may manage to put her in a
basket and bring her along. I think all children should be allowed
to develop their natural talent for eavesdropping.*

My love to you both,
BILL

_____

* Maxwell, considering the source of his own storytelling instinct, told Leonard Lopate in March 1995: "I sometimes feel the whole thing is a development of my love of eavesdropping as a child. There were no baby-sitters in my childhood, and my parents would take me out with them when they went for the evening, and I would fall asleep, but I always felt there was something I didn't know going on, and the truth is I don't think there was, but I hoped that there was, and I would fall into a state in which I was physically asleep but mentally alert to what people said. I was looking for stories, really."

WILLIAM MAXWELL TO FRANK O'CONNOR,
MARCH OR APRIL 1955:

Dear Frank:

Having written Congdon that we were taking The Teacher's Mass, I tried to call you and take the wind out of his sails by telling you first, but you weren't home. Hell of an afternoon not to be home in, but anyway, when I finished The Teacher's Mass I said what Josef Lhévinne said about Liszt's Campanella—"It's for the few." It's one thing to conceive of that kind of a story, but to carry it out successfully is for the damned few to be able to do. So while I was still brooding over this remarkable achievement, along comes the new story about the man who went to get the doctor, and that, in case you were in any doubt whatever about it, is nothing more nor less than a masterpiece.* I tell you this without waiting for my colleagues' reactions. I know a masterpiece when I see one, and so do they, fortunately.

Yours,
BILL

_____

* "Fish for Friday."

WILLIAM MAXWELL TO FRANK O'CONNOR, 1955:

Dear Frank:

That girl has gone, over hurdle after hurdle, leaving in each case one more man in love with her, and is now with Mr. Shawn.* I think it is safe to say that there will be no difficulties about the New Yorker's taking the story. If you have, in the meantime, thought of an arabesque here and there, fine, but nothing essential is lacking, so far as Gus or I could see.

The Paragon we all like, in principle, and think it is a story, and that it is pretty close to being all right, but that it could stand some more thinking about, and a little fixing here and there. See if you agree. As I understand the story, he is not a failure at the end, but still a paragon of sorts—a paragon 2nd class, instead of the paragon 1st class that he seemed along about page 2 to show every sign of becoming. But by page 13, he is pretty far down; so far, that (having made a bad marriage, and missed out even on a job with the county council) the narrator doesn't know, and neither does he, what he will do with the degree that he stubbornly continues to work for, when he does it. So shouldn't he, in order to be some kind of paragon and not a simple failure, be given a leg up? by you I mean? Shouldn't something good have happened—I don't suppose Aunt Mary would leave him a small legacy, and even if she did, it wouldn't probably in itself be enough—because if he is to stay in business as a paragon, something flashy must happen—an opening, an offer, perhaps the people at the university could change their minds about him, and offer him something that once he wouldn't have been too happy to take but that now is above his expectations? But about the university making it clear they didn't want him back (page 11)— why was that? Since the story has an Irish background, the reader's knowledge won't carry him as far as if, say, the boy flunked out of Harvard. It needs detail. Apparently he was dependant on the scholarship from the County Council, not a university scholarship, and therefore if the university didn't want him back, it must have been because of his behaviour, but was his behaviour that bad? It doesn't seem so, but the reader sees it through the narrator's eyes, of course, which is to say through yours, and it might well be, for all I know, that the university authorities were very straight-laced indeed. But it would help to say so. Also we didn't understand this sentence: "He still saw his friends in the university, but he didn't drink with them. When he did drink it was with the students". By friends, do you mean friends in the faculty, or what? Also, where did he get the money from to go—for all of them to go to England to visit his father in gaol? And shouldn't it be a little clearer what the wife is getting at, in A on page 14? I suppose it is merely that the father, whom he admires so, is all but a bigamist, or something to that effect, but it seems to suggest something undisclosed instead. There are a few other such points that seem to need more explicit handling. It is some time before the reader is sure that the family in England are not lawful—there has been no mention of a divorce between Jimmy's mother and father, but on the other hand, he isn't much struck by the circumstances that his father has a mistress and illegitimate daughter. He might only be struck with tolerant admiration, but shouldn't he be struck with something, on making this discovery? Instead of merely taking it in his stride? Also, he appears to refuse, or to try to refuse, the money to go to college, but then apparently he has accepted it, because both he and his mother begin living well. Wouldn't it be a good idea to say that he did in the end? And finally, would you take a good look (forgetting Jimmy and his troubles for the moment) at the narrator and his mother, who seemed to us a little skimped, and as a result, blurred in a way that your characters never are. She begins as a flighty-ish woman, or at least highly feminine one, (1st paragraph) and then goes on to become more and more sybilline, or at least on suspiciously solid grounds, morally speaking, as for example B on page 10. And the narrator is announced as a person who is never out of trouble, but none of his troubles are even named, and he seems, in the course of the story, to remain singularly unbitched up. Anyway, they both could do with a little of that supreme individuality that it is never, so far as I can see from here, difficult for you to provide your characters with. At all events, they almost always have it, as if from birth.

I thought of calling you about this, but decided it would be hard for you to remember afterward, so I have written this laborious communication. Suppose I call you on Monday, and we can talk about it then.

Love to you both,
BILL

———

* Shiela Hennessey of "Expectation of Life."

FRANK O'CONNOR TO WILLIAM MAXWELL,
APRIL 18, 1955:

136 Hicks Street
Brooklyn, 1.

April 18

Dear Bill,

I've looked at the last paragraph of 'Orphans' again in the light of what you and Gus say [in a telephone conversation], and I'm afraid that you *can't* continue the story beyond this point. It's a story that absolutely needs a full close even if it does sound like 'All together now, boys.' The only way I can think of which would remove the contrived air of a full close without running into the danger of anticlimax is by a last paragraph with a swift change of tense. Something like this:

> It was long years after this that she told me it was only then that she knew she had made up her mind. At that time she was living on a terrace in Cork, across the road from me, and Larry had settled into a business career. He was a morose man even then: I fancy he was a man who would never be exactly gay; and he had a sort of fixation on ~~the~~ his two children. ~~I used to see him taking them for walks, one by either hand, while Hilda waved at them~~

(34)

~~from the door.~~ He didn't talk much about Hilda, but on the one occasion when he did discuss her with me, it was to laugh incredulously at Hilda's sense of her own inadequacy. ~~Hilda always felt she wasn't doing all a wife should do~~ — Hilda, I fancy, always will think something like that.* But at least when he made fun of her it was clear that he no longer thought of her merely as Jim's girl, the one living link with his brother and ultimately with his mother and home. He sounded far too much like a real husband for that.

Actually this does let down the tension a bit, and gives the carry-over that Gus wants, and I'm not too sure but I'll adopt it whether you take the story or not.†

Yours,

FRANK

———

* Handwritten addition, at the bottom of the page, following "something like that": "; it is a way of women who take up a man as a cause."
† O'Connor did not choose to adopt this ending.

WILLIAM MAXWELL TO FRANK O'CONNOR,
MAY 2, 1955:

May 2, 1955

Dear Frank:

Gus just gave me back the manuscript of "Orphans," which he has been considering in the light of your letter of April 18, and he still feels it isn't right for The New Yorker. As I told you over the phone, we liked it fine, right up to the last paragraph, and I'm afraid I could have been clearer in talking about it, because we didn't at all mean that the story should have an epilogue such as the paragraph in your letter tacked onto it, but only that the girl's decision (which is not altogether easy to accept) is announced by you, which makes the second remove, instead of being felt, acted upon, announced, and explained by her; with the result that the reader, instead of putting the story down with the satisfied feeling that he knows the girl, inside and out, is—we were, anyway—left with a disappointing sense of the author's ingenuity. I know from talking with you that ingenuity is not what you felt or intended, since the story is not contrived but taken from life, so what is here is either a serious difference of opinion, or an unfortunate accidental effect. If you are satisfied with the story as it stands, then we certainly don't want you to tamper with it, and trust you to know whether or not it is right; also, that we wouldn't for the world dream of telling you how a story should or shouldn't be written. But if, on the other hand, you find you do see a way to go on a little and round out the action of the ending so that the focus is on her and not on you talking about her—in short to make it less explicitly diagrammed, we would be more than grateful to see it again. I am returning the manuscript to Don Congdon.

Love to you both,
BILL

Mr. Frank O'Connor
136 Hicks Street
Brooklyn, New York

FRANK O'CONNOR TO WILLIAM MAXWELL, MAY 11, 1955:

136 Hicks Street
Brooklyn, 1. N.Y.
ULSTER 8-8983

Dear Bill,

Here's Expectations, all pointed up. You don't have to use all or any of the emendations, but Harriet, who is the principal person in the story insists that it must be 'infatuations' and not 'affairs.' She says she wouldn't mind but it would break her family's heart.

Ever,

FRANK

WILLIAM MAXWELL TO FRANK O'CONNOR, MAY 13, 1955:

Dear Frank:

Since I've been prodding Gus to read the galleys of your stories before you and Harriet go abroad, I put Expectation of Life in type from the first version, and then, as I copied the changes on the margins, was free to admire how you changed something that was already in focus to hair-line focus, instead. It was a dreamlike experience, and if only the galleys could be published, with the corrections, it would teach a great many people who don't know now how to write and how to edit.

For reasons that Congdon will pass on to you, Orpheus in Exile didn't work out for The New Yorker. Privately, though I am supposed to wait before I express myself until the decision is arrived at, I feel sure that A Salesman's Romance will be bought. At least, if I had the doing, it would be. Orpheus seemed to us incomplete. Some day when you haven't anything better to do, I wish you'd call me and talk about it. Unless you are perfectly satisfied with it, in which case it would be foolish to.*

Love to you both,

BILL

P.S. I'm also sending your agent a renewal of the first reading agreement with that fellow Michael O'Donovan.†

———

* "Orpheus in Exile," about the power of alcohol to bring out hidden personalities (also called "Orpheus in Liquor" and "The Victim"), was that rarity, an

O'Connor story never published. Its protagonist is a quiet teacher when sober; after a few drinks, he is a frustrated musician who gets in trouble with the police.

† A first-reading agreement was the magazine's contractual procedure to assure themselves that they would get first look at favored writers' work. Upon signing a short but arcane agreement, O'Connor would offer the magazine first refusal of whatever he wrote that was longer than 5,000 words, for which he would be paid 25 percent more than the usual rate. If *The New Yorker* considered a piece and refused it, he was free to submit it elsewhere. The magazine could also add an additional payment, related to the cost-of-living index, paid quarterly. His agent, Don Congdon, thought these agreements were restrictive "nuisances," although the magazine occasionally granted O'Connor permission to offer writing elsewhere first. Between 1945 and 1967, *The New Yorker* published fifty-one of his stories and essays, more than any other American magazine, including *Harper's Bazaar, Mademoiselle, Esquire, Atlantic Monthly, The Saturday Evening Post,* and *Vogue.*

WILLIAM MAXWELL TO FRANK O'CONNOR,
BEFORE MAY 19, 1955:

Dear Frank:

Thank you for the delightful view of Harriet. I'm sending, today, a cost of living check to Matson's office for $1972.35, and thought I'd let you know, in case it might affect your traveling arrangements. It is too hot even to go around in your skin.

Love to you both,
BILL

P.S. A Bachelor's Story is scheduled for the issue of July 30, and Expectation of Life for August 20. And is O'Donovan behaving himself?

FRANK O'CONNOR TO WILLIAM MAXWELL, MAY 19, 1955:

136 Hicks Street
Brooklyn, 1. N.Y.

May 19th.

Dear Bill,

This is merely to satisfy Gus and yourself that I *can* profit by advice. I've tidied up all the structural faults, but I'm still vaguely dissatisfied. Harriet says it's a novel rather than a short story and she may be right.*

Anyway, after this I'll give you a rest. The only other story I've done is so scandalous that it can serve no purpose except to give you a laugh.†

We're supposed to sail on June 4th and after I've finished that trip from Dijon down to the Mediterranean I'll be in better form for stories.

Now, that I have all the money in the world, what's the chance of Gus and you, or either of you, having lunch with me before I sail?

Yours,
FRANK

———

* This might have been "The Paragon" or "Orphans." "The Paragon" was published by *Esquire* in October 1957. On July 6, 1956, Maxwell had written Congdon:

THE PARAGON still isn't right for us, and we've all spent a good deal of time beating our heads over it. I felt, mostly, a certain let down at the end, where it seemed to me that, having chosen to write a story about the paragon type, Frank could and should have managed to have something more interesting to say about it, in conclusion. Or rather, that he *did* have something more interesting to say, and the telephone rang and distracted him. Another of the editors felt that the story still slips off the track into mere explaining, quite often, after the boy's visit to his father. And Mrs. White, who read it for the first time in this version, has a note on it that I think might be helpful, so I am quoting it verbatim:

"I found most of it very interesting and think there could be a good story here. But it doesn't seem to me a new last page would do it, really. Isn't it a fundamental defect that this story is told by a narrator? So much of it—and the best part, too—is straight third person narrative, with dialogue, and with fundamental thoughts and attitudes and facts told by the narrator that he could never have been able to report, and that he could not even have heard from Jimmy, since some are observations and perceptions Jimmy would not have been able to make about himself. It seems to me that to be really sound, the story should be rewritten to remove the 'I' . . . I also feel that after Jimmy returns from visiting his father, the story slips away and becomes less interesting and convincing. It's as if he'd hurried over this last section. Perhaps if he rewrote it in the third person he could build up more the story of Jimmy's dissoluteness and his apparently haphazard marriage—this, too, is now quite undeveloped. The characters interest me a lot. I think that after the news of the father's embezzlement comes, the wind-up of what happened to Jimmy needs more work and more direct narration rather than exposition. I *wish* he would do it . . ."

Since we aren't able to commit ourselves to buying the story, this puts the final burden of deciding on Frank, but as you both know, we never urge writers to redo stories unless we are genuinely hopeful about the outcome.

† This story is untraced, but Harriet said that "scandalous" had a different connotation at the time; in O'Connor's view, the story would have upset only "nervous Nellies."

FRANK O'CONNOR TO WILLIAM MAXWELL,
LATE MAY–EARLY JUNE 1955:

Dear Bill,

The Bachelor reads nicely and I like the cut. Too much profanity in Fish for Friday, it's all in character but it weakens the story. Feel free to cut or alter any bad language that irritates you.

See you Thursday.

FRANK

WILLIAM MAXWELL TO FRANK O'CONNOR,
NOVEMBER 27, 1955:

Dear Frank:

As you will doubtless remember, we sometimes tear up the old first reading agreement and start over, with the same terms but a larger payment accompanying it. This year, I am happy to say, the check that accompanied yours to the Matson office was for $1600. Don't stay down there forever. I miss you.

Love to Harriet,
BILL

P.S. And to that dear man, Michael O'Donovan.

WILLIAM MAXWELL TO FRANK O'CONNOR, 1955:

Dear Frank—

If you stub your toe on a piece of editing, for God's sake do something about it.

Love to you both,
BILL

FRANK AND HARRIET O'CONNOR TO WILLIAM MAXWELL,
CHRISTMAS 1955:

Prayer for a Proper Literary Outlook.

Lord, may all we story-spinners
Die as we have lived like sinners
May our wives still live in terror
Knowing we persist in error.
May no offer seem inviting

To the serious forms of writing
May we have, and air, no knowledge,
Never get a job in college.
Never be successful when
We write criticism—Amen!

All good wishes and much gratitude to you and Gus.

FRANK (O'CONNOR)

P.S.—and may we all have an 11–3 lunch together *very* soon. We feel lonely for you.

Merry Christmas and love
HARRIET

1956

O'Connor continued to be in demand as a lecturer at American universities. On April 17, he gave a talk on the modern novel, "Ride to the Abyss," at the University of Virginia, and later described the lecture in a letter to his longtime Cork friend Nancy McCarthy: "There was a man there who turned out to be head of the English department and was exactly like Denis Breen. He snorted and pished during the whole lecture and finally when I replied to some academic question by saying 'Well, I'm not a scholar,' snorted 'You said it!' It was just like home."

In August, O'Connor made his annual pilgrimage to Dublin, Paris, and Cork. When he returned in September, he and Harriet again took up residence in Brooklyn Heights.

"The Man of the World," published in 1956, is a remarkable story, so highly regarded at *The New Yorker* that it was chosen as the lead story in their collection of their finest stories of the decade.

"A Salesman's Romance," "The Duke's Children," "The Man of the World," and "The Pariah" appeared first in *The New Yorker;* they did not take "Scholar and Artist" (an autobiographical piece), "The Paragon" (*Esquire*), and "The Ugly Duckling" (as "That Ryan Woman" in *The Saturday Evening Post*). *Stories by Frank O'Connor,* a paperback collection with a new introduction, appeared in 1956, as did *The Mirror in the Roadway.*

O'Connor's first editor, Gus Lobrano, died of cancer on March 1, at fifty-three. The Maxwells' younger daughter, "Brookie" (Emily Brooke), was born on October 15.

WILLIAM MAXWELL TO FRANK O'CONNOR, EARLY 1956:

Dear Frank:

I know about Lauzun's English period, but am not terribly impressed with his soldiering. I, who am no soldier, could have been a marshall of France under Louis XIV. I am impressed with Lauzun's life. Saint Simon I would like to hear about—next Wednesday.*

Love to you both,
BILL

------

* Antonin-Nompar de Caumont, duc de Lauzun (1633–1723), French courtier and soldier, led the unsuccessful Irish expedition to restore King James II to the throne in 1689–90. Louis de Rouvroy, duc de Saint-Simon (1675–1755), uncle of the French social philosopher, is known for his 1739–51 memoirs of the court of Louis XIV. When Louis XIV imprisoned Lauzun for a decade, Saint-Simon (later his brother-in-law) was his staunch advocate and dear friend.

FRANK O'CONNOR TO WILLIAM MAXWELL, EARLY 1956:

My dear Bill,

How DARE you dismiss Lauzun in that way? *After* the events you record he rescued the Royal Family from England, commanded the French army in Ireland and was the intimate pal of my pal Saint-Simon. I always refer to him in class in S.S.'s description 'Never having read anything but fairy tales, he knew nothing but what he had seen himself.' It is the only possible justification for a liberal education. And anybody who was the pal of Saint-Simon is as sacrosanct as anyone who can claim to be a pal of yours. It's the very definition of intelligence!

Yours ever,
FRANK (O'CONNOR)

P.S. I expect to be in town next week and I wish you'd save me one lunch date—Tuesday, Wednesday, Thursday *or* Friday.

F.

WILLIAM MAXWELL TO FRANK O'CONNOR,
JANUARY 9, 1956 (telegram):

=FRANK O'CONNOR=
=60 CORNHILL ANNAPOLIS MD=

I JUST REALIZED I DON'T KNOW WHICH WEEK IS NEXT WEEK. IF ITS THIS WEEK WE'RE LUNCHING ON THURSDAY IF NEXT WEEK ON WEDNESDAY. LOVE=

BILL MAXWELL

FRANK O'CONNOR TO WILLIAM MAXWELL,
JANUARY 9, 1956 (postcard):

60 Cornhill
Annapolis, Maryland

I had arranged to go up today in hopes of that lunch with you, but at the last moment I decided to remain and have another crack at the story I've been writing for you. It's still not good but it will be.

Please can Harriet and I indent for another date. I can't really argue with you yet because my books are still on the way from Europe. At least, they are at Baltimore, awaiting clearance and transport.

Ever,
FRANK.

WILLIAM MAXWELL TO FRANK O'CONNOR,
JANUARY 25, 1956:

January 25, 1956

Dear Frank:

In re this much fought over bone, if you have a mind to amplifying and redoing it, we have very much a mind to having another look at it.* It is a little thin, a little too free-wheeling as it stands, and in any case we had a feeling that you probably could (which feeling was corroborated by Don Congdon, over the phone) go on at greater length on the subject of your ambition to be taken seriously as a scholar. As the manuscript stands, the first page seemed over-extended, the second over-condensed. It might help if, on page two, you considered, along with Celtic scholarship (if you feel like it, that is) American and British, to which I seem to remember you have had exposures. The friendship of Russell and Bergin is enchanting. Are there others you know about? And anything further you have to say on the subjects of the attraction of scholars for writers and vice versa. What I really mean is Will you please enjoy yourself on this general theme, and let us see how it comes out.

That was such a good luncheon. I hated to leave you, as always. Brodkey went home a man inspired, he says, and sat down to his typewriter and wrote two marvelous, two inspired sentences, and then the doorbell rang, and he went to the door and opened it and there stood the man from Porlock. Brodkey roomed with him in college.† The new collection of your stories arrived this morning, and I've been entertaining myself by reading all the first sentences, pretending to myself that I don't know, for example, what comes after "There!" said the sergeant's wife, "You would hurry me."‡ An exquisite pleasure. I recommend it to you. I thank you for the book, which has a number of stories we didn't have at home, and should have had.

Love to you both,
BILL

Mr. Frank O'Connor
60 Cornhill
Annapolis
Maryland

———

* The "bone" was the autobiographical piece "Scholar and Artist" (*Kenyon Review*, 1965); "Russell and Bergin" were George Russell ("Æ") and Osborn Bergin, the greatest of Celtic scholars; see *My Father's Son*.
† Harold Brodkey (1930–96), American novelist and short-story writer. A frequent contributor to *The New Yorker*, he was Maxwell's close friend.
‡ The Vintage *Stories by Frank O'Connor*. Maxwell refers to the opening of "In the Train."

HARRIET O'CONNOR TO WILLIAM MAXWELL,
FEBRUARY 1956 (postcard):

Dear Sir:

This is to announce that my husband has disappeared—presumably to Ireland—though the police have been informed on the off chance his body will turn up in the Chesapeake Bay. Having checked his reference to Heine's—"Out of My Great Sorrows"— he has discovered that the verb *is* in the past tense—and feels he can no longer bear the light of day.* He did not wish to be remembered to you.

XXXX

HARRIET

———

* "Out of my great sorrows I have made little songs" concluded "A Salesman's Romance" in the March 3 issue; it was corrected to ". . . I made little songs" in *Domestic Relations*.

WILLIAM MAXWELL TO FRANK O'CONNOR,
LATE FEBRUARY 1956:

Dear Frank:

I opened a rough copy of the magazine on the train last night, and the first thing I saw, to my horror, was the italicized uncorrected quotation from Heine. Though I was wildly amused by Harriet's card, I forgot or failed to remember that action was required on that set of galleys. I don't suppose it will bring a flood of letters, but I am ashamed anyway of not taking better care of things. I wish this were only a letter of apology. Instead I have to tell you something quite terrible, which is as yet not generally known and so I will have to ask you not to repeat it. It's about Lobrano. That operation he went to Boston for revealed that he had cancer of the liver. His wife brought him home, kept it from him (since it had been such a great fear to him for years that he would have cancer) and in order to keep it from him had to keep it from everyone else. A very touching charade, in which we all unknowingly took part. The report yesterday was that he had only a few hours to live. I think it is more likely a matter of days. He had remained lucid the whole time, and affectionate, and trusting. I will tell you about it all when I see you.

My love to you both,
BILL

FRANK O'CONNOR TO WILLIAM MAXWELL,
ABOUT MARCH 10, 1956:

60 Cornhill,
Annapolis, Md.

Dear Bill,

I only got back from California yesterday, and I want to thank you for your letter telling me about Lobrano. I knew him very little, though what I knew I liked, but I can imagine that to you it has all come as a great shock. The disease Turgenev died of—it's always been something of a nightmare to me as well. God send us both something quick and quiet. I hope too that you may find as sensitive and intelligent a colleague to work with.

Harriet came back triumphant from California with her favourite among your books but I'm afraid you have a rival in Wallace Stegner.* I suspect that in her Expectation of Life mood she is now torn between the pair of you.

After three weeks of almost continuous talking, I find it wonderful to get back to my three pictures and my hundred books that don't talk back or ask silly questions. I hope I haven't misled you about my adorable Katherine Anne as she has misled me. She told me that Stanford was terrible and Michigan wonderful. And I believed her!†

Yours ever,

FRANK

---

* O'Connor was lecturing at Stanford, Berkeley, and the University of Michigan at Ann Arbor. Harriet's favorite of Maxwell's books was the 1937 novel *They Came Like Swallows*. Wallace Stegner (1909–92), American novelist and short-story writer, met O'Connor in 1956 at Stanford.

† Katherine Anne Porter taught at Stanford in 1949 and at the University of Michigan in 1953–54. Maxwell wrote me about meeting her early in 1956: "Michael decided that I ought to know Katherine Anne Porter, too. And took us to lunch. She must have been in her late fifties. Remarkably large, beautiful grey eyes. It turned out that we were both interested in roses, and I sent her a rosebush, which she planted beside the New England farmhouse she owned at the time." Writing to Glenway Westcott a year after the luncheon, Porter was still delighted with her Golden Damask rosebush.

WILLIAM MAXWELL TO FRANK O'CONNOR,
APRIL 23, 1956:

Dear Frank:

I didn't want to hold up the payment while we corresponded, so I did the preliminary editing and saved the quibbles for this letter. I know it's a first person story, and that in conversation people do not stop to consider whether or not there is any antecedent for their pronouns, but somebody somewhere along the line is going to write copious notes about the places I marked if I let them pass. So do give them a look, and fix what seems to need or would benefit from fixing.*

I had a report on your Charlottesville appearance. You were wonderful, it seems. I find it possible to believe that you were. I see, in fact, the flush and glitter as the appreciation began to bring out the performer in you, and I regret that I wasn't there to enjoy the fruit of it. Nancy Hale didn't kidnap you and Harriet, as I had hoped, because she is too shy, I guess. Probably it wasn't physically possible, anyway. Another time.†

I am counting on you to join Congdon and me for lunch on May 2, because we've never met, and surely you want us to start out on the right foot with each other?

And I trust that Harriet has already begun to forget that California writer who, just for the moment, of course, seemed—It's funny I can't remember his name, when I know it as well as I know my own. Sherman? Walter Sherman? No doubt it will come to me. Steegmuller? Well, some such name as that. She has forgotten all about him (and his books) hasn't she?

Love to you both,

BILL

If there is any editorial tinkering you feel inclined to tinker with, by all means tinker. It's a lovely story.

---

* "The Duke's Children."

† O'Connor's talk, "Ride to the Abyss," at the University of Virginia. Nancy Hale (1906–88) was an American novelist, short-story writer, literary critic, and art historian whose work appeared frequently in *The New Yorker*.

FRANK O'CONNOR TO WILLIAM MAXWELL,
LATE APRIL 1956:

60 Cornhill
Annapolis

Dear Bill,
I hope this meets your Goethean demand for "more light." My 'square' is really not a square as it's only two rows of small houses in a deserted lot; the remaining two sides are provided by houses on the farther sides of two roadways. Hence, postally it is still known as an avenue.

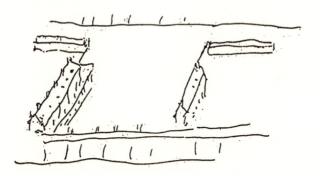

The ground plan of each house shows a tiny hallway, a small front room and a kitchen back of them. Nobody goes into the room in the story; everything takes place in the kitchen which has two doors opposite one another, one leading into the hallway, the other into the backyard. There is one window, beside the back door.

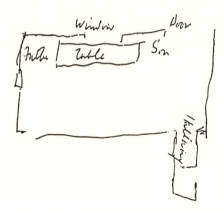

Does this illuminate and rejoice?*

I had promised myself lunch with you and Don Congdon IF I managed to finish the story I was doing for you. It has inspired me to a point when the story is *almost* right but there's still a small knot in the middle which would drive you crazy. Maybe despair will drive me to solve the problem tonight or tomorrow in which case I'll phone you and come.

But no story no lunch! I have to bully myself.

Harriet says she learned so much about you from Nancy Hale that she's lost hope.

Hooray, we have a flat in the Village as from September 1st and I shall be able to drop in and annoy you as much as I like.[†]

Ever,

FRANK

---

* In "The Duke's Children," the kitchen is the center of the Delaney household. O'Connor's references to "the Square" might have puzzled American readers. Recalling his requests for such detail, Maxwell told Charlie Rose in March 1995, "I used to say to Frank O'Connor, who was an oral writer—he was capable of marvelous descriptions, but it didn't interest him, he wanted to catch what he had caught—I would say to him, 'But what did it look like?' and he would tell me, out of kindness, and it would go into the story. Out of kindness to me, yes. He was a very affectionate man."

[†] They moved, instead, to Brooklyn Heights.

WILLIAM MAXWELL TO FRANK O'CONNOR,
MAY 3, 1956:

Dear Frank:

Thank you for maps, inserts, information, everything. There
are one or two small things, but they can be taken up in the final
proofs. Everything that was important you fixed. Will you give
me fair warning before you take off for Europe, so I can have them
ready in time for you to see. I don't think we'll be sitting on the
story, in any case.

A very pleasant lunch yesterday. Your sociable ghost saw to it
that there were no pauses, and now that your conscience has
proved to be of granite, I am confident that first the story and then
another lunch party will be forthcoming. Say the word. And love
to you both.

BILL

WILLIAM MAXWELL TO FRANK O'CONNOR,
ABOUT MAY 20, 1956:

Dear Frank:

Do you suppose you could have these back by Thursday, May
31, or the next day, at the latest. I held them back, expecting you
and Harriet to turn up here. Fond folly, it turned out to be. I hope
wherever you were there was good talking.*

Love,
BILL

------

* Maxwell enclosed proofs of "The Duke's Children." The O'Connors had been
at Harvard.

WILLIAM MAXWELL TO FRANK O'CONNOR,
MAY 29, 1956 (telegram):

=FRANK O'CONNOR=
  =60 CORNHILL ANNAPOLIS MD=

=FROM HERE IT LOOKS VERY MUCH AS IF YOUVE
EARNED YOUR WAY INTO HEAVEN=*
                                    =BILL MAXWELL=

———

* His reaction to "The Man of the World."

WILLIAM MAXWELL TO FRANK O'CONNOR,
EARLY JUNE 1956:

                                          Thursday
Dear Frank:
    Oh but you could have gone to Harvard by way of the pink
house.* I'm not even sure it isn't the quickest way. From the Geo.
Washington bridge you take the Taconic State Parkway (the signs
are also marked "to Albany") on up to Hawthorne Circle, and past
Millwood and the Kitchewan filling stations, and over a big
bridge over the reservoir, until you come to an overpass and a sign
that says "Yorktown Heights," at which point you leave the parkway and crossing back over it, via the overpass, find yourself in the
situation:

        [Maxwell drew a detailed map.]

I apologize for the fact that the top of the map isn't North. I
meant it to be and got lost in the facts of the case. I wondered also
if you would know what I was trying to say in the telegram. "This
is possibly the best story you have ever written" sounded too much

in the accents of posterity, or at least too pleased with my own judgment, but that is how I felt about it. I read it back and forth and around while I was reading it for the first time—Do you know that kind of reading, where you circulate among the words and double back to give your feelings time to catch up with you, and for enjoyment. Now he *has* got himself in a pickle, I said, and waited, and openmouthed watched you walk right over the pickle because it wasn't, for your purposes, even there. So beautiful and so moving. And perfection, beside everything else. My deepest congratulations to the writer—and the writer's wife. And my love, as usual.

BILL

———

* The Maxwells' house on Baptist Church Road in Yorktown Heights.

FRANK O'CONNOR TO WILLIAM MAXWELL, JUNE 1956:

60 Cornhill,
Annapolis, Md.

My Dear Bill,

This is not a revision, merely a rewrite with a few i's dotted and a few t's crossed which may be of use to you when you come to put it in proof.*

I accept your last letter as an invitation to drop in for a drink next time we're up your way, which I hope won't be too far away if I'm really going to Europe in middle August.

Harriet has sent you a copy of a book of stories by a new Irish writer whom I don't know. I like his work and I think you may like it too. It's interesting to me because it's a complete reversion to Joyce by a young man who obviously hasn't read a line by O'Flaherty or myself and doesn't conceal it very well.[†]

She says is there a house somewhere near you. We had agreed to take the flat of an editor who is supposed to be going to Asia, but as he doesn't answer letters we wonder if he's really going there or just wishing he were.

Blessings,
FRANK

———

* "The Man of the World."

† James Plunkett's *The Trusting and the Maimed* (Devin-Adair, 1955). In his introduction to the 1957 *Modern Irish Short Stories*, O'Connor said: "There is a new firmness and harshness in the work of James Plunkett which is obviously very deeply influenced by that of Joyce. Though he has still not solved for himself Joyce's problem of reconciling verisimilitude with artistic form, and though he spoils some of his best stories with forced symbolic contrivances, he is obviously a story-teller of high seriousness."

KATHARINE S. WHITE TO FRANK O'CONNOR,
JUNE 21, 1956:

Dear Mr. O'Connor:

I have been wanting to write you for some time now, to say what a delight and reassurance to all of us your recent stories have been—reassurance as to the quality of our fiction, I mean. "Man of the World" is one of the most perfect and most affecting short stories I have read. You are probably tired of hearing its praises by now, but I can't help adding my own word of delight and admiration. "The Duke's Children" is also a favorite of mine. To have you writing so often and so well has been one of my greatest comforts after taking over the responsibility of running the Fiction Department after Gus Lobrano's death.

I realize how much of a shock Gus's death must have been to you. It still seems unreal to me, and I can't be reconciled to it. When I turned over the job of heading up Fiction to him, in 1938, I of course thought he would be here long after I was, and it seems incredible that I am now having to try to fill in for him for a couple of years.

We are greatly in need of new editors and I thought I'd mention to you that there are some good opportunities here at this time. We need men with experience, who could step into a fiction editorship at once, and also younger men, who could arrive at this after a few years' work. If you have any names to suggest, I'd be most grateful. Bill Maxwell tells me that he has not happened to tell you about this, but he, too, hopes you may have some candidates to send. As it happens, we prefer men, not women, at this time.

Sincerely yours,
KATHARINE S. WHITE

Mr. Frank O'Connor
60 Cornhill
Annapolis, Md.

If you go through New York on your way abroad, I hope I'll catch a glimpse of you in the office. I'm temporarily in Maine but will be in New York on July 2nd.

WILLIAM MAXWELL TO FRANK O'CONNOR, JULY 6, 1956:

Dear Frank:

When I was a very young man, I had to go over a New Yorker proof with Edmund Wilson, who snorted from time to time and said in *his* youth he had been an editor on Vanity Fair, and that the editorial fallacy was changing things for the sake of changing things. Had I been older, I might have drawn him out, because he is always interesting no matter what he is talking about, but I just took it for a profound and witty remark, which it perhaps was. But *some* editors suffer from the fallacy of guardian angel–ism, and sincerely believe that they are put here on earth to protect authors from damaging their best efforts by after thoughts that are not an improvement. So I spent three intense, dedicated days going over your two versions of Man of the World, protecting what I feel is one of the most moving and beautiful stories of modern times from your itch to improve it. The corrections were, it seemed to me, of two different kinds—whether they added to the clarity of the story, in which case, with suitable prayers that the whole would not be affected by the change of the part, I left them; or they added to the explicitness of the story, in which case I struck off their heads. Because so many things had fused in the writing of the original version, the timing, the story-telling art, and the emotional effect, all of which were, really, beyond improving. In setting myself up so sacerdotally, I am not depriving you of the opportunity of having the last word—or myself either. Read it and see what you think.

Since this story is scheduled for the issue of July 28, we would need to have the corrected galleys back by Thursday, the 12th, if you can do that. There is no hurry on the galleys of The Pariah. And that was an invitation.

Love to you both,
BILL*

---

* On June 21, 1956, Maxwell had written Congdon that *The New Yorker* had turned down "The Ugly Duckling": "We all have the same feeling—that fresh and interesting though the idea is, the people are just not very interesting. It is somehow as if Frank's real interest was in the didactic part of the story, rather than the characters—that he *neglected,* I mean, to make them real. Because he can set stones to talking and revealing their hearts any time he chooses to."

FRANK O'CONNOR TO WILLIAM MAXWELL, JULY 7, 1956:

60 Cornhill,
Annapolis, Md.

Dear Bill,
Thanks for your labours on the proofs. I think the results justify the means.

I rushed up to New York over the weekend and rented at first sight a little flat in Brooklyn with a lovely view of the harbour. I hope to be in it before I go to Europe. Now, you must come and see us.

Yours,
FRANK

WILLIAM MAXWELL TO FRANK O'CONNOR,
JULY 12, 1956:

July 12, 1956

Dear Frank:

I am delighted about the flat with the view of the harbor. When I first moved to Yorktown Heights there were houses for rent everywhere, and one summer I played going to Jerusalem in them. But all that came to an end with the war, and rented houses are all but unheard of in our part of Westchester County. All very grieving because I would so much have liked to see your light burning as I went to bed. Tell Harriet I have been reading her book on the train with pleasure and I am planning to take it on my vacation. We are going to be at the seashore the first two weeks of August. I hope you will not time your arrival so as to miss us but in any case I plan to come and see you the minute you have moved.

Love,
B.

Mr. Frank O'Connor
60 Cornhill
Annapolis, Maryland

FRANK O'CONNOR TO WILLIAM MAXWELL,
MID-1956:

160 Columbia Heights,
Brooklyn, 1. N.Y.

Dear Bill,

I'm asking Don Congdon to send you two stories which you've probably seen before though there is something mysterious about one of them. I told you already about 'Lady Brenda.' Don's copy seems to have disappeared. My English agent sold it to an Advertising Annual, of all things, and nobody, least of all the author has ever seen it or heard of it since. It's one of my pet stories, and when I talked to you of it, you suggested that I send it on and give a report on it.

The other is a straightforward funny story which appeared in a digest form in a London evening paper twelve years ago. Both, of course, have been rewritten.

Yours ever,
FRANK.

WILLIAM MAXWELL TO FRANK O'CONNOR,
SEPTEMBER 5, 1956:

September 5, 1956

Dear Frank:

I have had so much delight from *The Mirror in the Roadway* that I think you must write in it when you get home—write for Bill Maxwell, I mean, because that's who it's for. No question about it. Most critical books and especially critical books about the novel bore me till my teeth water, the reason being, I think, that most critics are such hopeless readers. This book makes me see everything differently and want to start at the beginning and read them all over again. I can't thank you enough for writing it. When are you coming home?*

Love,
BILL

P.S. I called Harriet a few minutes ago and the phone rang and rang and that was all, which means nobody is looking at the boats in the harbor, which means there aren't any boats in the harbor, doesn't it.

Mr. Frank O'Connor
160 Columbia Heights
Brooklyn, New York

———

* O'Connor returned from Europe on September 19.

WILLIAM MAXWELL TO FRANK O'CONNOR,
LATE OCTOBER 1956:

Dear Michael:
I hope it's Annapolis and not lecturing that keeps you and Harriet from answering at Main 5-2670. I was hoping to celebrate Halloween in broad daylight with you.

Love,
BILL

WILLIAM MAXWELL TO HARRIET O'CONNOR,
NOVEMBER 1956:

Dear Harriet:
I wrote down lunch with the two of you, for November 21, subject to cancellation. Now we'll see if that will draw you north-

ward.* Is Michael working, for God's sake? Mrs. White is pale from lack of manuscripts, and keeps asking me about him. I tell her he is a frivolous, talk-loving man who only writes when locked in a room, and for money to buy drink, while his poor children go barefoot. I forgot to add in the snow, but I will next time. Love,

B.

————

* From Annapolis to New York.

1957

O'Connor's *Domestic Relations,* completed early in 1957 and published in September, collected new stories, all but one first printed in *The New Yorker.* It reminded Denis Johnston of *Dubliners,* although Johnston thought O'Connor's "sense of form and discipline" surpassed Joyce's. The book also returned to the thematic format of earlier collections; its scope is roughly chronological, from stories of a pre-school boy to adolescent romances, failed romances, and marriages which end only with a spouse's death. It began with six "Larry Delaney" stories (including "The Man of the World") which take him from a Mother's Boy of five to a seventeen-year-old Irish soldier.

In March 1957, the O'Connors went to a Copenhagen literary conference, stopping in Ireland en route, enabling them to visit Cork. Late in the year, they found that Harriet was pregnant.

Anthony Whittier interviewed O'Connor for *The Paris Review*'s "Writers at Work" series and sketched his subject at home: "O'Connor's apartment is in Brooklyn, where he lives with his pretty young American wife. The large white-walled modern living room has a wide corner view of lower Manhattan and New York Harbor. The Brooklyn Bridge sweeps away across the river from a point close at hand. On his table, just under the window looking out on the harbor, are a typewriter, a small litter of papers, and a pair of binoculars. The binoculars are for watching liners 'on their way to Ireland,' to which he returns once a year. He says he'd die if he didn't."

This year saw more stories accepted by *The New Yorker* than ever before: "The Study of History," "Daydreams," "Requiem," "A

Minority," "An Out-and-Out Free Gift," and "The Party," although "Private Property" was turned down for reasons unrelated to its merit.

FRANK O'CONNOR TO WILLIAM MAXWELL, JANUARY 1957:

160 Columbia Heights,
Brooklyn, 1. N.Y.

My Dear Bill,
I am sending you this, not by way of re-submitting it, but of showing you that I am very grateful for your criticism and am taking advantage of it.* I may develop on that later. I did this merely to make sure that your criticism was right. It was.

Yours,
MICHAEL

––––––

* "Daydreams."

WILLIAM MAXWELL TO FRANK O'CONNOR,
FEBRUARY 1957:

Dear Michael:
Where can you be? Not lecturing, I hope. Will you call me on Monday if you are around? Everybody is delighted with *Day Dreams,* as I suspected, and I have half a dozen quibbles to take up with you, before I send it off with the mail for the printer. Love to you both,

B.

WILLIAM MAXWELL TO FRANK O'CONNOR,
FEBRUARY 21, 1957:

Dear Michael:

Nassau, is it?* Well if you love me, take these galleys somewhere into a bit of shadow, and have a look at the scribbling.† And
if we could get them back by next Wednesday, I would consider it
God's blessing on everybody.

I'm so glad you got away. For the first time since I've known
you you looked really tired. And as for what tired you, allow me to
present you with what was written on Emmy's milk jug when she
was a child:

> For Every evil under the sun
> There is a remedy or there is none
> If there be one try and find it
> If there be none never mind it

Your friend,
BILL

Mr. Frank O'Connor
c/o S. Cargill
Box 1066
Nassau
Bahamas

———

* The O'Connors vacationed in Nassau for about a week in late February. Initially reluctant to go, O'Connor enjoyed himself; Harriet told me, "He was very
interested in the natives who had married Irish people who had been sent out
there as convicts."
† "The Study of History." On February 13, Maxwell had written Congdon about
"Private Property," later published in *Domestic Relations:* "I'm extremely sorry
but the vote is against PRIVATE PROPERTY. It's a perfectly good story, and in
theory The New Yorker can take anything that is good, by its own standards of
looking at things, but it almost never has published period pieces, and this applies particularly to stories about the Irish rebellion. I was immensely relieved
when Larry Delaney gave up politics, because I hope to see much more of him."

FRANK O'CONNOR TO WILLIAM MAXWELL,
LATE FEBRUARY 1957:

as from 160 Columbia Heights
    Brooklyn

Sunday

My dear Bill,
    Proofs herewith. Nothing to say but 'Guilty Guilty.' I've been
laid up with sunburn for God's sake, and Harriet has got herself
knocked out with a cocoanut! Save us one lunch next week: we're
supposed to leave on March 16th and I just wanted one gossip
without proofs to divert us. Any day will do us.

God bless
MICHAEL

WILLIAM MAXWELL TO DON CONGDON,
MARCH 25, 1957:

March 25, 1957

Dear Don:
    A couple of weeks before Frank O'Connor left, he mailed me a
story just for me to read, because it was out of the question for The
New Yorker, and it wasn't out of the question at all, and I told
him it wasn't, and he has probably since told you, and anyway, a
check for it will be coming along to you shortly.*

As ever,
BILL MAXWELL

———

* "A Minority."

WILLIAM MAXWELL TO DON CONGDON,
APRIL 3, 1957:

                                      April 3, 1957
Dear Don:
    A check for the account of Frank O'Connor.* I wish I could
think that at any moment during these next few months he would
sit down and write us a story, but I know damn well he won't.
Never mind, whenever he does, it is always like rain from Heaven.
                                      My best to you,
                                      WILLIAM MAXWELL

———

* For "A Minority."

FRANK O'CONNOR TO WILLIAM MAXWELL,
APRIL 17, 1957 (postcard from Adare, County Limerick):

You'd never think to look at this that it was once an O'Donovan
manor. However that was in the tenth century and as you know I
am not one to brood on old wrongs. Present ones are enough: for
instance an American wife who keeps saying: I think Bill would
like this!
                                      Love,
                                      MICHAEL

FRANK O'CONNOR TO WILLIAM MAXWELL,
APRIL 26, 1957 (postcard from Rome):

> To go to Rome
> Is endless labour, little gain;
> The Master that you seek in Rome
> You find at home, or seek in vain.

MICHAEL AND HARRIET*

———

* This is O'Connor's translation of an Irish epigram (showing the attitude to the imposition of Roman power) written in the eighth or ninth century. Another version of it is included in *Kings, Lords, & Commons,* as "A Word of Warning."

"I think on this trip," Harriet told me, "Michael took a picture of me sitting in front of the Vatican with my back turned to the Pope, who was speaking from the balcony, and he used to send it around proudly, saying 'What can you do with a Protestant like this who turns her back on the Holy Father?' "

FRANK O'CONNOR TO WILLIAM MAXWELL,
SEPTEMBER 5, 1957:

160 Columbia Heights,
Brooklyn
Main 5-2670

Dear Bill,

Here's your story at last.* As usual, you get fifty per cent of your way only. For once I think it's enough. Anything more would only spoil the story.

By this time you'll have had *Androcles and the Army.* There are several more to come, and I'll let you see them as they get typed on condition that you conspire with me against my agent who is firmly convinced that stories should be spaced out at regular intervals, not all written and fired in together as their irrepressible author writes them. That is because the author aforesaid believes with the old Indian woman who talked to Lord Edward Fitzgerald that humanity is 'all one Indian.'

I only wonder if you have the makings of a conspirator in you.

Harriet and I are both deeply offended because you never even sent us a card from wherever the blazes you were. It couldn't have been all that interesting. We are motoring to Boston next week to put my daughter in the hands of an educational adviser.[†] Once for all, if I lay hands on the car, will you allow me to call for a drink before *your* daughters have ceased to be one age with me and become interested in nothing but spotty midshipmen?

Ever,

MICHAEL

------

* Either "An Out-and-Out Free Gift" or "A Minority."
† O'Connor's elder daughter, Liadain, then sixteen. She described herself as "a particularly awkward teenager, I'd just arrived from Ireland and was trying to re-establish a relationship with my father after past family crises had caused so much hurt in all directions." Maxwell, she recalled, was "a lovely man . . . so natural and kind to me. A child, even a big one, will always remember someone like that."

FRANK O'CONNOR TO WILLIAM MAXWELL,
SEPTEMBER 9, 1957:

160 Columbia Heights,
Brooklyn, 1. N.Y.

Dear Bill,

This is CONSPIRACY. You are required to send this story back to me, with or without your comments. We've discussed the subject, but this isn't even supposed to be a story but a piece of pure lyricism in which the characters are regarded merely as voices in a bit of instrumental music. It's one of the odd things I do for my own satisfaction, without expecting anybody in the world to like it except myself. You will, in due course, get a copy from Don Congdon who, poor man, will not find any magazine that wants to print it.*

Yet, as you know, one has to write these things and one has to show them to the people one admires. It's a clause in the charter.

Yours,

MICHAEL

———

* "Music When Soft Voices Die," based on Harriet's memories of a trio of secretaries she had worked with in Annapolis. O'Connor's belief that no one would appreciate it was unfounded: *The New Yorker* published it on January 11, 1958.

WILLIAM MAXWELL TO DON CONGDON,
SEPTEMBER 11, 1957:

September 11, 1957

Dear Don:

I'm afraid you are going to have to break the news to O'Connor that we didn't like Androcles and the Army, which I happen to know is very dear to his heart.* Thank God he is of a forgiving disposition.

My best to you,

WILLIAM MAXWELL

———

* *The Atlantic Monthly* published it in May 1958.

WILLIAM MAXWELL TO FRANK O'CONNOR,
SEPTEMBER 26, 1957:

September 26, 1957

Dear Michael:
Galleys* and this and that.

BILL

———

* Of "An Out-and-Out Free Gift," then called "The Liar."

1958

Because of the birth of Hallie-Óg O'Donovan on June 25, and the beginnings of *The Château* and *An Only Child,* this was a memorable year for correspondence. Having teased Harriet about her preoccupation with her pregnancy, O'Connor began to write about *his* childhood, first as a novel, *Displaced Persons,* never finished, and then as autobiography.

In August and September, Maxwell and O'Connor reversed their established roles as editor and writer, as Maxwell gave O'Connor the manuscript that would become *The Château,* which he recalled in *The Paris Review:* "When I went to France the first time I promptly fell in love with it. I was forty years old. My wife had been there as a child, and we were always looking for two things she remembered but didn't know where they were—a church at the end of a streetcar line and a château with a green lawn in front of it. We came home after four months because our money ran out. I couldn't bear not to be there, and so I began to write a novel about it. And for ten years I lived perfectly happily in France, remembering every town we passed through, every street we were ever on, everything that ever happened, including the weather. Of course, I was faced with the extremely difficult problem of how all this self-indulgence could be made into a novel. . . . Frank O'Connor came out to our house in the country for the day, with his wife and baby, and in the course of the conversation he extracted from me the information that I had been working for eight years on a novel I was in despair over. 'Let me see it,' he said, and I was appalled. I was not in the habit of mixing my two lives. At that time the manuscript of what turned out to be *The Château* filled a good-sized grocery carton. I hadn't been able to make up my mind whether it should have an omniscient author or a first-person narrator, whether it should be told from the point of view of the French or the Americans traveling in France. I was afraid that it wasn't a novel at all but a travel diary. I told O'Connor that the manuscript was in such a shape that it was unreadable, but he assured me that he could read anything. He had been sufficiently trusting to let me see the rough draft of section after section of *An Only Child,* and I didn't feel like saying that it was one thing for me to see his unfinished work and another for him to see mine. He went off with the grocery carton in the backseat of his car, and read through the whole mess. Then he wrote me a wonderful letter in which he said he didn't understand what I was up to. There seemed to be two novels—which he then proceeded to discuss, in detail, as separate works. My relief was immense, because it is a lot easier to make two novels into one than it is to make one out of nothing whatever. So I went ahead and finished the book."

After O'Connor became ill in mid-year, he decided to return to Ireland with Harriet and Hallie-Óg. They sailed on September 23; when they arrived, they lived in a small apartment in Dublin for the next year.

His absorption in the controversy surrounding the late Sir Roger Casement (1864–1916), an Irish revolutionary whose reputation the British had attempted to impugn by forging sections of his diaries to depict him a notorious homosexual, had been long-standing, taking its impetus from Yeats's rage at discovering the forgeries. O'Connor had reviewed Alfred Noyes's book on Casement for *The New York Times Book Review* on November 17, 1957, under the title "At the Heart of the Martyr's Myth, a Haunting Mystery," and continued to protest in print against British treachery.

Nineteen fifty-eight saw "Music When Soft Voices Die," "A Great Man," "Sue," "Achilles' Heel," and "Child, I Know You're Going to Miss Me" in *The New Yorker;* they rejected "Androcles and the Army" (*Atlantic Monthly*) and "Lady Brenda" (*Harper's Bazaar*).

FRANK O'CONNOR TO WILLIAM MAXWELL,
MARCH 1958:

160 Columbia Heights
Brooklyn, 1.

Sunday

Dear Bill,

This was intended to be two, but at the last moment I decided to give the second story another chance. I'll have a go at it tomorrow.

I'm keeping the week free but for Tuesday afternoon at 3 when we go to see a half-hour film of 'Oedipus Complex' and then from there, if you feel like joining us, we should be free about 7. The address is 5. East 57th Street 5th Floor.

Blessings,
MICHAEL

FRANK O'CONNOR TO WILLIAM MAXWELL,
MARCH 23, 1958:

160 Columbia Heights,
Brooklyn, 1. N.Y.

March 23rd 1958

Dear Bill,

I keep my promises but 'in my fashion.' Two new ones instead of one old one.* I'm not abandoning that but clinging to it and praying for light.

Ever,
MICHAEL

———

* Possibly "Sue" and "Achilles' Heel."

WILLIAM MAXWELL TO FRANK O'CONNOR,
BEFORE APRIL 6, 1958:

Dear Michael:
I suspect you of being in Annapolis, since your phone rings and rings, and this is to tell you that all three stories went through, as the office expression is, and Mr. Shawn feels also that "Mass Island" is one of the finest you have ever written. What about three more?
Happy Easter to you both,

BILL

WILLIAM MAXWELL TO FRANK O'CONNOR,
APRIL 17, 1958:

Michael—
For you to read.* Don't rewrite them, if you love me.

B.

———

* Proofs of "A Great Man" and "The Mass Island."

WILLIAM MAXWELL AND ROGER ANGELL (interoffice memos to each other, sent on to Frank O'Connor on April 17, 1958):

Angell from Maxwell
A GREAT MAN — Frank O'Connor

For this. Would probably help to say whether the young Dr. married eventually, as I assume he did, and also I would like it if author added some more particular description of the heroine, who is now merely small and pretty. Seems a valid story, of a kind that only he can do.

Maxwell from Angell:*

Well, I like the main body of this story very well, and I'm for the piece. But I must admit to having been terribly confused at various points. I didn't realize until the end that all this being *told* to the "I" by a Dr. O'Malley, mostly because this isn't in quotes and because the second line of the story is sloppily written & confusing. I never did get straight who "Mick Mackey's Paddy" was, and how he happened to come back to take over the hospital. The "Michael John" in the middle of page 9 also stopped me cold. I guess that's the name of the person to whom O'Malley is talking, but it never appears before that and we don't know who he is. Nor do we know until the last para. that he *also* is a doctor. I find all this most confusing, particularly the business of two separate doctors reminiscing in the first-person in the same story. There is further indirection in the manner in which we learn (or I *guess* we learn it) that Margaret has left the small town and become the matron of a London hospital. And just to add a small complaint to all these larger ones, I had a hard time on page 2 figuring out that MacCarthy was also a doctor. I hope you and O'Connor can fix all this up, because I do like the story, if not the way it's told.

———

* Roger Angell recalled "[O'Connor's] pink Fenian face and his tweedy, smoky aura of energy and genius. I'm embarrassed to say that the only sample [of his talk] that comes back in memory was a passing, half-sighed comment that he dropped into a conversation about Yeats: 'Ah, yes, Yeats—he was a fearful masturbator.' " Of this letter, Angell wrote, ". . . Bill Maxwell's comments are followed, rather typically, by a longer, inferior comment of my own."

FRANK O'CONNOR TO WILLIAM MAXWELL,
AFTER APRIL 17, 1958:

160 Columbia Heights,
Brooklyn, 1. N.Y.

Dear Bill,
You see I do keep my promises, and I got a bang from the first part which assures me that this at least is right.* I owe this to you and to Roger Angell, and I'd be grateful if you passed on my thanks to him for his queries and suggestions.
You, as usual, I take for granted.

MICHAEL

_____

* "A Great Man."

FRANK O'CONNOR TO WILLIAM MAXWELL,
APRIL 22, 1958:

160 Columbia Heights,
Brooklyn, 1. N.Y.

April 22nd 1958

My Dear Bill,
The enclosed is excellent.* It merely makes me a little self-conscious about my persistence in the matter, and considerably more grateful to Mr. Shawn for the handsome way in which he has deferred to my weakness. Would you please give him my thanks and a promise not to be a nuisance again for another twelve years.

Yours ever,
MICHAEL

_____

* "The enclosed" was a letter, published under the heading of "Dept. of Correction and Amplification" on May 17, giving O'Connor's response to brief uncredited reviews of René MacColl's *Roger Casement: A New Judgment* and Alfred Noyes's *The Accusing Ghost of Roger Casement.* MacColl believed, as did the British government, that Casement was a traitor and homosexual. Noyes, like O'Connor, disagreed, and stated that the "Casement diaries" were British forgeries to discredit Casement so that he could be executed without public outcry.

FRANK O'CONNOR TO WILLIAM MAXWELL, SPRING 1958:

160 Columbia Heights
Brooklyn, 1. N.Y.

Dear Bill,
Right at last, I think, or will until tomorrow.* Meanwhile I'd better shoot it out while I still have the courage.

Ever,
MICHAEL

_____

* "I Know Where I'm Going."

WILLIAM MAXWELL TO DON CONGDON,
APRIL 28, 1958:

April 28, 1958
Dear Don:
Another check for the account of Frank O'Connor. I hope from now on he will write in fives instead of threes, since it works just as well from his point of view and better from ours. Or he could move up and do it in sevens.

My best to you,
BILL MAXWELL

WILLIAM MAXWELL TO FRANK O'CONNOR,
MAY 29, 1958:

May 29, 1958

Dear Michael:

I thought it might help you to have a set of galleys [of "Achilles' Heel"] with some of the questions that occurred to Shawn and the proofreader, by way of indicating what isn't clear to an American reader. And to add to Harriet's questions; though she, by this time, is more than half Irish, and I expect knows more about the way things are there than many people whose breakfast cream has been soured by the fairies.

Love to you both,
BILL

HARRIET O'CONNOR TO WILLIAM MAXWELL,
JUNE 6, 1958:

c/o Rich
Ferry Point Farm
Annapolis, Maryland

June 6, 1958

Dear Bill,

I suspect it is completely impossible to give sensible answers to all those questions on ACHILLES HEEL — so how about a general sketch of the situation with the hope that *that* will answer some of the questions?

First: the Bishop lives in a town on the Border between Eire (independent country) and Northern Ireland (part of Great Britain). There is as much a border as the one between Holland and Belgium for example; there are Customs barriers at both sides, and naturally, perpetual smuggling in both directions.

Second: Although Michael was thinking of the period after World War II, there are always certain things in short supply in both countries which will be smuggled. The North usually has plenty of industrial products and the South plenty of agricultural ones. Therefore, the South would be sending butter, eggs, ham and whiskey to the North and the North would be sending back petrol, tea and sugar. What Nellie was doing was to send things to the place where they were scarce. For example, she bought whiskey freely and cheaply in Eire and sent it to her pub in Northern Ireland where she could sell it at an exorbitant price. Then she bought tea cheaply in Northern Ireland and sent it to Eire where again she could get an exorbitant price for it. She was just running a two way black market.

Obviously the shopkeepers from whom she bought the things were in on what she was doing—but they were covered (as was she) by saying that the things were 'for the Palace'. And they could plead a natural reluctance to question anything the Bishop did—though it would be obvious to them that he couldn't possibly drink so much whiskey or eat so much butter.

Third: The Revenue Commissioners (Customs Officers would they be here?) in Northern Ireland and in Eire would work together—each trying to find out how so much goods, on which no duty had been paid, was getting from one country to the other. I think this is the point Miss Gould is missing—that this is a *two-way* smuggling operation.*

Miss Gould has a technical point in (B). However, remember that this is a small town in which everybody knows everybody else's business and they would all know that the Bishop wouldn't have enough money to buy all the stuff that was going into the Palace and that he couldn't use it in a hundred years. Therefore, it could pretty generally be concluded that the stuff was Nellie's and that she was selling it somewhere. However, Michael says he could change the word here from 'contraband' to something like 'her stores.'

In answer to Miss Gould's E, the Revenue couldn't come in and take the things out *until* Nellie admitted that they were, in fact, not the Bishop's, but hers and that she had been smuggling them into and out of the North. Obviously she could have balked the Revenue People by pleading that the stuff was her own personal possession, but this would have resulted in a case against her. Her only hope of avoiding prosecution was to cooperate with the Revenue people and to turn the stores over to them.

About (C) identity of the keg: kegs are marked with a name or trade mark burned in, but once the whiskey is transferred from keg to bottle it is not identifiable since bottles are used over and over again (not as in this country) and are plain without stamping of any kind.

Mr. Shawn's questions are mostly answered above—except for 4 about the 'licensed premises'. You have to have a license to run a Pub and Nellie of course had one—running the pub was perfectly legal, it was only the procurement of the stuff sold there that was illegal.

This is all very long winded and probably clears up nothing— but you know me—I always talk too much. Anyhow, we thought it best to send you this, and then if you have any questions about it, maybe you'll give us a call the first part of the week?

We're both fine—I'm finer than Michael is—Bless him I think he longs to escape to that green land and leave us all behind. But I won't let him.

Please tell Emmy that I'm getting great pleasure and comfort from her clothes—Please God we'll see you both again before too long.

Love from both of us,
MRS. FRANK O'CONNOR

---

* "Miss Gould" is Eleanor Gould Packard, who continues as a copy editor at *The New Yorker.*

WILLIAM MAXWELL TO HARRIET O'CONNOR,
JUNE 12, 1958:

Dear Harriet,

As you will see I snatched some paragraphs from your letter, and inserted them, with the intention that if Himself sees a sixth thumb or any other sort of awkwardness obtruding from the flow of story he will amend it; the problem, as I am sure you will agree, is to make him cast his eyes on it at all. Yes, yes, fine, I hear him saying, with his mind getting just comfortable in the root of an old tree growing up by the bank of a stream that flows God knows where. And with the intention that anything horrible can always be fixed the next time he rewrites the story. Well, that's the way he is. I don't know for sure that Mr. Shawn will understand the smuggling now, but I think he ought to, and from there it is only a step to raising my voice and risking my job and all that. I think it is pretty clear, and that's clear enough. If he has any ideas at the last minute, it will give me an excuse which I am sadly lacking for telephoning to you.

I'm glad you have him with you. The making of babies is something that requires two.* No double-entendre meant. If you smile, it's not my fault, but the fault of Kate and Brookie, who have kept us up between eleven and three or four for three nights running. First Brookie woke up and refused to go back to sleep, so Emmy went to bed in her room, with the window closed, in the kind of general discomfort she contrives for herself when I am not around, out of a belief that comfort isn't everything, and I couldn't get back to sleep because I never can when she is removed from beside me, and so thought about the New Yorker all night (TOO MUCH EDITING GOES ON HERE) and what should happen the following night but four violent thunderstorms in succession. At the end of the first one Brookie woke up, and stayed awake, and at the beginning of the fourth Kate woke up crying, because Lenny Lewisohn had that very day informed her that lightning comes right into the house and kills you. So I held her in my arms and tried to get her to enjoy the vegetable garden by lightning light, and her mother, more sensible, sent me to the bed in Brookie's room, where I lay awake listening to Brookie's night thoughts and thought about the New Yorker, while Emmy and Kate discussed electricity, with their noses an inch apart, and the heavens fell. The next morning as I was getting dressed, E said "Where *does* electricity come from?" And I said "Peekskill", which wasn't of course what she meant, though it was God's truth.

And that day at noon her father and brother came for lunch, and supper, and at ten o'clock, having taken them to the station, we went to bed, and Kate had diarrhea, which required a hot water bottle, singing, changing of diapers, waking up of Brookie, rocking, changing of babies, changing of beds, changing of bedrooms, singing of Green Grow the Rushes Oh and Savez Vous Plantez des Choux and The More it Snows, the More it Goes On Snowing, more changing of beds, more changing of diapers, more reflections on the nature of love as it appears in the midst of night life. I wouldn't have missed any of it, but it's tonight I am thinking of.

My love to you both,
BILL

———

* Harriet was then pregnant with Hallie-Óg ("Óg" being Irish for "young" or "small"), who was born on June 25.

WILLIAM MAXWELL TO THE O'CONNORS,
JULY 21, 1958 (postcard from Neskowin, Oregon):

Dear M and Dear H and Miss H,

It may be that green in Ireland, but it is just green green, and nice farms and nice people and nice weather and my nice vacation. Emmy has been putting out food for 15–18 for 5 days but now we are just our 6 selves. I hope herself is thriving, and that herself's

Ma is able to go up and downstairs. The Anthology* delights me and Tolstoi did not, so there you are—

Love from us both,

B.

———

* O'Connor's *Modern Irish Short Stories.*

FRANK O'CONNOR TO WILLIAM MAXWELL, AUGUST 1958:

236 Prince George St.
Annapolis

Dear Bill,

Welcome home! I wish you could say as much to me! At the moment Washington is my furthest, wildest dream. I shall be glad when this summer is over.

Hallie Óg is well. The other evening the following conversation took place between myself and an infant of three or four on a scooter.

In.   Hi!
Me   Hi!
In.   Hi. You're funny.
Me   What's funny about me?
In.   You're rolling a baby.
Me   Why shouldn't I roll a baby?
In.   *Men* don't roll babies.
Me   They do where I come from.
In.   Where's that?
Me   Ireland.
In.   They don't roll them on *sidewalks!*
Me   In Ireland they do.
In.   What's your name?*

(84)

The book has now broken down into complete jigsaw, all the little fragments charming but none seeming to fit another.[†] Ah me! It's the heat. It's Hallie's family. It's my family. I want the two Hallies to myself for at least a week, preferably on an Atlantic liner. I want to attend an International Writers' Conference in Naples in October and talk nothing but delicious shop for a week!

Love to Emmy,

MICHAEL

———

* Liadain commented, "He was not a typical Irish father. Howard Gossage told me that my father shamed the men of Dublin by being seen pushing a baby carriage 'right down the middle of Dublin.' "
[†] Then untitled, "the book" became *An Only Child.*

FRANK O'CONNOR TO WILLIAM MAXWELL,
AUGUST 1958:

236 Prince George Street
Annapolis, Md.
Colonial 8 - 2695

Dear Bill,

If this book ever gets done it'll be all your fault. I started on this draft after talking to you, and I've done four days hard labour.* If my spirit doesn't break under the chapter that faces me you'll get more.

Meanwhile, what about that novel? If it's too good it'll make me jealous and if it isn't it'll make me feel complacent, and one way is as good as another to encourage a discontented dilitairy sort of literary man.[†]

The pictures are for Emmy. Even if you don't like the Book, she'll be interested in the pictures.

We're going up somewhere about the 27th, and whether you want us or not, are coming out to see you.

> Love,
> MICHAEL

————

* O'Connor was working on "Child, I Know You're Going to Miss Me."
† "The novel" became *The Château.*

WILLIAM MAXWELL TO FRANK O'CONNOR, AUGUST 1958:

Dear Michael:

I don't know what's wrong with all this, but I don't know what to do (except to the attic with it).* Don't feel obliged to plow through it before you come, or read any after a drowsy numbness steals over you, and you wonder what Harriet and the baby are doing.

> My love to you both,
> B

————

* A section of *The Château* in an early version.

FRANK O'CONNOR TO WILLIAM MAXWELL, AUGUST 1958:

236 Prince George Street,
Annapolis

My Dear Bill,

I'd have written you before about the novel but I haven't known whether I was on my head or my heels. I normally read very fast; I found myself reading very slowly: I normally know where I am after a few chapters: I changed my mind half a dozen times in reading this: I took notes but they'd only make you laugh. And I STILL don't know where I am. The *clou* is missing, and a different *clou* means a different judgement. As Hallie says, there's no hope but the pair of us to be together for an evening over a bottle and gradually break down and sob in one another's arms.

My main trouble—caused perhaps by the fact that the first chapters have been rewritten with loving care—is that I got so fascinated by Roger and his wife that I saw inescapably one perfect novel, and when Mme. Viennot and the others turned up and tended to take the stage I shrugged them off impatiently. I *lived* with that pair for two days—my days, not novelist's days—and felt that no novelist before you had ever realised that the itinerary of an American couple in France was a novel in itself. Then I realised that this wasn't what you intended at all, and started to get involved in the Viennot circle; with terrible air pockets in which I collapsed into my original novel, which was obviously so much better but which you perversely refused to follow. Then the second novel began to possess me, and I began to wonder why on earth you didn't begin with Mme. Viennot. And this isn't right either, because you have a form in your head which derives from material that is still in your head, and till I know exactly what that is I won't know whether you've really brought it off or not. Neither will anybody else—you're like Hamlet, following the ghost, and as Horatio I can only stand back and wonder. The novel you see isn't either of the novels I see: the proof of that is that the really great scenes move from one part of the stage to the other—the mirror scene which first sold me on the Viennots, and the wonderful chapter when Roger pays his bill and they go off in a cloud of misunderstanding. For me, this is the high point of the book: the part where I really found myself with tears in my eyes and cursed myself for my own utter inadequacy as a writer—and yet *as a writer* I haven't the faintest idea how the effect was arrived at and I can only attribute it to those last chapters which you have written in your head and which I can't even begin to visualise.

So you'll have to meet me over a bottle and tell me, and then

I'll really know whether the moving in and out of the Mitchells' heads is—as I thought it in the first chapter when you move suddenly into the Broughton ménage—a failure of artistic tact, or, as I now suspect, a different form of composition to which I don't have the key. Because in that very chapter in which Roger pays the bill you deliberately create an effect and then—apparently with equal deliberation—destroy it, but what moves me is the combination of the two. In either of the ways in which I read the novel, Roger and the reader should be left with their suspicions, but we are not, and mysteriously it's dead right.

Anyhow, as you probably know, it's far ahead of any of your novels which I have read, and leaves me very humble as well as very stupid. Of one thing I am sure, if you finish it at all, it'll be a masterpiece.

And I *still* want to argue with you about it.

Love to Emmy,
MICHAEL

WILLIAM MAXWELL TO HARRIET O'CONNOR,
AUGUST 1958:

Dear H:

I was so upset by Michael's manuscript that I failed to tell you how intently we stood looking down at the snapshots of herself last night. Beautiful, the both of you. And the other daughter like a transposed chord in music, standing halfway between those older people in the story I had just been reading and the new one in your lap.* You realize, don't you, that these snapshots are going to cause me sooner or later to call the plumber and the carpenter and the electrician and start getting estimates. If it could only be twins so that nobody is left out, as somebody always is when there are three. Well, leg over leg and the dog gets to Dover.

Love,
B.

———

* The snapshots were of Hallie-Óg's christening in Annapolis and included "the other daughter," Liadain. The manuscript was "Child, I Know You're Going to Miss Me," which became the opening chapters of *An Only Child,* depicting the poverty of O'Connor's childhood, the agony of his mother's early life, and the effect his father's drinking had on the family.

WILLIAM MAXWELL TO FRANK O'CONNOR, AUGUST 1958:

Dear Michael:

My god what a long silence. You might as well be in California. Here it steams and stews, just the sort of weather to make you housebound. Angell and Henderson are both away, and so I have to be an editor instead of whatever it is I am ordinarily.* My desk is inundated with flash-floods of manuscript all day, and at night, last night, going home from the station, I drove through the most personal hail storm. Why me, I kept thinking as they bounced off the hood and the windshield. A great deal of water has gone over the Lewisohns' dam in the last week.† I was well into "The Way of All Flesh" and then got sidetracked by the claims (usually ignored) of family life. I mean I tried to be helpful. I can't say I was, really. In a cloudburst, running across the lawn to turn the car lights out, I slipped on the wet grass and landed on the back of my head. It could have resulted in a concussion, but it didn't. Only a stiff neck. And last night, after a nice comfortable Rum Collins, Emmy got up and went into the other part of the house to put the children to bed and I picked up the galleys of Muriel Spark's new novel.‡ After a while Brookie came and said could we talk, and so she sat on my lap and looked at a book that did not (being nursery rhymes) interest me as much as Muriel Spark had, so I waited and then suggested that—no, first, I said "Is Mommy reading to Kate?" and Brookie said she would go see. In a minute she came back and reported that they were talking. So pretty soon I suggested that Brookie take the nice book to bed with her and picked up Muriel Spark and read and pretty soon it occurred to me that I had read quite a long time. So I stopped and listened. Murmur, murmur, murmur. Still talking. So I read fifteen minutes longer and then got up and looked at the pork chops, and decided to turn them, and shortly afterward Emmy came out and began to set the table for supper. As I went down the hall Kate called to me to come and kiss her goodnight, and when I sat down on the bed she said "Mommy and I have been having a nice talk about babies." What Emmy said, later, was "She didn't leave a stone unturned." At breakfast Kate asked why I never sat on her side of the table so I picked up my egg and moved there. Gratefully. I guess, like Margaret Fuller, she has accepted the universe.

Love,

W

---

* Roger Angell and Robert Henderson, fellow fiction editors and fellow writers.
† The Lewisohns, next-door neighbors of the Maxwells in Yorktown Heights, actually had a dam, since a brook ran through their property.
‡ *Memento Mori.*

WILLIAM MAXWELL TO FRANK O'CONNOR,
SEPTEMBER 1958:*

You will think I have lost my mind, but I saw a way (I think) to do the novel your way—i.e., through the eyes of the Americans, and still explain what they were not in the position to know. I may try it, if it proves faithful to me. It is largely a matter of scissors and paste, in any case. But I keep feeling, on the last time through it, the old way, that the novelistic values aren't there, that it is only scene after scene after scene. And I do have a superstitious feeling that, being the simple son of your mother, you now and then see things correctly.

I hope you are aware that it isn't very long before you will be coming home. Love to those ladies,

BILL

---

* The first page of this letter is missing.

WILLIAM MAXWELL TO FRANK O'CONNOR,
SEPTEMBER 3, 1958:

Date: 9/3/58   Time: 4:18
For: Michael
From: Bill

Message: What about the galleys of Achilles' Heel? I started in,
and am now at page 60, and it seemed to be working.* That is, I
felt the material strengthening as the approach to it became consistently straightforward. Will you call me when you arrive? Love
to H.

                                                           B.

---

* Maxwell's revision of *The Château*.

FRANK O'CONNOR TO ALFRED A. KNOPF,
SEPTEMBER 21, 1958:

Practically on board the 'Mauretania.'

and at 52 Oak House,
Mespil Flats,
Sussex Road, Dublin.

                                        21st September 1958
Dear Alfred,
    Bill Maxwell brought the enclosed as a present for you, feeling
that as though you know of his book from me, you should know of

my book from him. We propose that you should publish us both more or less on the same day.

I also told him that if the business men on both sides didn't behave themselves I would have you appointed as his literary agent, and he agreed that you would show all of them something. Don't let them force us to such desperate expedients. We're all in literature because we like it.

All good wishes to Blanche.

Yours sincerely,
FRANK O'CONNOR

WILLIAM MAXWELL TO FRANK O'CONNOR, OCTOBER 1958:

Dear Michael,

Well, it doesn't work with the Americans alone. I got up to the very last part and it just trailed off. It wasn't a novel. All it proved was that I had been to Europe. It has to be counterpoint. So after a rigid, sleepless night I started in this morning to deal with—dispose of, is what I mean—the false clues, of which there are hundreds, and I think I have something. ("Achilles' Heel" going to press tomorrow; they just put the galleys on my desk.) With every novel you have to divest yourself of the no longer useful or appropriate machinery of the previous ones, and the psychological probing of the Americans serves no purpose, probably, since they aren't going to change as a result of their experiences in France; at least, not on that level. I read and reread your letter, and curse you for not sending me those notes, because a word will suddenly leap out at me, mean something tangential, be enormously helpful.

Meanwhile, I sent Don a check for $2,030.73 yesterday—Cost of Living Adjustment payment for the last quarter. Try not to let it make you despondent. It's only money, and it doesn't mean a thing.* And I wait patiently for that period to end during which the people travellers leave behind them sit in the waiting room in limbo until suddenly their reality is restored to them, at which moment you will sit you down and write me a letter, I trust. Love to the three of you,

B.

———

* Harriet commented to me, "Bill thought that Michael thought being paid for doing something that you love, writing stories, was somehow wrong, and if you got too much money for it maybe you weren't a very good writer. So he always made a joke about it. Michael was almost superstitious about money, having been so poor for so long, and Bill knew that, so this is purely ironic."

WILLIAM MAXWELL TO FRANK AND HARRIET O'CONNOR, OCTOBER 15, 1958:

Dear Michael and Harriet,

I see I'll have to go after you, through the fog and the rain. First of all, I have to report that there may be a house for you to rent next fall on the Baptist Church Road. It is not a sure thing, I am fishing for it. Some people up the road with a good deal of money decided to make a guest cottage out of a barn. But being perfectionists, they have sunk more money into it than they intended (with perfectly wonderful results, aesthetically speaking—it is so good I would be ready to take it for you sight unseen (by you); it's on a hilltop, with a field on one side and the woods on the other, and has three bedrooms and a downstairs room where himself would be able to work in peace—) and may have to rent it, but they wanted to use it first, next summer, for the purpose it was planned. It turns out that the husband of the family is addicted to the stories of a fellow named O'Connor. I know you would rather he were addicted to Friday Night poker games but everything has a price attached to it in this world, and the price of this cottage might be an admiring landlord. Anyway, I will keep my eye on the cork, and report any bobbing.

The more I thought about the material I have, about your education, Michael, the more I felt the need of a concluding scene of some vividness, which I would have extracted from your inside coat pocket when you were here if you hadn't been involved in too much else for vaudeville magic. But what I would like now, please, is that scene of your appearance on the platform, when you delivered a speech in Gaelic and were then confronted with the question period. Will you give it the works, and then mail it to me? You were going to do it anyway, you said, so I don't feel I am pushing you. Just asking for one more thing, as you are about to settle in your chair in peace.

I got them off to Switzerland yesterday, and realized, with a sense of shock, that I could—though I probably won't quite—finish it in one more chapter, and that it is no more a novel than my hat is.* But if I get them on the boat train, I can then go back and see what's what, knowing from page one the material that lies ahead. It isn't that nothing happens, so much as that I can't decide how much or how little to reveal, and that the less I tell the more it seems like, but will the reader stand for it? I tried having the French people reveal most of the things I had told as narrator, and you know, it was so un-French. Well, we'll see. Koshland called yesterday to say that Alfred wondered if I knew how much more of your autobiography there was than the galleys he has seen, and I said it was, what he had was a third, roughly, somewhere between a third and a fourth of the book. I take it this was for drawing up a contract. Finally we got everything signed, the ship is safely harbored, and thank God you were around, because some real silliness might have resulted from the confusion.†

Brookie is two today, and had her birthday party yesterday, because I was home. It was quite calm, as children's parties go. She astonished her mother by remarking in a sad voice on her way through the kitchen, a week or so ago, "I don't have any friends." This is so far from the truth that I wonder if she could have meant "I *wish* I didn't have any friends," since somebody is always hugging, kissing, squeezing, showing signs of a barely suppressed desire to EAT her up with love.

The fall colors are at their height, the garden is all but finished, the weather is lovely. Summer one day, winter the next. All
the winter constellations back from their summer vacation. Let
me know how it is with you. It seems many years.

Love,

BILL

------

* The characters Maxwell "got off to Switzerland" were his youthful American
travellers, eventually named Harold and Barbara Rhodes.
† William A. Koshland is now Chairman Emeritus of Alfred A. Knopf, Inc. In
1958, he was Assistant Treasurer and Secretary.

FRANK O'CONNOR TO WILLIAM MAXWELL,
LATE OCTOBER 1958:

52 Oak House,
Sussex Road,
Dublin

Dearest Man,
    As Mother used to say whenever she got mad with someone:
'That you may be grey!' Can't I even leave you for a couple of
months without your getting some dotty notions into your head?
Of course, it's not a novel! Novels were written exclusively by Jane
Austen and Turgenev, and the secret died with them, but the sub-
stitutes have a lot to be said for them. I dread your counterpointing, not because I think you can't do it, but because I fear you
won't let well enough alone. I wish, instead of re-writing immediately you felt dissatisfied, you had put it away for a few weeks,
and re-read it some evening you were feeling really brilliant. You
would then see what I saw; that the virtue of the novel was in its
apparent thinness and ingenuousness. It has a sort of Yankee quality that I sometimes get from a Frost poem of somebody with a

slightly idiotic smile saying 'Of course, I'm not a real writer, and I don't understand how to do this sort of thing as Faulkner and Hemingway do, but I hope you won't find it too bad' until he's lured the reader into saying 'No, of course he's not as good as Faulkner, but it's not bad at all, and except for the fact that it ISN'T a novel, as he admits himself, you'd really say it was quite good. Personally, I'm almost inclined to say that in its own rather simple-minded way, it's a tour-de-force. *Almost* a masterpiece, in fact; or am I exaggerating?' I may, of course, be talking through my hat, but what occurs to me is that the thing I fear in the counterpointing is that you'll put out your full strength, without realizing that when you aren't putting out your full strength you are quite strong enough for the purposes of fiction. I know it's a case of pot and kettle, but, as an artist, you can afford to be rather less exacting with yourself. With that book, I should feel like using the counterpoint for four or five stories, just leaving the essentials for the two Americans to digest.

On the other hand, I'm the one to talk. Harriet asks if I can't leave you for a couple of months without getting myself into a state. Ireland seems very strange, and I realise now that it may be months before I begin to feel myself into it. If I could draw I would do you and Emmy a picture of the two of us this afternoon with two copies of the New Yorker that arrived with your letter, sitting at either side of the table while Hallie Óg kicked up both legs to the ceiling and crowed in vain for attention. Living in Dublin is different from holidaying in Dublin and living here is something I haven't done for ten years and don't know if I can ever do happily again. It's not a question of the temporary forgetfulness of friends that comes of travel and new scenery; it's the remembering them so clearly that they blot out the scene for hours at a time. (And you, to make things worse, have a review in the paper!)*

I know exactly what's wrong with the three chapters of the autobiography you have, and in one day in Brooklyn I'd get it right. Here, it'll probably take me a couple of weeks. On my way from the liner, I went up to the little cabin in Blarney Lane which I described in the first part and found a demolition order nailed above the door. I went in and talked to the old woman who lives there. She was very gloomy, leaving the little place she'd been in thirty years, and afraid they wouldn't give her an alternative place. 'Oh, sir,' she moaned, 'I can't sleep at night with my mind.' Everyone's trouble is his own. On the liner as we waited to go aboard the tender one small girl, not much older than Kate turned her face to the wall and howled like a banshee without ceasing. In my usual silly way I tried to comfort her but she only howled louder. Then Hallie went to her grandmother and asked what was wrong. Grandma said 'She wants to go back to Chicago.' Hallie is beginning to bear a strong resemblance to the child. She has a song to a mournful air that runs 'Oh, please take me back to Baptist Church Road.' Our block of flats is largely occupied by Americans who crowd together like cattle in a gale. The final touch is that, like Mother, she has found a young man she says is like you, though, apart from the fact that he's a good writer, I can see no resemblance.

Her only concession is that she permits me to tell Emmy that the kids are more charming even than she remembers them. A group of little boys plays mud pies outside our window, and micturate the liquid. Yesterday, they ran out of liquid so they called on a little girl who was passing and who cheerfully provided the necessary quantity.

We shall settle down. I had forgotten how beautiful the city was, and I have been storing up bits of it to show you when you come. Until after Christmas is about as long as we can wait to see you. If you don't come then I shall have to dig up a teaching engagement in South Carolina.

You don't, I fancy, need those proofs of the autobiography. I feel I shall never be able to face them till the second part is right. 'Oh, God! God! God!' as the little hen says. 'There are going to be no more eggs!'†

Love to Emmy and the family,
MICHAEL

———

* Maxwell reviewed Virginia Woolf's *Granite and Rainbow* in the October 11 issue.

† In *My Father's Son,* O'Connor remembered Æ wanting to know "how the writing was going": "Usually it was going badly. In those days I wrote in brief excited fits that might be followed by months of idleness and depression, or—what was worse—of fruitless and exhausting labour on some subject I was not mature enough to tackle. . . . Once I must really have exasperated him, for he said: 'You know, you remind me of an old hen who has just laid an egg and is going round complaining. Did you ever hear a hen that has laid an egg? She says, "Oh God! God! God! God! There are going to be no more eggs!" That's what she says, you know.' "

WILLIAM MAXWELL TO FRANK O'CONNOR,
NOVEMBER 6, 1958:

Dear Michael,

Ah, my goodness, what a comforting letter. I really thought you had forgotten us. Ideally, we ought to have these galleys back by the 20th of November, since it is running in the issue of December 6th.* I have made a few changes, to satisfy Mr. Shawn's idea of clarity, but anything that I thought you would care about, I have had them put in pencil, on these galleys. Only a few need any comment:

Galley 2, note one: There is a slight hiatus here, which it didn't occur to me to do anything about, since I know how I feel about Mozart and how you feel, but to a more literal way of thinking, to say that a person has gaiety on galley one isn't enough by way of preparation for referring to them on galley two as "these men and women of Mozartean temperaments." In short, Shawn simply didn't follow you or understand the point you were making. I think a couple of sentences would bring the whole thing out, and make it better than it now is. Would you look at it carefully?

Note 2 and note 3: I assumed from the evidence that O'Brien

and Redmond were Irish politicians, but when Shawn asked who they were and I looked them up in the Century Encyclopedia of Names, I was embarrassed by the richness of information. What I have written in in pencil may not at all be the most significant things that one could say by way of identifying them, so would you fix it so that it is satisfactory, and reads like what you would have answered if somebody asked you who they were. Also, though it isn't important, it might be interesting to explain why the Redmondites were known as Molly Maguires, unless of course it is more complicated to tell than it is interesting to read about.

Note 4: It is possible to interpret differently the facts here, and I really don't know whether your father switched from the O'Brien band to the Redmond band and back again or what. Could you clear this up, if the pencilled insertions don't make it clear?

Note 5: This immigrant/emigrant business depends on where they are supposed to pine, by the people at home in Ireland or by Americans, and I don't know and you do, fortunately.

I wish we could go over these in the back yard, under the apple trees, because I know how hard it is for you to concentrate on something you aren't working on at the moment. As for that, where is my scene? The ending of my piece on your self-education? If it weren't for the fact that I know it is necessary for you to touch Irish ground every so often, I would never have let you go beyond my reach. It isn't, though, merely the editorial vanity; it's just that I know you need me, at this point, as I know I need you.

I am hard at work on my book, in the spirit of a sleepwalker. It comes out a little clearer, and not clear enough, but since I am again doing what I have done so many times without knowing why, I say There must be a reason, and go on, hoping for it to be revealed. If not, it will run down, and I will go back to the other way.

How I loved those children making mud pies. A smooch for Harriet,

B

_____

* "Child, I Know You're Going to Miss Me." The results of Maxwell's requests for clarification are visible in the early pages of *An Only Child*. For instance, O'Connor now described William O'Brien and John Redmond, warring leaders after Parnell's fall, as "two rival Irish politicians with little to distinguish them except their personalities—flamboyant in O'Brien and frigid in Redmond."

FRANK AND HARRIET O'CONNOR TO WILLIAM MAXWELL,
NOVEMBER 12, 1958:

52 Oak House,
Sussex Road,
Dublin.

November 12th 1958.

My Dear Bill,
    Here are the proofs, and if they aren't much good they are at least not as bad as the proofs of the education chapters would have been if they had been under way. By the time you get them again—which should be within the next couple of weeks—they will, I hope, have some life in them.
    I have been instructed to say that if anything arrives from Ireland in the next month it is not to be opened before Christmas. Harriet is gloomy. It's partly a bad attack of colitis and anaemia, partly her inability to get anything done in this country under a fortnight, but principally, I suspect, that she can find no one to enthuse over Hallie Óg, owing to the fact that, as in China and India, babies are twelve a penny (though since the adoption act the price has gone up like everything else here) and that glorious baby can be paraded through all the principal streets without anyone's saying as much as 'What a pretty child!' This, you will agree, is hard on a mother of one.
    However, the doctor who diagnosed her case and came up with the same answers I've been giving her for years, is a great relief as he has a nice straightforward approach to medicine and be-

sides bears a strong resemblance to—guess who! Whatever about Harriet, Emmie should certainly feel in Dublin like a much-married woman.

Hallie Óg, on the other hand, adores Dublin. Her landscape which had been severely restricted to ~~grey~~ skies and clouds has now become filled with leaves, and when you put her in her perambulator she instantly begins to roll her head from side to side, looking for them. At her first sight of a fire she burst into floods of tears, but has now discovered that flames are as full of interest as leaves and smells.

I shall say no more about the novel till you have something to show me. I know that state all too well—Hamlet following the Ghost. My ingenious theory that Hamlet was really a novelist looking for a subject has never been taken with sufficient seriousness by the English faculties.

Love to all,
MICHAEL

P.S. [from Harriet] Himself having gone off to Belfast for the day, after making a lot of funereal jokes about being arrested at the Border (and consequently plunging me into a classic state of the jitters) I'll take the liberty of adding to this before I mail it. *Actually* we're surviving remarkably well, considering that this whole country is about the size and organization of a corrupt Maryland county. The only thing I really mind is the constant criticizing indulged in by the whole populace. Bad enough to tell me I ought to *enjoy* washing diapers, but when a man who can't put two sentences together tells Michael that this or that story of his 'wasn't really very successful,' I begin to fume! However, it *is* a beautiful city, and Himself *does* get his pint of Guinness every evening and think how we'll appreciate Baptist Church Rd. when we finally get back.

Please tell Emmy that Hallie-Óg wears her blue Persian coat every day and looks delectable. And give my love to Kate to whom I shall send a colored postcard shortly.

We both miss both of you—terribly!
XX

FRANK O'CONNOR TO WILLIAM MAXWELL,
NOVEMBER 14, 1958:

52 Oak House,
Sussex Road, Dublin.

Nov. 14, 1958

NEXT DAY

Bill,

The word 'jingle' is wrong. I ran up to Belfast on the train yesterday, and suddenly I saw a real jingle and realised that the correct word is still 'covered car', a vehicle known only in Cork.

I was going into the Enemy's territory and expected to be arrested at any minute, and suddenly too I almost wished they would arrest me and save me from the nightmare I was involved in.* I shall die of acute meticulosis contracted in the service of the New Yorker and ye won't even give me a pension.

My epitaph—

> Once I was light as a fawn
>> I called things whatever I pleased;
> But then I ran into Bill Shawn—
>> Now life and precision have ceased.

Ah, me!

MICHAEL

————

* O'Connor could have been arrested in Belfast because his ex-wife, Evelyn, had a warrant for his arrest for contempt of court as a result of their disagreements over the custody of his son Myles. He was thus reluctant to enter British territory, but went to Belfast for a BBC (Northern Ireland) broadcast of the story "Public Opinion" on November 13.

FRANK O'CONNOR TO WILLIAM MAXWELL,
NOVEMBER 26, 1958:

52 Oak House,
Sussex Road,
Dublin.

Dear Bill,

As I promised these chapters of the Book I send them, but
with no particular pride.* They are nearer what I want to do, but
they aren't what I want to do which is really intellectual slapstick.
This is where I long for the form of the story, so that I could project that kid as though he had absolutely no relation to myself,
and I could laugh my head off at him and give him an occasional
hard kick to show my genuine affection. It's a bad trade.

Harriet is still very unwell with this wretched colitis, which
she keeps on confusing with Dublin. Dublin has its drawbacks,
but the bellyache and nausea it produces are of a different kind.
But women do not distinguish. The Emmanuels were here last
week and Janine said 'You are not happy here. Michael is not really happy. So you say 'It is finished. We go.'† But I am not sure
that I don't cheer up at the numerous legends of Brendan Behan,
whose 'Quare Fellow' you should see. He is now a wealthy man. A
few weeks ago he entertained some friends of ours to dinner, produced four pounds of boiled mutton, took off his boots and put
them at either side of the mutton and shouted 'Beatrice, bring in
the f—— champagne.' Which his wife did. But his doctor is devoted to him. Eighteen months ago he had to put Behan, who suf-
fers from diabetes, in a ward with two old men dying with cancer,
and when the priest appeared Behan shouted 'Jesus, this f—— is
following me round' and ran out of the ward in his night shirt
screaming for the doctor—'Rory, Rory, the druids are after me!'
As a result the old men got back their nerve, are still alive and
Behan visits them regularly to promote some fresh blasphemy. I
think when you come I must introduce you. We shall give the

girls ear-plugs instead of corsages, and you and I will order the dinner.‡

Blessings,
MICHAEL

———

* "I Know Where I'm Going" and "The One Day of the Year."
† O'Connor had met the French poet Pierre Emmanuel at Harvard.
‡ Harriet told me, "Michael knew Brendan fairly well. I met him once. They were walking down by the canal, and Brendan, who was absolutely cheerfully inebriated and scatological, said, 'I've never met the wife,' and Michael said to himself, 'I don't know that I want to bring him up,' but he did, and it was extraordinary. From the time they got out of the elevator at our floor and I came to the door, Brendan never said another bad word. He had a cup of tea and met Hallie-Óg. Then Michael escorted him down to the front door, and he went back to his usual language! A *very* nice man."

WILLIAM MAXWELL TO FRANK O'CONNOR,
LATE 1958:

Dear Michael:
    Too bad. What a letter writer you are. Mme. de S. will have to take a back seat, when your correspondence complet is published in nine elegant feuilletons.* Love,

W.

———

* Madame de Sévigné, whose correspondence amounted to more than 1,500 letters.

WILLIAM MAXWELL TO FRANK O'CONNOR,
DECEMBER 1, 1958:

Dear Michael,

In the end, after a careful line-by-line study of the two manuscripts, I decided to dump them both on my colleagues.* My own
feeling is that the one you gave me before you sailed is slightly
more affecting, the newer slightly more polished writing, but that
there is substantially very little difference between them. I wish I
had persuaded you to blow at that scene at the end—that is to say,
dramatize it a little more—but that is all I wish. Except that Mr.
Shawn will say yes to it. That I wish with all my heart.

Don't be cross with me, will you, for sending more money to
Congdon? It's none of my doing, you know. The bookkeeping department comes up with these things. This time it is the renewal
of your first reading agreement, and the check that accompanies it
is for $2500. Next year, as Mr. Truax always begs me to tell every-
body, it may be an even hundred.†

I am now on page 380 of Hamlet's Conversations with the
Ghost, and not too much more time, but meanwhile there is
Christmas lying across my path, and I am never one to paint instead of going to my mother's funeral, alas, and all that it brings
with it in the way of justified interruption, but maybe the book
will write itself if I keep out of its way. I am insanely optimistic,
at the moment. I don't believe you can be sanely optimistic. It
isn't optimism then. And if you should ever be moved to build a
doll-house for Hallie-Óg, beware the sin of pride (this one is
copied from a 17th century one I saw in a book) and beware again
of the Mansard. The secret, whatever it is, apparently died with
the old boy. It's absolute hell, and keeping us both from sleeping
at night. While you are leading the proper life of a writer, I am
leading the life of a carpenter.

We both think Hallie-Óg is the most BEAUTIFUL baby we
ever saw. She puts both of ours to shame, and our memory is recent. I must say, you take very good pictures. It is colder than the
hinges of hell on the Baptist Church Road, and I didn't quite get

the vegetable garden plowed up or the burlap screens up between the north wind and the rose bushes before the ground froze and I myself came down with a bloody awful cold, the aftermath of too exquisite a Thanksgiving. I am almost myself, and never was so bad off that I couldn't crawl to the typewriter. Yesterday when Emmy came home from the supermarket, Brookie refused to get out of the car and Emmy said impatiently "Brookie, what are you waiting for?" and was put to shame by the answer: "I am waiting for Christmas." Kate's talk is about nothing but giants, witches, and fairies, and often puts me in mind of Yeats. Last night she asked for an Andersen story, which had a particularly morbid beginning—the death of the dear father, which I read rapidly and skipping, hoping that nothing would sink in, but a page or two farther on she interrupted me to say that she hoped I wouldn't die until she got married. I assured her I wouldn't. She wanted to know why I wouldn't and I gave her various good reasons. In the end, she said quite calmly, "In any case, it will be all right if Mommy doesn't die too." She doesn't fancy being an orphan, it seems. But what an incorruptible sense of her own best interests!

I hope Harriet's colitis is better. I used to have it mildly, and remember it as a kind of vicious circle. I mean it's its own cause, but gradually goes away. High strung people have to pay for it, is what it amounts to. Give her a kiss for me, and my profound congratulations on having produced a perfect female creature.

Emmy sends love to you both, with mine,

BILL

———

* Versions of "Go Where Glory Waits Thee."
† R. Hawley Truax, Vice-President of The New Yorker Magazine, Inc., who signed first-reading agreements.

WILLIAM MAXWELL TO FRANK O'CONNOR,
DECEMBER 11, 1958:

December 11, 1958

Dear Michael,

Here is the final proof of THE MASS ISLAND, which we are planning to run on the 10th of January. That means that we ought to have it back by December 23rd, if you can possibly manage it.

Where you are concerned I seem to have the gift of tongues and I always understand everything in your stories, up to the point where I'm asked to explain it, and then I'm in trouble. With this one, Shawn has asked for explanations, and I have in a number of places put in what I assume to be the right ones, subject to your changing and approval. He said, about this story, "The total effect was wonderful, but I could not follow the action. I didn't know, quite, where anything was or what was going on. All the ambiguity impaired my enjoyment of the extremely important, and moving, final scene. Couldn't it be made a *little* clearer?"

So that is what I have tried to do, since his detailed questions seem to me, on the whole, ones which any ordinary reader might well ask.*

At (1) I have had them go upstairs, since a minute later they come down and when last heard from they were standing by the front door, though by indirection one supposes they are in the room where the corpse was laid out.

At (2) the whole story becomes considerably easier to follow with the sentence I have inserted here, and, as a story, it presents both geographical and cultural mysteries that you, because the material is so familiar to you, aren't perhaps conscious of.

(3) Shawn says "Where does this take place, and when?" Hence the insert, which you are to fix if it isn't right.

(4) You don't actually know until (4a) that Father Hamilton came along with Father Jackson. This is the sort of thing which used to make Mr. Ross very nervous.

At (5) and (5a) Shawn was made nervous because in the paragraph just above you have shown Father Hanafey cagily suggesting that *Jackson* mention to Mr. Fogarty that his brother wanted to be buried on the Mass Island, but in the actual scene it appears that Father Hanafey himself brought the matter up. This is not only contradictory but presumably out of character, Shawn feels.

He also thought it would help if at (6) you made it clear that the church was Father Hanafey's, since, after an initial, it could be any church.

At (7) you remember I queried the phrase "took it to the fair." It turns out that nobody understands it, alas. Isn't it better, since that is so, to cut?

At (8) Shawn is troubled because, he says, he had no idea that all the arrangements mentioned just below could be accomplished that night and that the funeral would take place the next morning. The whole scene at the Keneallys' doesn't make any sense unless you understand that the funeral *is* taking place the next morning, but, nevertheless, for clarity's sake it might be a good idea to have some such insert as the one I have suggested here.

At (9) Shawn says "Surely the scene here should be described a bit? Where it is taking place, for example, and what Mr. Fogarty did or said that scared 'even Jackson.' " I have attempted a kind of dummy fix, in the hope that you will improve on it.[†] But Shawn is right, I do think. The scene is a little underwritten. I have also inserted at (10) a hearse and a funeral car because Shawn didn't realize, on the next galley, that it was the funeral procession that you were writing about, and that they are from Dublin. You say toward the end of galley 9 "the Dublin driver" and that, of course, is a horrendous piece of indirection which I have corrected on galley 7. If, of course, the hearse and the funeral car are not from Dublin, then you'd better account for that Dublin driver, old socks.

At (10a) I have also made it clear that the two cars are a funeral procession and at (11) Shawn pointed out that there are actually three priests involved in the story and that you haven't said that Father Hanafey did not go to the Mass Island, so it takes some time before the reader is able to pick up which two actually did go and, for purposes of clarity, there is no reason not to say so here. Also, since Shawn had forgotten that Father Jackson once went to

the mountain village with Fogarty, I have put in an, I hope, un-
obtrusive reminder.

All this makes me I can't tell you how homesick for you, because it would be such pleasure to be sitting down at my table
ironing it out with you and arriving, as we so often have, at one
brilliant stroke after another that not only solves the problem but
improves the story. How I detest all forms of separation.

Love to Harriet,

BILL

------

* In 1983, Maxwell explained these pages to me:

> There are two kinds of readers. Readers who, when they don't under-
> stand it, they're patient until they do understand it. But when you're
> editing a magazine, you feel obliged to read for the reader, and remove
> what seem like pointless difficulties.
>
> By myself I'm not too concerned about this kind of detail, but as an
> editor I had to be, and I had to convey those queries I thought were sen-
> sible. So this is really when Michael and I were all through, and an out-
> side person comes in, with his difficulties.
>
> [As] a *New Yorker* story tends to go from sentence to sentence,
> they're [the queries] so that you don't have to double back on your
> trail—having found out a piece of information out of place, you go back
> and reread and say, "Oh, that's what was happening. . . . Oh, he was
> there. . . . Oh, this is what happened." It's so that as you read along you
> understand the situation and don't have to double back.

† A "dummy fix," Maxwell explained, means "Don't leave this. Fix it yourself, in
your own language, so that it fits in, but, for God's sake, don't leave it."

WILLIAM MAXWELL TO FRANK O'CONNOR,
DECEMBER 15, 1958 (telegram):

> TO: FRANK O'CONNOR
> 52 OAK HOUSE
> MESPIL FLATS
> SUSSEX ROAD
> DUBLIN
> IRELAND

> SHAWN SAYS QUOTE THE INVISIBLE PRESENCES
> UNQUOTE IS FULL OF WONDERFUL THINGS AND HAS
> YOUR STAMP ON IT AND THE NEW YORKER MUST
> HAVE IT, BUT THAT AS IT STANDS IT IS LONG FOR
> US, AND THAT IF YOU WILL LET US TRY FOR A
> SHORTENED VERSION OF ABOUT TWENTY-FIVE
> PAGES, TO BE OF COURSE SUBMITTED TO YOU FOR
> YOUR APPROVAL, YOU WILL MAKE HIM VERY HAPPY
> STOP   ARE YOU WILLING QUESTION IT WOULD BE
> A LABOR OF LOVE, SO FAR AS I AM CONCERNED DASH

FRANK O'CONNOR TO WILLIAM MAXWELL (handwritten
draft on the back of Maxwell's letter of December 11):

Dear Bill,

You must write a new fable about the Cruel Taskmaster and
the Fairy Godmother, and how the C.T. broke the child's spell but
then the F.G. came along and said 'Now this is how we do it.' The
catch in the fable will be the two will be the same.

All the Big Fellow's points are surely OK with me [?] but tell
him for me that I have faced West, prostrated myself and beaten
my forehead ten times on the floor. You have answered all of them
beautifully but I am still sore about the name 'Dublin' which

never, as you say, should have been allowed to stray into the story at all—God forgive me.

I was delighted with your cable of course, but I still feel you have already enough work on your hands.

This vacation, I suspect, was a mistake, with Harriet ill, Hallie Óg ill and myself down with a cold. I began last week to think of emigrating to the South Sea islands.

M

It struck Jackson as sheer sentimentality. It wasn't even as if Fogarty came from the place.*

———

* These two sentences from "The Mass Island," perhaps created in response to Shawn's queries, were handwritten upside down at the bottom of the page.

WILLIAM MAXWELL TO FRANK O'CONNOR,
DECEMBER 17, 1958:

Dear Michael,

Emmy read me your cable over the phone. Own work is helped and stimulated is the answer. If I weren't working on this, I would be working on something that gives me less pleasure and excitement, and in any case it will be done on the New Yorker's time, not the novel's. So I am wholly happy to be able to go ahead with it.*

The dollhouse is all but done, and Emmy finished the sugar-candy house (the witch's house, with the witch coming out the front door, and Hansel and Gretel outside helping themselves to a little of the architecture) last night and I persuaded her to let the children see it instead of waiting for Kate's birthday, which will have its own excitement, and it takes such a little anyway to launch her in the general direction of the moon. They came in from playing with the Schwartzes, and Brookie said "A candy house," and Kate didn't say anything. She just looked and looked and looked and looked, getting paler and paler. Because of course the effect of living entirely in one's imagination is tiring, but one doesn't realize it until, for a moment, it isn't necessary, and when the real world and the imaginary coincide and one can sit down, one discovers that one has worked much too long without stopping to rest. Brookie's finger became full of electricity, and she pointed to the candies, getting closer and closer but not quite (being forbidden to) touching them. Kate lay full length along the dining room table, with her head down, still looking. As of this morning, the cookie fence was still intact, though Emmy regrets the later addition of gumdrops. Too much. It was right before. It is my fault for not stopping her. But it is still all right, of course, and I didn't stop her because the gumdrops were a childhood memory, the house always had gumdrops on it, she said, and what was the whole thing but a recreation of what used to be, and not the last one there will be, I dare say. But it was and is very pretty. The yard is white icing covered with a dust of colored this and that, and the walk is candy gravel, the chimney of candy stones, the shutters pieces of Hershey's chocolate bar, the doorframe candy canes, and lollypops are set in the wall, in among the hard candies. I had one exquisite moment, with it, when Brookie accidentally touched the white icing, and withdrew her hand in distress, and I said, "Lick it," and she did, dubiously, and *then* the look that came over her face. Straight out of the Brothers Grimm, it was.

Love to you three,
B.

------

* O'Connor's cable no longer exists, but Harriet explained, "Michael felt guilty that he was sending Bill bits and pieces of the autobiography for advice when Bill was trying frantically to finish his novel. The cable may have read something like 'Feel guilty. Forget my rubbish. Do your own work.' "

WILLIAM MAXWELL TO THE O'CONNORS,
AFTER DECEMBER 25, 1958:

Dear Man, Dear Woman, and Dear Child:

I am not such a fool as not to recognize a coat that has magic woven into it.* I suppose that in the Aran Islands it is used for other purposes, but this coat is a Writing Coat, and when you write in it, all sorts of new connections occur to you, and you understand suddenly what this and that are really about. It also contains memories of a beautiful evening, when I got soaking wet and had to be dressed out in Somebody Else's clothes, from head to foot. It also reminds me of you. It has been many years since any garment gave me so much pleasure. But how you showered us all! Emmy's stole is so becoming to her, as she sails out into the Baptist Church Road, and the dolls are charming. So much so that they abide on top of the book case, for the time being, in Kate's room, because those dolls they are allowed to play with they undress. All the dolls in the house lie around naked, with their clothes in one big trunk. We are hoping that this is just a stage.

Since you have all Annapolis to worry about Hallie-Óg's gastric infection, I am putting my faith in that doctor you mentioned. But I will be relieved to learn that the most beautiful of babies is all right again. Both of ours have had delicate stomachs, and periods of difficulty with them. The main thing is that, if it prolongs itself, she should have lots of vitamins, and if you have trouble getting the kind you want, you know who to write to to have send them to you. Not that we are a tower of health at our house. I think with small children you open the door to Pandora's Box. Emmy is also thinking of tropical islands and emigrating. It is so cold day after day, between zero and ten above. I am mostly kept going by my delight in the journal of the brothers Goncourt. And a terrible desire to get that book done that is taking place in the study.

My father is better, and may linger, may go suddenly. I implore him (in my mind) to wait until I get my book done.

I sat next to West today at the Century and it is the first time

I have ever talked to him, and I thought him exceedingly nice.[†] And nice to talk to. So shy, isn't he? And then gradually, he begins to emerge from it and be himself. You must remember all about the Casement forgeries, so you can tell me about them in detail.

Christmas was happy and calm. Just when the children had finished opening their presents and were beginning to quarrel over the crayons, the uncles arrived, with more presents and themselves, which the girls prefer to any present that ever was, and when the children were bedded down for their naps, we had Christmas dinner at the kitchen table, everybody knowing everybody so well, and it was relaxed and lovely, and then we opened our presents and the babies went on sleeping, and we went for a walk, and then while one uncle and Emmy and the children were in the kitchen, one uncle and I were in the darkened living room, listening to Die Winterreise. Then more food, more talk, all of it pleasant and happy. That fable of the Cruel Taskmaster and the Fairy Godmother—maybe you think that didn't stop me in my tracks.

Love,

B

------

* Harriet remembered, "This was a bawneen coat, collarless, buttonless, of white wool, which was worn by the Aran Island fishermen. Michael had one which he always wore when he was writing and thought Bill should have one, too."

[†] Anthony West (1914–87), novelist and literary critic, whom the O'Connors had met at Carmel Snow's.

1959

O'Connor devoted much of his energy to a book of translations of early Irish poems, *Kings, Lords, & Commons.* When published, it was banned in Ireland in reaction to his vigorous rendering of Brian Merriman's poem *The Midnight Court.* (The original, uncensored, remained in print.) In September, the O'Connors returned to Brooklyn Heights, and lived at 2 Pierrepont Street.

The New Yorker published two autobiographical pieces, "I Know Where I'm Going" and "The One Day of the Year," as well as "The Mass Island."

WILLIAM MAXWELL TO FRANK O'CONNOR,
JANUARY 28, 1959:

Dear Michael,

I distinctly remember asking Harriet to write me your telephone number, and probably she did and it is within four feet of me, but I can't lay my hand on it, and neither can the telephone company provide any number for you, so I am deprived of the pleasure of talking to you about I Know Where I'm Going, which suddenly found itself, as the French say, in the issue after next. There should be time, however, between now and next Thursday for you to cable collect (EDYORKER) if there is anything on these galleys that doesn't meet with your approval. I thought there would be time to get them to you, and I still don't know what the rush was, but I took advantage of it to leave practically everything the way you had it.

Beautiful snapshot of her serene highness. It has, I thought, a little the look of that picture of your mother. Tell Harriet that when Kate was a baby and wouldn't go to sleep at night we let her cry an hour for several nights running, and it never made any difference, so we gave it up and attacked the problem another way—half an hour of singing, half an hour of reading, half an hour of coming and going, etc. but at least no crying, and now she reads to herself until she is ready to have the light out and calls "Finished" cheerfully, and that's that (or almost). With Brookie, when the pattern started repeating itself, I spanked her for fifteen minutes steadily, mildly, on the bottom, through three diapers, while she raged at me (after keeping her mother coming and going for two hours and forty minutes) and that night I won. The next time, I didn't. If you lose, you win and if you win, you lose, and it couldn't matter less, but there is no truth in discipline; just convenience. This is probably not quite how Emmy would describe it, so maybe Harriet had better send us that questionnaire. You of course, have never been near children and don't know the first thing about them.

I am keeping to that afternoon schedule, and am hopeful. I am too superstitious to say more.

I am perfectly sure you have a telephone. What in God's name is it?

Love to you both,
BILL

FRANK O'CONNOR TO WILLIAM MAXWELL,
FEBRUARY 1959 (draft of cable):

Oingel

Maxwell
EDYORKER

Proofs fine you're an eyengel the name is Delaney but phone number 66803.* Find another excuse to call.

Love
MICHAEL

———

* "Delaney," no relation to Larry, was the name under which the telephone was listed, probably that of the previous tenant.

WILLIAM MAXWELL TO FRANK O'CONNOR,
AFTER MARCH 15, 1959:

Dear Michael,
Well it went off to the makeup department this morning.* Two weeks ago it was ready, and I put it in my out basket and then remembered that I had a later version which I had meant to compare, and so I took it home instead, and my eyes got bigger and bigger as I started to read the manuscript. By that time I was thoroughly familiar with the material, of course, and every place that I had been stopped by or wondered about had been fixed by you. It was uncanny. So I sharpened some pencils and went to it again. The worst that you will think of the result is that it is disastrous, the best, probably, that it has been tampered with. But what I was after was something that read as if it hadn't been lifted from an autobiography but was complete in itself. This meant sacrificing some anecdotes that were relevant and keeping in some that weren't particularly, and you are going to miss things that you

were fond of, but it seemed to me to read very well. It has such a kind of sustained sadness hanging over it. The family is reduced because in these chapters you could refer back to previous scenes and episodes, which you can't do in the New Yorker piece. They won't be there; you would have to retell them, which is a bore. So it comes out pretty much the account of a child's search for education, with very few side shoots. It seemed to me beautifully written, and moving. And you know, of course, that things that don't seem right are to be fixed; nothing is final.

But now what I wonder about is you. You haven't been twiddling your thumbs, I am sure. Have you been holding back the new chapters until this was out of the way? If so, it would be an ideal time to let me see them.

By this time you must have heard that Pat Knopf is going to start a house of his own. I was distressed, because I like him, and counted on his being there in the years to come. I have no idea what happened. It doesn't seem likely that there was a bang-up quarrel, because they must all three understand each other and be used to quarreling by this time. More likely he and his father had different ideas of where the publishing business was going and what to do about it. I assume that the Vintage Press will stay with the old man. Too bad, though.[†]

I am about half way through a fairly final revision of the book, in spite of fantastic interruptions. I am not sure that it makes any more sense than when you saw it, but it seems to fall into simpler lines. By the end of the year, I think.

My love to you both,
BILL

----

* "Go Where Glory Waits Thee."
[†] "Pat" was Alfred A. Knopf, Jr., Alfred and Blanche Knopf's only son and a vice-president of the company. His resignation to establish Atheneum with Simon Michael Bessie and Hiram Haydn was front-page news in *The New York Times.*

WILLIAM MAXWELL TO FRANK AND HARRIET O'CONNOR,
BEFORE MARCH 29, 1959:

Dear Michael and Harriet,

Well though it is in general evenly matched, I have one advantage over you. When, like today, I felt homesick for the sound of your voices, I could go over to 6th Avenue and buy a record of Michael reading Joyce (whom he hates, *he says*), which is more than you can do in Dublin when you are homesick, as I insist on your being, for me. I also discovered, to my surprise, that there is a recording of the Old One, reading the Lake Isle of Innisfree.* For years I had been grieving that I would never hear the sound of his voice, and there it was. So that's what I am going home to. A week ago last Monday I came down with what seemed to be a nervous stomach, and I have been living on milk and cream and oat meal (Irish, not Quaker, thank God) and junket ever since. I think I am about cured. The only symptoms I have are just what I have when I am suddenly very hungry, and considering the fare I have been living on, why shouldn't I be is what I ask myself. Meanwhile, in the face of roast beef, Idaho potatoes, lamb chops, chicken fricassee, and everything else that makes life worth living, I have been an absolute philosopher.

Hallie-Óg grows on us. She is the one of all the children in the two framed collections of snapshots in our bedroom that Emmy's eyes and mine always light on. I find myself more and more attached to her all the time.

Happy Easter is what I sat down to say.

BILL

---

* A record of Yeats reading his poetry was issued by Spoken Arts.

FRANK O'CONNOR TO WILLIAM MAXWELL, APRIL 1959:

52 Oak House,
Mespil Flats,
Dublin

My Dear Bill,

Alas, I have been doing worse than twiddling my thumbs; I have been, in my son's phrase, looking at my sneakers. The case is altered, as the Elizabethans used to say, and I have to listen to Hallie telling me that there's really no reason why we shouldn't settle in Dublin—it's so nice for children, and it's all part country and so on—while I explain gloomily that I seem to find it impossible to write a story. My old friend A.E. used to say that writers should avoid extremes because like fish they burn when put into warm water, and when put back into their native element shiver and say it's impossible to live in and they must get back to where it's warm.

You needn't be afraid of how I shall receive your recasting of the autobiographical piece. Probably as with Yeats' revisions of my poems I shall be fascinated that anyone of that talent should see so much in my rhymes, and then go my own way—having stolen whatever was stealable. I've rewritten that piece two or three times, and, instead of working over your version, I shall probably send you mine to see if there's anything in it that appeals to you. All I know of it that you will like is the opening where I've transferred the background and lighting to the first couple of paragraphs. As for the rest, as you say, it's sad, and I can only hope that the fourth part, which I'll send you will be silly and amusing enough to balance it.

Pa and Ma are here, and after two days with Hallie Óg decided that it would be very helpful to us in our need of a holiday if they brought her back to Annapolis and left us free. At which point I sternly said 'No', knowing that Big Hallie would start breaking her heart within a week, and within a fortnight we would both be careening back for a summer in Maryland. But I'm still not certain they won't kidnap her. The latest snapshot will show you why. All the same I regret that holiday we might have together in Italy. It might have brought some light into that damned book. I took the family up to Sligo to see how Yeats was getting on, and even he seemed to be disgruntled. Kavanagh the ex-poet ran into me soon after I came home, and the following conversation took place exactly as recorded.

K.	I see you do be writing for a paper called the New Yorker.
Me.	I do.
K.	I dare say for a piece in a paper like that you might get big money.
Me.	Begod, you might.
K.	I dare say you might get $500.
Me.	You might, indeed.
K.	You might even get $1000?
Me.	Still, I'd say $500 wouldn't be too bad, wouldn't you?

Now, Rhein or Rhine could make a lot of that conversation, don't you think?* It happened I was shy of meeting Mr. K, having already taken him as model for a story I'd broadcast a few days before. The conversation I had composed for him was—

K.	I dare say for a large view like that you would get a lot of money.
Stranger.	That's what I'd hope for.
K.	You might get five pounds.
Stranger.	Or more.
K.	You might get ten?
Stranger.	More than that.
K.	Begod, the whole country isn't worth that.

Anyway, it shows you the high standard of intellectual conversation now to be enjoyed in Ireland.

I'm correcting the final proofs of the Collected Translations.[†] They at least are good and Alfred is doing me proud in the way of lay-out. I'll be glad when I can let you have that to reassure you that I'm not an out-and-out waste of time.

Hallie sends her love.

MICHAEL

Tell Brendan that his little poem on his father made me wonder why we bother to write 80,000 words when it can all be said in a dozen or two.[‡]

---

* "Rhein or Rhine" was J. B. Rhine (1895–1980), a parapsychologist who conducted early ESP experiments.

† This might suggest that O'Connor thought little of Patrick Kavanagh, but in a review of Kavanagh's *Collected Poems* for *The Spectator,* O'Connor called him "our greatest living poet, and I don't mean Alas!" The "Collected Translations" were *Kings, Lords, & Commons.*

‡ Brendan Gill's poem "Bad Dream," thirty-four words long, appeared in the March 7 issue.

WILLIAM MAXWELL TO FRANK O'CONNOR,
LATE APRIL 1959:

Dear Michael,

I sent you the galleys this morning, with a mash note from Emmy clipped to them, and look forward to the newest version. But explain to Harriet please that you can't settle in Dublin because you can [handwritten addition: 't*] manage without me, which she will understand means that I can't manage without you, and since she loves me, that will be the end of it. It also happens to be the truth. I am managing very badly these days, if manage is at all the word I should use. How badly you will realize when I tell you that it was only last Saturday that I finally sat down and played the record with Yeats' voice on it, for the first time. To think that it was once possible to sit and listen to him telling how he came to write this or that. And people were his friends. By the time he had talked three minutes, I was convinced of something I know isn't true—that prose doesn't matter a damn, only poetry. Only *his* poetry. I am meeting Emmy on the 4:40. She has again been looking at schools and apartments, and will be so uplifted when I present her with a picture of Hallie Óg.

I spent the weekend going over an early novel for Vintage— They Came Like Swallows, which title I cribbed (with encouragement) from Himself, of course.* And I was moved helplessly by the material, which will only cease to move me when I am dead, I suppose, but also discouraged that it wasn't better. I wrote it when I was twenty-four or five, and all the judgments are so harsh and, as I eventually discovered, in many cases quite wrong. But there was nothing I could do short of rewriting it out of existence, except here and there to do the small detail work that pulls a character back into recognizable human focus, and to restore a grand scene that I mistakenly deleted, in which I was impertinent to my father, who, of course, had a minute before been impertinent to me. I think you will like it. I was something under ten at the time.

Love to you both,

BILL

[Handwritten addition:] *What a sad Freudian slip!

———

* W. B. Yeats's "Coole Park, 1929."

WILLIAM MAXWELL TO FRANK O'CONNOR, MAY 12, 1959:

Dear Michael:

The bookkeeping department has issued a check for The Invisible Presences*, and I was going to sit on it until I heard from you, but my more sensible side says that if I were going to hear from you about it, that is, that you didn't want it to appear in this form, I would have already.* So I will send it along, and if you are uneasy, write me right away and I will call Don. Or write him. I feel that this is only the interim version, and that I have ahead of me the exquisite pleasure of copying all sorts of exquisite improvements into the margins of the galleys, from the manuscript that is perhaps even this minute on its way to me.

I had sadly to turn down an invitation to Sunday lunch from the Old One.† When I explained that I could neither eat nor drink, he was most understanding. And what on earth would be the point of going to lunch with the Old One and not eating or drinking? It gives me no trouble, my stomach, unless I drink a glass of wine or put my foot over the line, and have a cup of vichyssoise or something interesting like that, so don't waste any sympathy on me, and since all our problems seem nearly solved now, it shouldn't be of any great duration. But what a thing to happen to a pleasure loving man!

A kiss for Harriet (kissing doesn't bother me in the least, I'm happy to tell you) and my most respectful leg to Hallie-Óg, and where would you be spending the summer? in Dublin?

B

[Handwritten:] *$3,493.75, tell H. I know money doesn't interest you but it interests wives.

---

* The original title of "Go Where Glory Waits Thee," published in *The New Yorker* on March 26, 1960, and O'Connor's earliest title for his autobiography, rejected as sounding overly religious. (Another title, *Mother's Boy,* was discarded when O'Connor was told that it would suggest effeminacy to American readers.) The "Invisible Presences" themselves, the heroic models O'Connor read of (and attempted to emulate) in British school stories, are explained in *An Only Child.*
† Alfred A. Knopf (1892–1984), publisher and epicure. He gave a party for his authors every September; Harriet described them as gastronomical "command performances."

FRANK O'CONNOR TO WILLIAM MAXWELL, MAY 12, 1959:

52 Oak House,
Mespil Flats,
Dublin.

May 12th.

Dear Bill,

After all the loving care you had put into the proofs I feel guilty at returning you this horrid mass of scribbles. I fear that, as you say, we are necessary to one another, so when you give me ideas you mustn't blame me for seizing on them. I first corrected the proofs, and then rewrote the whole thing, so that you would have something like a clean copy to work on and alternatives you might care to fall back on, as well as a general outline to show how the inserts and transpositions are supposed to fit into one another. It is entirely for your convenience and has no other significance. I haven't increased the length of the piece and have almost always accepted your cuts joyously and felt inspired to make some of my own. Where I have restored a passage you omitted it has only been for the purpose of pegging a date or a transition. The most important insertions are the introduction—all my own work—and the last paragraph—your original suggestion which at the time I didn't feel strong enough to do. Even now, it's not absolutely right, and having changed it in the typescript I have gone back to the proofs and changed it again there, for the better I think. Curiously, for the first time I've been feeling vaguely happy about the whole section of the book, as one does about a child that's not yet born but who, one feels, will be all right.

I have also changed names to avoid giving pain. It is always an astonishment to me to find how the New Yorker gets round Ireland, even in the provinces. The only confusion of idiom I see is in my words 'store' and 'file.' As I've noted on the proofs a store with us is not a shop but what you might perhaps call a warehouse. It is really a railway station with six or eight platforms where the goods trains are run in to be loaded and unloaded. A file is a tall wire spike with a head like a bishop's crozier—Hallie calls it a 'spindle' which sounds improbable.

Please, if you're not distracted with boredom, go over the thing again, and don't be afraid to ask me to do the same. I envy you working over 'They Came Like Swallows.' Not that I think you'll be able to improve much in it. 'Oh, won't I?' say you, turning back to your proofs.

Love to Emmie.

MICHAEL

WILLIAM MAXWELL TO FRANK O'CONNOR, MAY 18, 1959:

Dear Michael,

I studied the manuscript and the galleys, made a lot of changes, and then, after thinking a little, put the piece in escrow until you get back in the fall, when we can sit down and discuss it, and fix it together. I was hurrying things along in case it had to be published because of the book coming out, but apparently you are not intending to bring the autobiography out this fall, so we have all time's delight to reconcile our cross-purposes. You continue, quite properly, to treat it as a section of a larger work, and I continue, quite properly and naturally, to tug and yank at it and pull the wool over the reader's eyes so that it will appear to have been written as an isolated piece. It should appear your way in the book and (roughly) my way in the New Yorker. The new title and the new ending are both better than the old ones. It was mostly the cuts I questioned. And the new beginning replaces something that is closer to the heart of the matter, and so maybe should be tinkered with by the both of us. But also putting it aside allows you to do whatever else you feel like doing to it without having the feeling that it is being torn out of your hands before you are quite ready to let go of it.

Meanwhile, what comes next?

Love to you both,
BILL

Minnie O'Donovan and
her son at four months
(see page 265)

A young Frank
O'Connor, portrait by
Æ (George Russell)

O'Connor, Harriet, and Hallie-Óg on the Brooklyn Promenade

O'Connor, Harriet, and Hallie-Óg in Cluny, France

O'Connor and Hallie-Óg, Ireland, 1959

Frank O'Connor,
photograph by
G. Paul Bishop

O'Connor addressing a raccoon at the Bread Loaf Writers' Conference
(see pages 263–64)

Relaxing in Yorktown Heights: Maxwell and O'Connor,
with Katie, Brookie, and Hallie-Óg

Hallie-Óg

Brookie and Katie

William Maxwell,
photograph by
Consuelo Kanaga,
1945

William and Emily Maxwell in the late 1940s

Maxwell reading to Katie and Brookie

William and Emily
Maxwell, with
Brookie and Katie

William Maxwell, photograph by Alfred Knopf

Frank O'Connor, photograph by Alfred Knopf

WILLIAM MAXWELL TO HARRIET O'CONNOR,
AUGUST 12, 1959:

                                        August 12, 1959
Dear Harriet,
    If you think Himself won't sleep after reading this, you have
my permission to throw it in the wastebasket without showing it
to him.* But I *think* he owes me a letter, and I know he owes me
a new section of that autobiography. When exactly are you coming home?
                                        Your loving,
                                        W.

_____

* Clippings about Sir Roger Casement.

HARRIET O'CONNOR TO WILLIAM MAXWELL,
LATE AUGUST 1959:

                                           Thursday
Dearest William,
    How did you guess what had been keeping him up—and
away from work? A two page letter to the Spectator, describing
how the diaries were forged went off today, and I pray we may hear
no more on this subject for a bit.* But oh how I long for September 13 when we leave this enervating, malicious, beguiling impossible bloody country. He can't work here—it gives all of us
perpetual stomach aches, it looks so lovely. Anyhow, please God,
we arrive in NY on September 18, go to Annapolis for the weekend to leave Hallie-Óg with her grandparents—and then off to
look for a place to live. Which brings me to the most important
question. Where will you be? Have you decided to stay in Yorktown Heights? If you have, is the house that you mentioned going
to be for rent? If you haven't—where will you be? What did

Emmy find that day she went in to look at places in the city? I've been reading the classified section of the NYTimes with interest—and dismay. I keep wondering about places on the Hudson—just up from the George Washington Bridge—what is that part of the world called? Is it Yonkers? Is it awful? Cyrilly has a friend who lives in Hopewell, N.J.—8 miles from Princeton—which tempts Michael—but I'd sooner be North of the city than South.[†] Liadain will be with us—which means at least two bedrooms as well as a study and living room, and I suspect anything that size in the city would be exorbitant. Anyhow, tell us your plans—it would be very nice to be not too far from you.

We had an absolutely imbecilic time in France. I had nightmares about it for weeks ahead of time and then it turned out to be wonderful fun. Hallie-Óg learned to walk by herself—ate cheese, olives, fried potatoes—and flirted with Priests from one end of Burgundy to the other—Himself admired Romanesque churches and drank every variety of Burgundy—*I* ate everything that had been forbidden all winter with no bad results at all (I suspect that you and I have the same disease and that it all originates in the worrier and not in the middle at all—but I'll talk to you about that when I see you.). We even had a surprise bonus of a visit from Myles who was adorable and took us all in hand for four days. We were something like a travelling vaudeville show and completely mystified the French who speculated about us in French that I could understand—tho they didn't know it. Of course I've been completely converted and am now almost as big a Francophile as Michael—nobody seemed to mind when Hallie-Óg had a screeching fit in the restaurant—they all let me go first in queues—Priests played with her—there was even a touching workman in those blue overalls who patted her so tenderly on the top of the head that he reminded me of 'Seymour' when he burned his hand by leaving it too long on Franny's downy pate when she was a baby.[‡] There's so much bubble and life in the French atmosphere—Dublin seems even more sexless than usual in contrast. Ah well—soon we'll be away from it and probably lonesome for the very things that are driving us demented at the moment.

But most of all—we're looking forward to seeing you two. Please be available about the 24th of September—there's an awful lot of talking to catch up on. And Hallie-Óg says to tell Kate and Brookie that she has LOTS to tell them—she tries to tell her parents but they are too dumb to understand her—but she's sure that K and B will know exactly what she's saying.

love to you both
MA

---

* O'Connor's dissenting response to Brian Inglis's March 6 review of *The Black Diaries of Roger Casement,* "Saintly Sinner," was published on August 28. "Michael *did* go on about the subject for a long time," Harriet said. "If he were alive now, he would be raging at the notion that they have just said, 'The diaries are authentic. We got an English handwriting expert in to look at them, and *he* said they were.'"

† Cyrilly Abels, first the managing editor of *Mademoiselle,* where O'Connor had published stories, later his American agent when he had become dissatisfied with the Matson Agency.

‡ The O'Connors were in France from July 30 to August 17. Harriet's reference is to J. D. Salinger's "Raise High the Roof Beam, Carpenters."

FRANK O'CONNOR TO WILLIAM MAXWELL,
LATE AUGUST 1959 (on the reverse of Harriet's letter above):

Bill.   Of course what I need is you—a course. I have two of the best stories you ever read all neatly jotted down, and I can't face typing them, and won't, till I'm settled somewhere in or near N.Y. Here I become too involved in other people's moods and business and politics. Instead of writing, I sit admiring Hallie Óg, who has become big and greatly addicted to walking. She likes museums and calls all sculpture 'baba' but prefers cathedrals and abbeys where the echoes are really worth rousing. Talking about novels, I re-read my own, and in my mood of general untalentedness was delighted with it. You'd better finish yours before I get back or I'll get to Knopfies before you. The Casement thing is an extraordinary repeat of the Dreyfus case. Now the diaries are there to see, the national heroes say they are clumsy forgeries, René MacColl says they are authentic, and the 'Spectator' says 'Frank O'Connor is correct in saying that there are interpolations, but the interpolations are the work of Casement himself.' I invite you to study one. "After dinner talked two Richigaros muchachos—one a fine chap. He pulled stiff and fingered it laughing. Would have gone on and other too. (Keys on chain in left pocket) looking for cigarettes." As an editor I invite you to support me that 'keys' is the object of the verb 'pulled' but you don't have to. I felt I had to go on record as saying that I didn't give a damn about what any handwriting expert said; the evidence is there in that sentence as it is all over the shop if anybody wants to read it. I can see Elizabeth's* attraction for you, as I can Colette's—all those lovely smells and colours that stop Hallie Óg dead in front of every shop. What I don't understand is how you can tolerate me, with my nose and eyes ruined by bad tobacco.

MICHAEL

----

* Elizabeth Bowen.

WILLIAM MAXWELL TO FRANK O'CONNOR,
LATE AUGUST 1959:

Dear Michael:

It's quite simple how I can tolerate you—all those lovely smells and colors won't keep the human race going, and you with your nose and eyes ruined by bad tobacco (so you say; I wouldn't have) *are* the human race. I wonder that this simple fact has never occurred to you.

Love,
BILL

WILLIAM AND EMILY MAXWELL TO THE O'CONNORS,
SEPTEMBER 17, 1959 (telegram):

MR. AND MRS. MICHAEL O'DONOVAN
(FRANK O'CONNOR)
C/O RICH
FERRY POINT FARM
ANNAPOLIS
MARYLAND

WELCOME HOME

BILL AND EMMY

WILLIAM MAXWELL TO HARRIET O'CONNOR,
BETWEEN SEPTEMBER 18 AND OCTOBER 19, 1959:

Hooray! And think of H.O. being old enough to travel without
her Ma. I have been needing himself something terrible. I needed
him to explain about the Trouble. I just finished reading Elizabeth
Bowen's The Last September and I can't figure out from the con-
text why on earth they burned those houses down, unless possibly
there was ample precedent. 6C sounds up in the air.* Have you
got beds to sleep them all? And what a pleasure to have a reunion
with your furniture, books, and pictures, to say nothing of the
record player. We'll be waiting for you. Love,

B.

---

* The O'Connors had arrived; 6C was their apartment at 2 Pierrepont Street,
Brooklyn, where they moved in on October 19, 1959. Liadain, then eighteen,
lived with them for a few months.

WILLIAM MAXWELL TO FRANK O'CONNOR,
NOVEMBER 1959:

Michael:

I'm working away at that piece now, and you know it would be duck soup if only you weren't such a good writer. I get it all neatly lined up and look around for you, and lo, you've got out for a cup of coffee. I put it back the way you had it and you come back in wiping a smile off your lips. It is very *instructive.*

I sent Don Congdon another check, saying to myself this will make himself morbid or I don't know Arkansas. $2500, roughly. Adjustment for the whole year of the cost of living adjustment. There is no news because I have too much to say. Love to H and Queen Mab and you,

B.

WILLIAM MAXWELL TO FRANK O'CONNOR,
NOVEMBER 30, 1959:

Dear Michael,

What I suspected would happen did happen. Those inserts made it enough better that they couldn't bear to run it back of the book, and so they tore the schedule to smithereens, and it is running in the December 19th issue.* See that you find some melancholy explanation for all this, because it doesn't do for a writer to feel appreciated. Apart from the little bit of description that Shawn asked for, on the last galley, there is nothing here that will take any time or thought for you to look through. I'll be talking to you later in the week.

Love to all three of those girls.
B.

_____

* "The One Day of the Year."

FRANK O'CONNOR TO WILLIAM MAXWELL,
DECEMBER 2, 1959:

2 Pierrepont Street,
Brooklyn, 1. N.Y.

December 2.

Dear Bill,

Enclosed proofs which I shall probably deliver as I don't trust
the U.S. mails with serious manuscripts.* The Boss' point is well
taken, though I think it's not worth explaining, and it would be
better if you gave a local equivalent that the reader could pass over
without getting bogged down in irrelevant descriptions.

I have, of course, rewritten the damn thing since you saw it,
and two or three bits have become clear—why we couldn't shop in
a good store and why wrens were killed, with a typical bit of
Mother's fastidiousness. You can stick them in if they help and
forget them if they don't.

Shall I or shall I not drop in the M.S. of the third part of the
Autobiography? It's quite useless for the paper, and I hate asking
advice gratuitously as you might say. And if I do, I like to pass it
over en famille, over a glass of wine, if the man drinks wine, and
over the smell of it if he doesn't.

Yours,
MICHAEL

———

* "The One Day of the Year."

WILLIAM MAXWELL TO DON CONGDON,
DECEMBER 8, 1959:

December 8, 1959

Dear Don:

I can't tell you how happy I am to be sending you checks for the account of Frank O'Connor again. That was a long intermission. "The One Day of the Year" is in next week's New Yorker, and I think you ought to read it there instead of in galleys because of several interesting additions he made after it was set up. The other two pieces haven't been edited yet. One of them is called "Variations on a Theme of William Maxwell"—which is of course too intramural to do. So it is simply story MV2309, but you can call it "Variations" on your records if that is any easier. . . .

My best to you,
BILL MAXWELL

1960

In April, O'Connor completed *An Only Child,* which examined his first twenty years. In September, the O'Connors travelled to Copenhagen for a conference, where he spoke on "The Writer and the Welfare State." When they returned to America late in the fall, he wrote "The Weeping Children" and "The American Wife." He had been invited to teach at Stanford University by Wallace Stegner; the three O'Connors arrived in California at the end of December, and classes began on January 4.

In 1960, "Go Where Glory Waits Thee" and "A Set of Variations on a Borrowed Theme" were published in *The New Yorker.* The latter, although its genesis was in a story O'Connor's son Myles told him in 1959, has a particular connection to the O'Connor-Maxwell friendship. The first five versions of this story (drafts discarded by O'Connor and rescued from the wastebasket by Harriet)—about an elderly woman, her own family grown, who takes in two foster children and makes them her own—were titled "Variations on a Theme by William Maxwell." In 1983, Maxwell wrote me:

"I remember talking Michael out of using my name in the title for a story, but what I said that gave rise to the story in the first place I have at this late date no idea. I reread the story, and the only thing I can find that offers a clue to it is the fact that I had a younger brother whose birth preceded my mother's death by three days, and during the years when we lived under the same roof I was a kind of substitute mother to him. It is possible that I told Michael about this and that it went through one sea change and another in his mind and came out in the form of that beautiful story."

In 1995, Harriet added, "I can't remember the occasion but clearly remember the conversation which prompted the title. The three of us were talking about motherhood, in a general, rather philosophical way, and Bill said he thought motherhood was a conscious choice rather than a matter of biology. Michael was delighted and said something like 'Of course, you're right. It's a vocation—something you take on deliberately.' I suspect he already had the bones of the story in his mind and felt Bill's comment helped him to see it more clearly."

WILLIAM MAXWELL TO FRANK O'CONNOR,
JANUARY 11, 1960:

January 11, 1960

Mr. Frank O'Connor
6C
2 Pierrepont Street
Brooklyn Heights, New York

Dear Michael:
Some hairsplitting for your attention.*

Love,
BILL

---

* Maxwell enclosed the author's proof of "Go Where Glory Waits Thee."

WILLIAM MAXWELL TO FRANK O'CONNOR, MARCH 1960:

Michael:

The New Yorker is starting on a new system of returning original manuscripts three years after the appearance of the story in the magazine. The Study of History appeared in the issue of March 9, 1957, and Day Dreams in the issue of March 23, 1957, and if you present them to Harvard, they will set a value on them, and you can deduct that from your income tax return.

Love,
WILLIE

WILLIAM MAXWELL TO FRANK AND HARRIET O'CONNOR, SEPTEMBER 26, 1960:

Dear Michael and Harriet:

I suppose it will turn up, the minute it is no use, but that yellow slip of paper disappeared, during the time when my effects were moved to Roger Angell's office and then back again, after my office was painted. So I had to wait until Elizabeth got to Dublin, to reach you. Emmy's brother spent two summers in Denmark. The first summer he loved everything about it, and the second summer he learned how to read the Danish newspapers and discovered, to his horror, that he was in the most complacent country in the entire world. He never went back. All the same, I wouldn't mind a look around, my ownself. But no speeches. That would have to be agreed on, before I set foot in the country.*

And without you I got nowhere at all with "Displaced Persons."† Or rather, I got into such a rage, over the telephone, that I saw that unless I gave way I would be in an even greater one, and among the displaced, looking for a publisher. I didn't mind that so much as I minded the thought of how unpleasant the unpleasantness was going to be. In short, I was a coward.

We are moved back to town, and going to the country week-ends. This means that Friday is frantic and Sunday is frantic, and Saturday is nowhere. Bluebell came back with us, and we could have brought a small elephant with about as much ease. She has never been kerbed, Maeve says, and doubtless she never will.[‡] And she didn't at all understand what we were doing in somebody's strange house, and whined in the night, sure that we had put the potted plants all back in the car and gone home without her. Even the sight of me in my pyjamas with a rolled up newspaper in my hand wasn't reassuring. I could have been a hallucination.

We also introduced a nice calm colored woman into the house last night. I don't yet know whether it is the calm of lethargy or the calm of calmness or the eye in the center of the whirlwind. Kate was shocked; she had been expecting a small, wall-eyed Scotswoman, who was most friendly and willing to do everything and liked children and liked Kate, but whose references revealed that she had been fired from her two last places for coming home drunk and not feeling like doing any work all the next day. All of which we had neglected to tell Kate. "But her skin is so dark," she said plaintively, having never heard, from us, at least, of the Civil War. Just natural prejudice. Nice woman, though. I hope she's there to stay. I sat reading my paper at breakfast as if I had fallen through a hole into the previous generation.[§]

I miss you both terribly. I miss being able to pick up the phone and hear your voices. I hope you are enjoying your freedom from the angel tyrant, and that the angel tyrant is sufficiently ruling the roost that she doesn't behave like a child in Kipling.[‖] Our angel tyrants have taken to socking each other like little boys. Hard, I mean. Kate is learning to read. She can read about a dozen words. And she said to Emmy that yesterday at school it wasn't fair how some of the children got to go to the reading table and she didn't. Dog, fish, Bill, Brookie, girl, a, the, Brearley, baby, ballet shoes, ball, duck, she can read. And more.[#] Emmy draws pictures with the word beside them, on a fragment of grocery list, and leaves them beside her bed to find when she wakes up in the morning. She comes to the table reading. Emmy falls asleep constantly, from exhaustion, the exhaustion of having finally hired a maid. I have never seen her like this.

Love,

B

———

* "Elizabeth" is Elizabeth Cullinan (b. 1933), author of *House of Gold, The Time of Adam, Yellow Roses,* and *A Change of Scene,* who began working at *The New Yorker* in 1955 and became Maxwell's secretary in 1956. She recalled, "Working for William Maxwell was the most wonderful fun. He took, or so it seemed to me, only pleasure in what he did, and I was engulfed in this. And all I had to do was to walk things here or there, and make copies of his letters (he typed the originals himself), which in those days meant not passing paper through a machine, but retyping the letters, which I loved doing. It was, in fact, my education though not in any conscious way; I just absorbed a certain attitude along with a tremendous amount of detail about what made stories work or not work. I also typed a couple of drafts of *The Château,* which was kind of my senior thesis, invaluable for the close look at how a long manuscript changed, how things got moved around or replaced—all that sort of thing which I sat and soaked up." When she spent a year in Dublin, she was aided by the O'Connors, and was "enormously grateful to Michael and Harriet, and to William Maxwell who'd engineered this."

The O'Connors had been at a writers' conference in Copenhagen (September 7–12). "Ownself" is Maxwell's echo of the incident restored to *They Came Like Swallows,* where Bunny Morison is "impertinent" to his father.

† *Displaced Persons,* Maxwell noted, was the title O'Connor offered him for what became *The Château.*

‡ Maeve Brennan (1917–93), Dublin-born, published short fiction and occasional prose in *The New Yorker* from 1949, collected as *In and Out of Never-Never Land, The Long-Winded Lady,* and *Christmas Eve.*

§ Katharine Maxwell explained, "I remember at this age, five years old, that the label 'colored people' referred to ordinary people I'd seen all my life who were only faintly tanner than our family. I thought a word like 'colored' should apply to people who were green, pink, blue, orange, violet, and so on. So I'm sure I didn't perceive this woman as looking significantly different than our family except for a few shades of tan."

‖ Hallie-Óg stayed with her grandparents in Annapolis while her parents were in Denmark.

Katharine Maxwell remembered that the first word she read was "Bill," and that she was "so proud" because it was her father's name.

1961

In January, the O'Connors moved to Palo Alto, where he taught the spring semester at Stanford. Here, he lectured four times a week on the nineteenth-century novel and, as at Harvard and Northwestern, offered a twice-weekly writing seminar. Larry McMurtry and Ken Kesey were among his students.

Both O'Connor and Maxwell had major publications in the spring. Writing of *An Only Child* in the *Saturday Review,* Granville Hicks compared O'Connor to Turgenev and praised his "perfect lucidity." In 1948, O'Connor had published a study of Shakespeare, *The Road to Stratford.* Revised and enlarged, it appeared in America as *Shakespeare's Progress,* winning accolades for its singular ingenuity. Reviewing *The Château* in *The Reporter,* Elizabeth Bowen wrote, "I can think of few novels, of my day certainly, that have as much romantic authority as *The Château,* fewer still so adult in vitality, so alight with humor."

In California, O'Connor suffered a "slight stroke," which frightened him. He and Harriet returned to New York by train, sending Hallie-Óg by airplane. He was anxious to go home again, and, as it turned out, never returned to America. In Ireland, he began working with David Greene of Trinity College on a book of translations of early Irish verse. Two complex late stories, "The Weeping Children" and "The American Wife," appeared in *The New Yorker.*

In 1983, Thomas Flanagan recalled his close friend: "The O'Connor whom I knew was . . . at once charming and imperious, with a crest of white, thinning hair, a bristling moustache, piercing brown eyes behind thick glasses, and had the manner of a wary conquistador. He was a bit of a dandy, conscious of the effects of dress, and his jackets of Donegal tweed and Galway tweed were offset by a single exotic touch—a leather-thonged bolo tie, dark-hued, fiery Navajo turquoise. As if saying, 'Damn your eyes, I am back home with foreign decorations.' "

WILLIAM MAXWELL TO FRANK O'CONNOR,
JANUARY 4, 1961:

Dear Michael:

Very forlorn to go over the pages of "The Weeping Children" and not end by picking up the phone and calling you. I was hoping that there was going to be something that *would* justify my picking up the phone and calling you, but we had done our work too well and there was nothing. By now you must be settled in, with something like a routine. I hope you have found a face to lecture to. That fickle Harriet—no, not fickle exactly, susceptible— that susceptible Harriet is, I am sure, already giving Wally Stegner the affection that rightly belongs to me. Wherever she goes there is always one of me. Very distressing, but I don't see what is to be done about it. One would think that in Denmark, but no. Most of all in Denmark.

We have inadvertently slipped out of gear. Tonight will be the fourth social engagement in a row. No, two of the four were somebody dropping in and staying for dinner. But fourth evening with people. I do not know how people survive who do this every night. I look forward to Thursday evening after supper as if it were the light that indicates a clearing in the forest.

Sunday evening, Brookie appeared with Teddy wrapped in yellow swaddling clothes and announced "Teddy is Christ." Yes? I said. "Where are the halos?" she said. So I made them both halos, out of shirt cardboard, with a tab running down behind their collar, and then Kate appeared and wanted one too, and Brookie said "You can't. There can't be two Marys," and in the end she was prevailed upon to be Joseph, and so they walked around the apartment in a group, Joseph with a stick brought in from Gracie Square, and the halos covered with yellow New Yorker typewriter paper, and the interesting thing is that halos seemed as natural to them as ribbons or bangs. The next night when I got home Emmy said "Brookie is in her room, tired out. I think she may have fallen asleep." And so she had, in the dark, with her arm around Teddy, lying on her side, with her halo sticking out of her bathrobe collar. I wonder if we could buy or rent that empty church near you in Brooklyn and revive the Manichean heresy?

I have been still another time to the Brooklyn museum, this time to see the Egyptian show that I had hoped to see in your company, and after walking through it with some pleasure I decided I might as well see the permanent Egyptian collection on the third floor and so went up and found myself in the most extraordinary series of rooms I have found since we walked into the Musée Guimet. How poverty-stricken it makes the Egyptian room of the Metropolitan look. And shabby and like something that should have been in the Museum of Natural History. Everywhere I turned, something astonishing or something beautiful. So I took back a number of unkind things I have thought and said about Brooklyn, since that afternoon at the Academy of Music.

We are about to surrender Bluebell permanently to Maeve Brennan, and there is talk of acquiring Bluebell's niece, who is the same breed but has an albino mother, and so the puppy is variously described as peach-colored or as the color of a polar bear. E has read a book which said big dogs are more of a problem in the city than little dogs, which is clearly true, but on the other hand she doesn't like little dogs and she does like big ones. I am trying to remain passive, having learned that when I put my shoulder to the wheel or cut the Gordian knot it only leads to a mistake, the wrong decision, the hiring of just the maid we shouldn't have hired. On the other hand, I have a very low tolerance for suspense. It's why I cannot read mystery novels.

Are you all right? Are you happy? Is the sun shining on you? (It is here.) Are you glad you came?

> Love from us all to all three of you,
>
> BILL

FRANK O'CONNOR TO WILLIAM MAXWELL,
JANUARY 11, 1961:

4102 Amaranta Way,
Palo Alto, California

Dear Bill,

I did once know you, didn't I? And a girl called Emmie? It seems so long ago. We arrived here on December 30th in broiling sunshine, sat in the garden among the oranges and lemons to get a tan and caught the cruellest colds ever, all three of us.

I HATE teaching. I always did, I discover. I have an interesting writing group. Two of them are writing what seem to be novels, and as I gather official connection between the school and the magazine has been broken off owing to one of the usual statutory misunderstandings, I reserve the right to pick out anything I please and send it to you for your unofficial opinion. Where literature is concerned I refuse to recognize statutory misunderstandings.

This is Wednesday, and I have given notice that I shall have nothing to do with my classes until Monday. This in the wild hope that it will give me an opportunity to write a story. I am in that abstract stage of wanting to write a story, not a particular story but ANY story, just to prove to myself that I am still alive.

Harriet is sitting in a corner fuming over an incident in class—academic class of a hundred and more—the other day. One of the girls came up and said a number of the students wished to meet my wife. I said 'She'll be honoured but why do you want to meet her?' She said 'Because we admire her work so much—she is Ayn Rand, isn't she?'*

It's hot and I sit in the open air with my writing group and drop names, and I pine for Brooklyn.

You've had the damned book by now. The jacket alone has kept me off it.[†]

When is the novel?

Love to Emmie

MICHAEL

————

* Ayn Rand, whose propaganda fiction the O'Connors loathed, was married to another "Frank O'Connor" (born Charles Francis O'Connor in Ohio), to whom she had dedicated *The Fountainhead* and *Atlas Shrugged.*

[†] The American edition of *An Only Child* had a dark-brown cover ornamented with a floral sprig.

WILLIAM MAXWELL TO FRANK O'CONNOR,
JANUARY 17, 1961:

Tuesday Jan 17

Dear Michael:

We crossed in the mail. If I don't hear from you for a certain length of time I begin to get fidgety. I am keeping your letter in my safe deposit box, for the next time this situation occurs (as it will inevitably) and then I can show you the words I HATE TEACHING. I wish those two works in progress were less remarkable. You may end up convinced that you like teaching instead. But for your sake I can't help being relieved that the group is interesting. It doesn't take as much to make you turn your face to the wall as it does some people. Yesterday I turned my face to the wall. Maeve took Bluebell for good, and we got a puppy from some friends of the Cheevers, who it turns out live a fairly relaxed life. That is to say, *they say* that the oldest girl (quite old, a teenager) used to sleep with a half grown sheep, and that the mynah bird's droppings ended up in the table silver drawer, that sort of thing. Anyway, the puppy had not had its permanent shots and when Emmy took it to a vet's for a preliminary checkup he hit the ceiling and said that the puppy showed signs of distemper. So I took it to Speyer hospital, where they said they didn't think it did have distemper, but said to watch it for a couple of weeks, gave it a temporary shot, and sent it home. Well it is the color of a Yorktown Heights deer or a young lion, but a Labrador, and very sweet, but a little timid, after having been left for six weeks in a kennel, and having seen a dog and a cat die of distemper I would just as soon (yesterday) have died myself rather than live through it. Today I am hopeful as usual. As people who give up at the drop of the hat always are. Anyway, it either was paper trained already or we have paper trained it. It is partial to Kate, who loves it more than life itself. Everybody has colds except E and me. The rugs were all rolled up and the apartment looked like Buchenwald, but we put them back in last night, in a burst of confidence in the dog, which so far seems justified. Exhausting, though. Just like having a baby. Broken nights' sleep and listening (E) and great interest in defecation.

If by "the damned book" you mean the bound autobiography, I haven't had it. The Lawrence books arrived about three weeks after you mailed them. I have been reading, with wild pleasure, Forster's Guidebook to Alexandria, which he wrote just after Howards End.* I can now find my way around that city blindfold in the dark, though I don't know just what I will do with this knowledge.

As for the usual statutory misunderstandings, I had to think and think to remember what could be the cause of the current one, and then it came to me. Something Rachel MacKenzie told me, about Harriet's friend What's 'is name.† He did Something He Shouldn't Have. But I am sure she has long since forgiven him and I never was even cross about it, and I doubt if anybody else knows about it, except possibly Shawn, who has many too many reins in his hands to care. What it reminds me of is Brookie's Sulking Curtain, which she resorts to officially because of hurt feelings but actually only when spoken to about something she *knows* was naughty. Anything you can say that will suggest that nobody is cross at anybody will be appreciated. It is now Tuesday, and I hope to God you actually did write that story. My novel is the same week as your book. I think it's the 20th, but anyway somewhere in there. It is strange to think of last Sunday's sleet beating against the windows of your forsaken apartment. Do you ever think how much the objects must miss you? Or how much I do?

Love to H and to HO and to you,

B

---

* Maxwell's lead review of *Alexandria: A History and a Guide*, "Mr. Forster's Pageant," was published in the February 18, 1961, *New Yorker* and is reprinted in *The Outermost Dream.*
† Rachel MacKenzie (1909–80), a fiction editor at *The New Yorker*, wrote *Risk* (1970), an account of her open-heart surgery, and *The Wine of Astonishment* (1974).

WILLIAM MAXWELL TO FRANK O'CONNOR,
JANUARY 23, 1961:

Monday

Dear Michael:

Well it was just handed to me. I don't know the name of that white wildflower that looks like Queen Anne's lace and isn't, but the other is brown-eyed Susan, and I hope they both grow in Ireland. Under different names, of course. As if in a dream I looked to see if my name was really in the front of it, and as in a dream it was. All the pictures are splendid. The frontispiece is so clear, it is like having the original. The one on the back of the dust jacket is just as valuable. The eyes, the eyes explain everything. You are already quite there, inside that hood. Looking at her mouth, I would give a good deal to protect her from what is still to come. But she could have gone through all that and not had you for a son. I am sure she is more than content. Good picture of you as a man, too, but then you should be ashamed of yourself for always taking such handsome pictures. It's not fair to the likes of other people that have to have their pictures on dust jackets. I turned to the last section first and seem to find a great deal there that is new to me. In fact there are some pages where I *think* you didn't leave one sentence standing on another. I was happy to see you had put back the foreskins.* And I wish you were here so that I could show you the calendar that Elizabeth sent me, with the picture of Casement on it. Though there is no real resemblance, he reminded me of Emmy's brother. Such handsome men haven't a chance in the world of happiness. In the Greek army, in the Golden Age, he would have been given a medal for his beauty. With us he gets quicklime.

We are going to see "Rhinoceros" tonight, against my better judgment. E has a cold. Everybody has, except the new puppy and me, and the puppy has some sort of intestinal infection and is only half paper-trained. We have had her a week now, and I don't know how many colored crayons she has swallowed. Enough to give anybody enteritis. I think the German girl is going to leave before we get the puppy housebroken. In the manner of Germans, she loves the puppy when it is good and says that dreadful puppy when it is bad. Since she and Brookie are not getting on, I can face her departure, myself, but not the picture of E coping. A visit from my father-in-law beginning Wednesday. Emmy's older brother and new wife shortly after that. And I forget what else. If only I had been permitted to sit a little longer in the waiting room of the S.P.C.A., I would have finished a book review, radio and all. As it is, I am your devoted,

B

---

* An imaginary lost shipment of "One Bale Foreskins" that O'Connor, a young messenger boy for the Great Southern and Western Railway, was asked to trace as a joke at his expense.

EMILY MAXWELL TO HARRIET O'CONNOR,
LATE JANUARY 1961:

Harriet dear,

We loved Michael's letter and having bits of him appear—the new story and the critical piece in the N.Y. Times about private reading.* I picture you and Hallie Óg, brown, under an orange tree half in blossom and half in fruit, not missing our Russian blizzards at all. My little vase from Burgundy stands on my desk, holding narcissi that got too heavy for their bowl, reminding me of nice things to come. Things are not as gloomy as that, but at mild sixes and sevens. Kate has been home for a week with bronchitis, Brookie has a cough, and we have a 5 months old Labrador puppy. *Not* housebroken & with diarrhea. Thea, the German girl, is very cross with the puppy and says it is so spoiled! I wonder how we ever had the courage. But she is beautiful, honey-colored, and good, except that she eats of course all the crayons, button-eyes, hairpins, & slippers, & a great deal else, she can find. Bill is just finishing a review of Forster's Guidebook to Alexandria, and we are trying to get to "Rhinoceros" tonight, if it stops snowing.

Brookie's pinafore is another little breath from France—all those *fresh* vegetables, & it is just right, a little big, so she can use it next year again, and very becoming. And Kate took her pencil box to school the first chance she got.

Now comes the sad bad news. We have decided to go to Oregon this summer, & can't do both financially. We are both very sad because it was so tempting, but maybe we can still hope to do it another year. I hope you can find someone else!

Tell Michael I am so grateful to him for showing us the Soviet translations of Chekhov. They are so different from any I've ever read.

With much love to you both & Hallie Óg—

EMMY

———

* "Discovery and Rediscovery Within the Covers of a Book," which O'Connor originally called "The Modesty of Literature," in the January 15 *New York Times Book Review.*

WILLIAM MAXWELL TO FRANK O'CONNOR, MARCH 1961:

Dear Michael:

Ça commence. How reluctant people are to do simple justice to an accomplishment.* You'd think praise had to come out through the rectum. Well, what I have on *my* mind is what lies ahead. Nobody has ever tried it, and nobody but you could do it. And I need to read it.

The American Wife is going to press this week, after which there will not be *any* stories by you waiting to be published. In other words, put up or shut up, as the man said.

Oh I wish you were here instead of there.

B.

———

* An early review of *An Only Child.* Maxwell might have been referring to Patrick O'Donovan (no relation) in *The New Republic* (March 13), who praised O'Connor only after sharing his reservations. Reminded of this in 1995, Maxwell said, "Anybody who didn't think *An Only Child* was a masterpiece was a fool and should be hung up by his thumbs."

FRANK O'CONNOR TO WILLIAM MAXWELL, APRIL 2, 1961:

4102 Amaranta Way,
Palo Alto, Calif.

My Dear Willie,

Slackness in writing is due to (a) shame and (b) overwork. However they manage it these American institutions do work you to train oil as they say in Cork. So yesterday when I got a nice letter offering me $15,000 to teach next year in upstate New York, Hallie sat down and wrote a firm reply. Then she said 'Sign that or I'll divorce you.' So I signed. When term ended last week I decided to write to you and then thought that I had only a week before the nightmare began again, so I wrote a chapter of the autobiography, part two, as per instructions. I have just finished and re-read it, and it's awful. I wouldn't show it to an enemy, but I have a feeling that when I've re-written it half a dozen times (how? in this mess I've got myself into?) it'll be something. At least, it will remind me that all literature is escape, and to hell with critics.

Hallie and Hallie Óg are off to Easter Sunday church, Hallie Óg in what she calls Katie-Brookie's dress so I have the house to myself for once. I don't like the house, which is California-style, meaning that it's a wooden hut with glass walls and wooden screens, and I keep promising myself an Irish-style one with thick bricks and solid doorways. Houses like these were designed by pansies for childless couples.

I enclose a review of The Château, which is rather superior for this dreadfully provincial press of ours—item, Brendan Behan is drunk again; Joe de Maggio is seeing Marilyn Munro again; the Chronicle keeps you in touch with the great world of culture. As I keep on quoting to you from that marvellous old Gaelic poem 'This house is empty tonight; if only there were one poet in it it would be a full house.' Actually we have a poet, Yvor Winters, and in the kindness of his heart he gave me an offprint of his essay on Yeats, which shows that Yeats was ignorant and wouldn't even get a Pass in Stanford. Which may be true.* Seeing that I have a class of a hundred, I couldn't grade the papers, but I saw one on Lawrence and Joyce entitled 'The Nightingale and the Bird of Gold' which only got a B, so I changed it to an A and told the marker that any student who quoted Yeats so appositely deserved an A for that alone. (I needn't say it was actually a really good paper.)

I got a delightful letter from a man on the N.Y. called Anthony Bailey about the book, and I shall reply to it if ever I shift this load of work off my shoulders for an hour. If you know Bailey, thank him for me, and tell him I wish I had written his letter about Childers instead of the piece I did write.†

Tomorrow school begins again, and I must be reading Dickens, but Hallie, who is the original Pollyanna assures me that now I shall be able to count the days, and the days will be longer, and I shall be so inspired I shall be writing like mad. Christ is risen, brother. In church this morning the parson said as he shook hands with a Dear Old Lady 'Christ is risen' and she replied with a delighted expression 'Oh, he is?'

That is how I feel!

My love to Emmie and the Care—I like those Irishisms which are so much more to the point than our miserable literary equivalents. As for you, you don't know how well off you are—'O to be in Brooklyn now that April's there!'

Ever,
MICHAEL

----

* *The Château* was reviewed by Jackson Burgess on March 26. Winters's characteristically hostile essay on Yeats may have been "The Poetry of W. B. Yeats" in the April 1960 *Twentieth Century Literature.*

† O'Connor had written admiringly of Erskine Childers, "one of the great romantic figures" of the Irish Troubles and author of *The Riddle of the Sands,* in *An Only Child.* Bailey's March 20 letter to O'Connor was about Childers.

WILLIAM MAXWELL TO FRANK O'CONNOR, APRIL 5, 1961:

Wednesday

Dear Michael:

When I picked up the phone to call Anthony Bailey it turned out he had flown the coop. He's in England. I sent your message after him. (63 The Droveway, Hove 4, Sussex) and a young Irishman named Sean O'Criadain pleased me yesterday by saying with all the seriousness at his command that the autobiography was great writing. Proving that there are exceptions, or there is at least one prophet who is not unhonored in his own country. And how can the new chapter of the autobiography be anything but awful, with me so far away, too far away to look up from it and say It's marvelous, which I'm quite sure it is. Upstate New York indeed. Who do they think they are? Has anybody told you about a book of Mrs. Yvor Winters called "The Wife of Martin Guerre"? I recommend it to you. Also her poetry, which I know better than her husband's. And speaking of poets, I read the chapters from the autobiography about the three neighbor women aloud to Robert Fitzgerald, who was on his way home to Florence from a teaching stint in Seattle, and when I finished, he said quietly "That's not ever going to be done any better by anybody." Neither, I think, is his translation of the Odyssey.*

I took Kate to the planetarium last Friday afternoon, and as usual I was rushing things a bit. After fifteen minutes she asked politely, in a whisper, if it was almost over. But then lay back across my lap as if it was the real sky the man was manipulating with his dials. I was very happy. It was just right for my age, knowledge, and time of life. When he filled the sky with stars and they began to *revolve,* my eyes filled with extremely sentimental tears.

In an effort to seize disappointment by the forelock, I continue to look on the dark side of things, so far as The Château is concerned. They printed 7500 and ran out of copies and have just printed 4000 more, and this is so like what happened with the Folded Leaf that I thought history was repeating itself, but then I talked to Himself this morning, and he sounded as if he had the situation well in hand. So maybe he does. It's all so queer, and besides, I cannot remember a word of the book, so I don't know what to expect. Except, from force of habit, the worst.

And it is not April in Brooklyn, I don't suppose, because it is February on East End Avenue. I wake up, rush to the window, see that it is 40 degrees, and that is what it stays all day. With, usually, wind and rain, and a general round of abuse from all concerned. Walking the dog, I am cold and sometimes soaked. And you don't really deceive me. You like teaching. It creeps out of your letter. It's all right. I forgive you. I love editing. We'll have to answer for it on Judgment Day, but by then we will be dead. When do you come? Late May? Early June? They will find a way to keep you there. Paper work. Late June. Never mind. Next year I intend to spend entirely in the uninterrupted felicity of your company.

Love to all three of you,
BILL

---

* Maxwell, in *The Paris Review,* on Fitzgerald, poet and translator: "When I was at Harvard I got to know Robert Fitzgerald, and I used to show my poems to him. In spite of the fact that I was older than he was—I was a graduate student and he was a sophomore—I had enormous respect for him. He was better educated than I was, and intransigent, and he despised anything that wasn't first-rate. One day he looked at my poem and then he looked at me, rather in the way you look at children who present a problem, and he said, 'Why don't you write prose?' I was so happy that he thought I could write anything that I just turned to and wrote prose—as if he'd given me permission to try. The prose took the form of fiction because I do like stories and don't have a very firm grasp on ideas."

WILLIAM MAXWELL TO FRANK O'CONNOR,
AFTER APRIL 20, 1961:

Thursday

Dear Michael:

Rachel MacKenzie was kind enough to present me, the first thing this morning, with a snapshot of you listening in the most sympathetic way in the world to an upset raccoon. It is now under the glass top of my desk, along with AE's portrait, which it beautifully complements. It has made my day.

Also, it turned out that, with your infinitely greater experience of civil wars, you had anticipated the gloom that settled down over the whole Eastern Seaboard. Wonderful how easy it is to keep Americans in ignorance of what is going on in Florida.* They have never been able to take Florida seriously since there was a real estate boom in the late twenties and it suddenly collapsed, just as they were selling housing lots with Venetian mooring posts thrown in, and you couldn't lose. My old man lost exactly what it cost him to pay his ½ share of putting my two brothers and me through college, thus lightening for me, considerably, my sense of obligation and gratitude. I mean, if he had it to throw away . . .

My goodness, I miss you. We had to go through Kate's tonsillectomy without a single call to JA 2-5210. Kate and her tonsils were separated on Tuesday at roughly ten-thirty, by a surgeon who makes a specialty of being both more humane and more psychological in his approach. As usual, this is one step forward and two steps back. The step forward is that Emmy was allowed to stay with Kate in the hospital. The step backwards is that we are on the threshold of a new age in which any difference between human beings and Pavlov's dogs will not be very important. Emmy took Kate to see the surgeon at his office and he charmed her with tricks, and again at the hospital more tricks (Daddy took a violent dislike to the surgeon; Daddy can't do any tricks) and after she was suitably dressed and he was suitably dressed he came back for her and hand in hand off they were to (I'm afraid in her mind) a party in the operating room, though she had been told that it could hurt afterward. Not however that it would hurt like hell. Half an hour later he called down that she had gone under. Forty minutes later he appeared in his business suit and explained the technique: You walk up and down, talking and introducing the child to the anesthetist, showing her machines, etc., because if she stands still the anxiety increases, and if you hurry them they fight it but if you wait there is a moment when they will hand themselves to you and there you are. She got up on the operating table with a smile and took the anesthetic beautifully. She would be down in an hour. . . . She was down in two hours, the last hour being not exactly free from anxiety for her parents, and was wheeled in, and put in a cot, with what looked like a thread of dried blood (as if she had been shot in the head) at the corner of her mouth; a scratch from the clamps. From then on, about every ten minutes, she woke up, sat up, looked around wildly for her mother, and brought her hand to her mouth in the most horrifying Grand Guignol gesture. So much for the party upstairs. Emmy stroked her head and she fell back asleep. In the night E woke up and saw Kate climbing over the side of the crib, and jumped up in time to catch her; she was going to the bathroom. E was terrified. In the morning I came and got them and today is the second day and though she has given up food for the rest of her life, she is cheer-

ful and smiling and has a good color. She has made no unkind remarks about her friend the surgeon, who knows how to do tricks;
she has made no unnecessary remarks of any kind, and her air of silence keeps reminding me of the princess who had seven brothers
who were turned into swans and who had to weave seven shirts for
them in silence for seven years. . . . The surgical job, it seems, was
excellent; we were in good hands; if only the surgeon had not
walked out of the room while Emmy was saying "I have just two
questions I want to ask" I would have loved him. As it is, he can
go fuck himself. And as for the world of the future, perhaps nobody will know that the technique that works so successfully is a
parody of the trust that was once instinctively placed, not always
correctly but always with love. I hope you will shudder with me.

Yours, while there is still time,

B.

———

* The Bay of Pigs invasion.

FRANK O'CONNOR TO WILLIAM MAXWELL, MAY 1961:

4102 Amaranta Way,
Palo Alto, Calif.

> I am asking another of the class, Gurney Norman, to send
> you a story though I feel sure it won't do. At present I am
> reading a very interesting novel by Chu on the theme
> 'Romantic China's dead and gone; it's with Sun-Yat-Sen in
> the grave.'

My Dear Willie,
    You are an egotist! No other word fits it. You write in grief
and indignation about how the specialist was so nice when he took
out Katie's tonsils, and I conceal from you how brutal the special-

ist was when he took the cancer out of my hand! How I longed for my old insincere specialist friend in Dublin who would never have allowed me to lie there on the table for half an hour while he chattered to the old lady in the next room about her imaginary grievances, but would have chattered to me about my real ones. I didn't ask for sympathy; just a little personal attention. Now, when Gogarty operated on Sean O'Faolain's wife he left the tonsils on a plate to be presented to O'Faolain when he called. THAT would have shown you.

And, then, the other day, putting on an old coat that I hadn't worn for a year I pulled out a roll of film which I had forgotten and Hallie took it away to have it developed. Here are some of the results. [. . .] I think I'm almost as clever a photographer as Emmy—not so good on form perhaps, but better on content.

Dammit, don't you realise that each week I say to myself something like 'Twelve more lectures, eight more seminars, and then I'll be in Brooklyn again, arguing with THAT FELLOW about somebody else's story'? Today, I felt so close that I started on a second section of the autobiography—the first, as I told you, was terrible. Then we drove up to San Francisco along the Skyline Boulevard, went to the Zoo and saw the monkeys. Hallie and Hallie Óg went on the Merry-Go-Round, and I sat on the side and felt sentimental, because I suddenly realised that I had never been on a Merry-Go-Round.

At present I am trying to restore peace in the home. I let Hallie off to go to the movies, and she went to Bergman's Virgin Spring and came in in a terrible state. Then she picked up Iris Murdoch's last novel which, she swore, had been well reviewed in the N.Y. and cursed all the way through and threatened to write a letter to Shawn. This morning after breakfast I persuaded her to read the review, and she collapsed because it wasn't favourable at all. Now, I am reading the book to see whether she and Malcolm are right. (I don't think they are.)*

On the way back we passed a restaurant that described itself as 'Me 'n Ed's Pizza Pies Ye Olde Publick House.' Hallie has at last resigned herself to the fact that I won't live here—she has seen such beautiful houses—but Hallie Óg has no intention of leaving and when she is told she is going to New York and Annapolis says 'Just for a couple of days. Then we come back to Canningfornia.' We have also been adopted by a cat called 'Ginger', and there is further dissension because I won't be parted from ~~her~~ and Hallie Senior won't even consider bringing ~~her~~ him with us. What does one do?

Love to Emmy,

(It's a he.) MICHAEL

———

* In "To Everyone, with Love," Donald Malcolm had reviewed Murdoch's *A Severed Head* in the May 6 *New Yorker.* He praised her ironically as "a conscientious craftswoman" of dubious accomplishment: "For its size and weight, [the novel] contains an astonishing number of carefully wrought and involute relations. Indeed, perhaps never in the course of humane letters have so many intimacies been so variously accomplished by so few."

WILLIAM MAXWELL TO FRANK O'CONNOR, MAY 1961:

Wednesday

Dear Michael:

Yes, of course, painful though it is to be found out. An egotist I certainly am. Didn't I rush off, two days after I got your letter, and have a lump removed from my shoulder, just so you wouldn't get ahead of me. I can't say that this operation was worth describing. In fact, I couldn't even feel it, and so I am not quite able not to worry about your hand. Is it all right? Was it very painful? Where was it, in the palm or the back? And which hand? Anyway, it never would have happened if you had stayed in Brooklyn. . . .

There was something queer about that Murdoch review. I thought, on first reading, that the last paragraph contradicted all the unfavorable things the rest of the review said, and was complaining about it to Emmy, who said no, it was all unfavorable, which, I guess, it is. But it is clear who has the brains in the family, and it isn't Harriet and me. We *always* know what we feel before we have time to know what we think. Hmm. Back on the

subject of me again, thinly disguised as "us". Oh damn your eyes.
[. . .]

Alfred just called to congratulate me on how the novel was selling what turned out to be much less than I assumed. You know how good news has a way of wilting on Alfred's tongue. About twelve thousand copies had left the warehouse. Or in other words four thousand less than I thought. Meanwhile I am exhausted. I don't know from what, but I think my unconscious has been working for a chain of Doubleday bookstores in the disguise of a bored young man who doesn't give a damn what novel the ladies who come in buy. I hope you are not showing any such signs of weakness. Never mind Freud and all that. If I were to be jealous of anybody or any book, it would certainly be of you and that one. And if by the time you get back here you have still never been on a Merry-Go-Round, we have a date. It is not considered outré for grownups to ride on the one in Central Park, and I will take Brookie and you can take Her Majesty, and we will ride four abreast. I promise you you will enjoy it.

A kiss for Harriet, and come straight home, do you hear? don't dally along the way drinking up the prescription.*

B

———

* Maxwell's whimsical allusion to "The Man of the House."

WILLIAM MAXWELL TO HARRIET O'CONNOR,
JUNE 12, 1961 (telegram):

MRS. MICHAEL O'DONOVAN
=4102 AMARANTA WAY PALO ALTO CALIF=

I THINK I WILL JUST ABOUT MAKE IT. I AM HAVING
LUNCH WITH YOU BOTH ON THE NINETEENTH, IN
CASE I DON'T SEE YOU BEFORE THAT. LOVE

BILL

WILLIAM MAXWELL TO HALLIE-ÓG O'CONNOR,
AUGUST–SEPTEMBER 1961:

Dear Hallie-Óg:

It seems your parents have given up answering letters. Living among the Irish, who as everybody knows, are charming but critical, terribly critical, they have pulled in their horns, thrown away the typewriter and emptied the bottle of ink down the kitchen sink, and broken the points of all the pencils. If you don't answer this I will have no choice but to give up too, optimistic though I am by nature, and try patience.

You will be interested to know that Katie-Brookie got hit by a swing. In the park. How many times has your mother said, "Watch out, baby! The swing! For God's sake watch out for the swing!"? Roughly five thousand. And do you? No. Did Brookie (it was her forehead that got in the way, and Kate's swing it got in the way of)? No. So there I was in my new study that used to be the breakfast room and I heard them coming back from the park sooner than I expected them, and then I heard your Aunt Emily saying in a very queer voice my name. And then as I ran through the dining room I heard "Brookie's been hit by a swing." Frankly, my dear child, I thought Katie-Brookie had become just Katie. But there she was in her mother's arms, blood from—I won't go into it. Just you keep away from swings, do you hear? A nice man, a doctor, saw it happen in the park and came up in the elevator to ask if he could do something, and asked for a cold cloth and washed her face so we could see the extent of the damage, and then we went to New York Hospital in a taxi and they took x-rays of her head and gave her a shot in the behind just after we had promised they wouldn't, and said are you sleepy for a while and then made us go out in the hall, and unfortunately she wasn't very sleepy and minded very much that her mother was not there and she cried, and it took them forty five minutes instead of the ten they said it would take, but in the end she got sewed up, five stitches, which her doctor, Dr. Singer, is going to take out this afternoon at five o'clock, and she is going to take them to school tomorrow if he will let her. Blue stitches, they are. I'm afraid all this has made her rather proud. But what can you do? People keep asking her what happened and she tells them and they are amazed and she feels very proud. I am very proud of her for having such a thick head. The swing was metal, and Katie is a tremendous swinger, and I wouldn't be surprised if with her in it that swing would go through a stone wall.

I don't suppose they have told you when they are coming home? No. No. That would be too much to expect. Well, enjoy yourself. And if they won't do what you want them to do, you know how to get them to do it. Don't be nice. There is nothing in it. Your loving uncle, and Katie-Brookie's only father,

BILL

WILLIAM MAXWELL TO HARRIET O'CONNOR,
AFTER SEPTEMBER 18, 1961:

Dear Harriet:

I begin to see what Michael meant by that lack of enthusiasm for O'Connor O'Brien only that isn't how you spell his name. One N? I don't know which I am more furious at, whoever started the current fracas, or the Belgians, or Hammarskjöld for being such a fool as to think he wouldn't be shot down.* Oh god it is so maddening. And on top of everything else, you don't come home, like I planned for you to do. I am not even sure I have the right address.

All during the most recent and most humid hot spell of the whole summer I ran along beside Kate's bicycle with my hand on the seat to keep her from toppling. She got the idea at last, the last weekend we were in the country. It was partly that the seat was too high. I lowered it and she rode right off. Then she learned how to stop and start, and finally how to turn around. And then she lost her head and ran into a fence and burst into tears and said "Why are you so mean to me?" when it was all her idea in the first place and I had done nothing but praise and encourage and *support* her. The whole history of the war between the sexes.

One of the things you are missing by not being here is the current hullabaloo raised by Updike's review in last Sunday's Times Book Section. He *said* that the Franny of *Franny* is not the Franny of *Zooey*. And furthermore that the Franny of *Franny* was not even a member of the Glass family. I didn't get any work done at all yesterday. I just sat and listened. The truth is, I suspect, but can't prove it, that the difference, and there probably is some, is that Salinger created the Glass family after he wrote *Franny,* so naturally he didn't know as much about them then as he did after he had made them up. Something like that.[†]

It is lovely being in town. I have got the breakfast room for my study, and we are eating in the dining room, which makes every meal seem like company. There is supposed to be a hurricane tonight or tomorrow. Maybe. I miss coming to see you in Brooklyn Heights. I miss you. All three of you. Terribly. Love,

B.

----

[*] Dag Hammarskjöld, then Secretary General of the United Nations, died on September 18, when his plane crashed en route to a meeting with Moise Tshombe in Rhodesia. Conor Cruise O'Brien (b. 1917), Irish literary critic and political theorist, was then Hammarskjöld's special representative to the United Nations peacekeeping mission to the Congo.
[†] Updike's review of *Franny and Zooey* appeared on September 17; it is reprinted in his 1965 *Assorted Prose.*

FRANK O'CONNOR TO WILLIAM MAXWELL,
BEFORE OCTOBER 10, 1961:

52 Cherry House,
Mespil Flats, Dublin.

My Dear Bill,
　　When I burden you with letters it is in the main that life is so
pleasant; when I don't—it is in the main that I am living in Ireland again. My burden is that of the old tinker woman in Colum's
poem—'O to have a little house, to own the hearth and stool and
all.'* The older I get the more I feel like a superior tramp who at
one time never has with him more than he can carry. I never have
with me the extra manuscript with which I could for a while be
unfaithful to my task of the moment, and so my task becomes a
wearisome marriage, becomes resentful at not being made jealous
and develops an appalling frigidity. Oh, that room of one's own
that V.W. pined for, thinking it a deprivation that only women
knew!
　　I'd buy a house here tomorrow, just to install a duplicate set of
essential books, essential manuscripts and essential gramophone
records, but Ireland within the last year has become enormously
wealthy and expensive, mainly I gather due to an incursion of
Germans who are dodging the atom bomb. We live in two
rooms—all sleeping together in one—and people insist on dropping in. First the friend of Hallie's girlhood who stayed ten days,
then the friend of my boyhood who stayed three weeks, this week
Hallie's parents coming to ensure that the sadistic tendencies they
have always suspected in me are not being taken out on their
grandchild. [. . .] Hallie Óg goes under protest to the only
Montessori school that will take heretics like herself, she having
been turned down for the superior one because the Archbishop
thinks Protestants of three excessively dangerous to faith and
morals. Even where she is she seems to learn peculiar things, sings
hymns consisting of 'Holy Mary, Holy Mary' repeated ad nauseam
and asks me in an awed voice, 'Daddy, are you a Proddy stink?' At

the same time we are all very upset at the segregation you practise in that barbarous country of yours. I have not once exploded in print; indeed, I seem such a changed man that I have been offered a handsome job and haven't yet quite engineered myself out of it, but NEXT WEEK the B.B.C. is doing a television interview of me in my native city, and I think even you will be astonished if I don't say something that will require my immediate return to Brooklyn, house or no house.

Elizabeth seems to have slipped back to N.Y. without even seeing me, which may be as well, as it would have made me home-sick, and I am sick enough as things are. I wanted her to meet my friend, Binchy, the philologist, who has now become an ardent N.Y. reader but is very upset by the fact that the paper is slipping and he has discovered several examples of the non-reflexive use of 'avail'—'avail of the opportunity'. I think it's a subject for a circular, don't you?[†] And when those 6,000 copies of Salinger get distributed, do see that I get one.[‡] I must write a chapter on him for my short story book, but I don't know what to say. Do you?

The first part of the new Autobiography is done but frigid, frigid. I have nothing with which to deceive it.

Love to Emmy,

MICHAEL

---

* "An Old Woman of the Roads."

[†] Daniel Binchy, who first met O'Connor in 1927.

[‡] In *Time*'s September 15 cover story on Salinger, Jack Skow wrote that William Shawn was so flattered by having *Franny and Zooey* dedicated to him that, ". . . graciously bowing in reply," he had "ordered that *The New Yorker* give away 6,000 copies of the book this Christmas."

WILLIAM MAXWELL TO FRANK O'CONNOR,
NOVEMBER 1961:

Dear Michael:

If I have a complaint against you (and I don't, really, I am only
resorting to a figure of speech) it is that you don't value yourself
sufficiently highly. For example. Those six thousand copies of
Salinger. Now the natives have long ago learned not to believe a
word that they read in TIME, and I think of you as a native, and it
is true that to all intents and purposes you are, but now and then
a slight . . . Well, we won't make more of it than it is worth.
There was, briefly, some idea downstairs in the business department that *they* might—not Shawn—distribute copies of the book
at Christmas, as a sort of promotion deal, as in other years they
have distributed copies of New Yorker cartoon books (but never
books by New Yorker writers) and they decided in the end not to,
but though the first rumor reached the ears of TIME INC. the second didn't. So what really happened, you can tell anybody who
asks about it, is that Shawn sent out *one copy* of Franny and Zooey,
to a New Yorker writer much beloved and cherished, named Frank
O'Connor. And trying to get into the act, I added tear sheets of
Seymour and Raise High the Roof Beam, just in case you were
thinking of reading all the Glass stories and didn't have copies of
them. If you also would like a copy of "Nine Stories" all I have to
do is walk across the street to pick it up in paperback. If you really
don't know what to say, don't say it. But I have never known you
to be sincerely at a loss for an opinion. One thing I would suggest,
though, is that you let me read it for questions of fact. The order
in which the stories were written—that kind of thing; most pieces
about Salinger get something wrong, and so contain fallacious de-
ductions, through no fault of the writer, but because the information isn't available to him. And I would like that not to happen to
you.

Elizabeth is here in a manner of speaking. I hear her heels
clicking, and all day long she does things for me, and no one could
say she isn't cheerful, but her heart is I think pacing the length

and breadth of O'Connell Street. If the first part of the autobiography II is done, why isn't it here where I can read it?

Having got such quick action, and from both of you, out of my letter to HO, I will know, from now on, who to address my complaints to. There cracks the whip.

Love,

B

WILLIAM MAXWELL TO FRANK AND HARRIET O'CONNOR,
CHRISTMAS 1961:*

Herself drew it and Katie-Brookie colored it, leaving a few thumbprints to prove that it isn't a four-color process. If you were here, Michael, I would wheedle a Christmas story out of you. (That particular sleight of hand performance I will never forget as long as I live.) The children each have half an hour a day at the piano with me, in addition to their regular lesson, and it astonishes me to discover that you can (to all intents and purposes) get knee deep in incest through the medium of a musical instrument. On the debit side, I am sorry to inform you that the Russian bookshop has stopped carrying most of those English translations. I couldn't get Chekhov for Humphrey.† Only a couple of small volumes of Pushkin. Everything else is Tolstoi—though the atmosphere is still unfriendly, of course. Certain things never change. Christmas does, but then let us hope that the more it does the more it's the same thing. My 'mot' for today.

Love from us all.

B.

———

* Emily Maxwell drew this card, as she did every year. It showed a little boy holding up in a pyramid shape a Christmas tree, a ballet dancer, a star, a pony, Noah's ark, and other holiday bounties.

† Humphrey Noyes, one of Emily's two brothers, a poet and psychotherapist.

1962

O'Connor worked diligently on the reminiscences that would become the second volume of his autobiography, published posthumously as *My Father's Son. An Only Child* was difficult to follow. As Maxwell wrote: "In certain ways, there *is* no going on from volume 1. Not only because it is a classic, but because there is nowhere higher to go in the realm that it deals with. . . ." Writing of his adult life also required that O'Connor relive painful memories, many of which he did not wish to make public. In the spring he began writing weekly essays, no longer in disguise as "Ben Mayo," for the *Sunday Independent,* as well as describing "The Holy Places of Ireland" for *Holiday.* He also completed *The Little Monasteries,* translations of early Irish poems. On July 5, Trinity College awarded him an honorary doctorate of letters, long overdue and, astonishingly, the only academic honor he ever received.

WILLIAM MAXWELL TO FRANK O'CONNOR,
LATE MARCH 1962:

Dear Michael:

Poor incinerated creature. So human and fallible his bottom looks. And if you mean Samuel Beckett, I do, very much.* St. Thomas à I have no feeling about, one way or the other. This is largely the fault of L. Olivier, who isn't as good an actor as he used to be, or I am getting more particular. Both, I dare say.† In the

Century Club there is a large book full of illustrations from the museum in Pompeii that ladies are not allowed into. I must say I was pleased to see that I had so much in common with the Romans. On the face of it, I would have said not. But that is because Roman sculpture always looks as if it had been made by a machine, of a machine, and for a machine.

When are you going to let me see part II? I prefer to think that you are in no position to tell whether it is awful or not, having just written it. And if there is an alarming object in this world it is a writer delighted with something he has just written. There is no worse sign. Even if it is awful, it doesn't matter, because I will beat you and beat you till you get it right, do you hear? Because the material is there, and when have you ever failed to come through as a writer? It has got to work. For God's sake stop teasing me, and let me read it.

I am on page 290 of Katherine Anne's new novel, a borrowed copy.[‡] It comes out next week, with a party at '21. It's fine. I don't want to do anything but read it. Not because of the style, though it is well written, but because I am so interested in the people. Would you like me to send you a copy?

The Yeats show I went to mournfully, as an act of piety toward a missing, a long and maddeningly missing friend.[§] It was beautiful. They look as if he had painted not with a palette knife but with a nail file. "The Old Days" was marvelous. Such life, and such color.

It seems I need you not only to finish my novels but to get them started. I have a character, a central figure, a man shaving, but the son of a bitch won't do anything.

We are going to Oregon in July, and next summer, I really think, it will be Europe. If it isn't, it will be because the Life force is running low. This noon I sat looking at a book full of photographs of Brooklyn Heights. There was even a picture of one of your favorite churches. Ah well, if I had known what you were up to, I would have slapped a habeas corpus on you and kept you from leaving the country.

This is Easter vacation, and we are in Yorktown Heights until Sunday. Lovely bright weather, skunk cabbages, and the tips of daffodils showing. Kate has a cold and is learning to play the xylophone. Brookie is running all over the neighborhood, and swearing most shockingly when she has trouble with her plastic sewing machine. The house is full of children, and Emmy is happy. She loves the country the way I used to. The dog is happiest of all. The New York Central is unchanged. I miss walking by the river, the first and last act of most of my city days.

Water, said Freud softly in his beard. Just what is it about you and water. (knowing the answer, having invented the whole thing, though not the womb)

> Love to you both,
> B.

---

* This is in response to a postcard that no longer exists which the O'Connors sent Maxwell from Pompeii.

† Beginning in October 1961, Sir Laurence Olivier played the title role in an American production of Jean Anouilh's *Becket*.

‡ *Ship of Fools,* published intentionally on April 1.

§ The paintings of Jack B. Yeats (1871–1957), the poet's brother.

FRANK O'CONNOR TO LOUISE BOGAN, MARCH 31, 1962:*

34 Court Flats
Wilton Place
Dublin, Ireland

March 31, 1962

Dear Miss Bogan,

I do hope that Bill Maxwell told you I've been abroad for the last few weeks, and waiting to get at a typewriter to reply to your letter.

Naturally, I was thrilled by it, less for the money—though that always comes in very handy—than for the honor of being associated with so many of the writers I most admire. My only hesitation about accepting is the difficulty of getting to America—and back—(particularly back)—and particularly in view of the fact that we are already committed to a trip to America in October when I've accepted an invitation to lecture at Dartmouth.

Except for my wife, I am the world's worst air traveller, always insist on flying the plane myself and am then sick for a week, so whenever it is at all possible I prefer to go by boat. As you can imagine I've been pestering the shipping companies, but unfortunately in this benighted country I am condemned to slow ships. The best offer I've been able to get is a ship from Galway that takes eight days; the Mauretania, which isn't so bad doesn't, alas, get in until the afternoon of the 24th. Bill will explain to you privately the reasons why I can't just go to Southampton and pick up the Elizabeth or the United States and make the journey in four and a half days.[†] Even as things stand, the shipping companies are reluctant to offer me a passage back, just when the tourist tide turns, and at the best it looks like taking a whole month off from work and the family.

I feel sure that I could make it, somehow, even if I have to fly the damned plane myself, but it wouldn't be fair to you to accept without warning you of the concatenation of mischances that might befall. And if you felt that you'd prefer not to risk the possibility of my not making it, I should sympathize and understand.

Anyhow, when we come to New York in the Fall I shall insist on Bill's effecting an introduction so that I can thank you in person, and not leave you with the impression of an elderly cowardy-custard afraid of a short plane trip.

Yours sincerely,

FRANK O'CONNOR

Miss Louise Bogan
Chairman, Committee on Grants for Literature
The National Institute of Arts and Letters
633 West 155 Street
New York, New York, U.S.A.

* Louise Bogan (1897–1970), poet and poetry critic for *The New Yorker* from 1931 to 1969, had written O'Connor on March 8 that he had been chosen to receive an Arts and Letters Grant of $2,000 (along with seventeen others, including Daniel Fuchs, John Hawkes, and Galway Kinnell). The awards ceremony was planned for May 24. O'Connor could not come to New York and was asked to send a brief statement for the manuscript exhibition that also opened on May 24. His "Progress Report" follows.

† O'Connor's ex-wife had legally prevented him from entering England.

PROGRESS REPORT

The most important thing about this Prize is that it is given me by my peers and masters. I think that what any writer worth talking of values most is the approval of other writers, for though I have met good writers happy enough with little in the way of public recognition, I have never met a really successful writer who wasn't hungry for the praise of writers who had had no success; or as a publisher once put it to me 'We have to publish a *few* good writers because the successful ones want to see their own names on the same list.' (The publisher was not Alfred Knopf.)

It is secondary, though important, that the prize will enable me to continue for a while my attempts at making Early Irish Literature intelligible in our time. This task, too, may be partly vanity, because W. B. Yeats was one of the first to praise my translations, and he published two volumes of them at his own press. It is also partly piety, because it was the first literary task that I set myself. Irish literature of the 8th and 9th centuries, like Irish literature of the early 20th century, is important because it is better than what was being done anywhere else, to my knowledge; but it is still the province of ~~scholars~~ philologists, and it is not the business of philologists to answer questions that should be answered by literary historians and critics. When they do, the answers can be very wide of the mark. When I was a boy I made manuscript anthologies of Irish poetry to read while I was walking; now that

I am approaching the age of 60 I am still making anthologies of Irish poetry, though walking has become more difficult.

The best thanks I can offer my friends of the National Institute of Arts and Letters is to copy some of the translations I have been working on during the last few months. The latest—which used to haunt me in the country in America—was written about the year 800.

In the Woods.

A hedge of trees is all around;
    The blackbird's praise I shall not hide;
Above my book, so smoothly lined,
    The birds are singing far and wide.

In a green cloak of bushy boughs
    The cuckoo chants his melodies—
Be good to me, God, on Judgment Day!
    For I write well among the trees.

The second is dedicated to Malcolm Cowley because I recited the Irish to him on New Year's Eve, 1961 in Stanford but was too inebriated to translate it properly. It dates from about 850.

The Ex-Poet

Once the ex-poet, Cuirither,
And I were lovers—there's no cure,
And I am left to bear the pain,
Knowing we shall not meet again.

South of the church there stands a stone
Where the ex-poet sat alone;
I sit there too at close of day
In twilight when I come to pray.

No woman now shall be his mate,
No son nor daughter share his fate,

No thigh beside his thigh repose—
Solitary the ex-poet goes.

The final verse is supposed to be spoken by the same girl, the poet Liadain, asked to prove that she had overcome her passion for Cuirither by spending the night with him.

The Pleasure of Virtue.

Though I and my love Cuirither
Had practised virtue for a year,
Left together for one night,
Our thoughts would stray before daylight.

After that, I can only hope that my friends in America will agree that in Irish Literature I've found a rival not unworthy of them, and will not find me insincere when I send them my love.

FRANK O'CONNOR

WILLIAM MAXWELL TO FRANK O'CONNOR, APRIL 2, 1962:

Dear Michael:

Now look what I've gone and done. I read this with such pleasure (and Proust is not my man, not in the sense that you are, I mean) and found myself asking Moss if I could send it to you. You are to take the imposition lightly, and if it bores you, for God's sake don't read it.*

Emmy and I went to a party for Katherine Anne at 21 yesterday, mostly so I could tell you all about it, but there was nothing to tell. I expected to see the beau monde and instead ran straight into a boy who was raised on Baptist Church Road and is working for Collier's. Publishers and publicity people, as usual. They have worked out a system for getting each other drunk. KA was exhausted from the massive hullabaloo, had been vomiting all day,

and was in a state of impermeable excitement. It was like shout-
ing at somebody through the thick plate glass of a restaurant window. I couldn't see that anything had been done for her pleasure,
only her apotheosis, which she was bravely enduring. Emmy was
taken with the surroundings and would have stayed for dinner on
one of the lower floors but I took her firmly by the elbow and ush-
ered her to a table at Longchamps instead. Just as expensive but
they aren't rude to you.

Love to Harriet,

B.

---

* Howard Moss (1922–87), poetry editor of *The New Yorker* since 1948, had
written *The Magic Lantern of Marcel Proust*.

FRANK O'CONNOR TO WILLIAM MAXWELL, APRIL 5, 1962:

34 Court Flats,
Wilton Place,
Dublin.

April 5th.

Dear Bill,
    Thanks for Moss's book received a few moments before. I'll
write about it when I've had a chance of reading it. All I know
from a first glance is that you like Moss better than me. You
wouldn't let me get away with a phrase like 'an abstract concept of
the mind.'
    The B.B.C. did a half hour program on me in Cork last No-
vember. It took a week and they paid me $150. On the road back
to Dublin I got drunk and spent $175 on one of Proust's girls
whom I saw hanging in an antique shop in a country town, while
Harriet screamed murder at me from the background. She now
lights fires under her—our chimney smokes.

Life is difficult everywhere. My last note to you was from Pompeii, and when I get back our girl Elizabeth asks if she can introduce me to a journalist who has got my dander up by writing ignorantly of Scandinavia.* Don't tell anyone in the office, please. It would upset her, and anyhow, I shall go on as if I were you, in loco parentis.

There is only one man in each town one can learn from, and he's always moving. I told you many times about Binchy, your alter ego in Dublin. Now he's got a professorship in Harvard, and if I go back to America you'll get a fellowship in Rome. You'll meet him in the Fall but don't worry. He is good-looking but he won't run away with Emmy.

I've written personally to Louise Bogan about the prize, but how the hell do you explain personally that you're terrified out of your wits of aeroplanes? I'll probably go through with it if I have to—after all I never missed going to London during the Blitz except the one time when I was taken off the boat by police, but it's nothing to look forward to, and I am principally planning on spending October and November in New York and seeing you all. Don't forget to write to me if any one you know has a flat to rent up to Christmas. You may even get me writing seriously again. At the moment I seem to do nothing but verse translations, which are beautiful but vaguely alarming, like the first hints of delirium tremens.

Love to all,

MICHAEL

———

* The note from Pompeii may have been the postcard of the "poor incinerated creature" Maxwell spoke of in March.

WILLIAM MAXWELL TO FRANK O'CONNOR,
APRIL 10, 1962 (telegram):

> MICHAEL ODONOVAN
> 34 COURT FLATS
> WILTON PLACE
> DUBLIN 2
> ==NO I WONT GET A FELLOWSHIP IN ROME
> COME BACK COME BACK==W

FRANK O'CONNOR TO WILLIAM MAXWELL,
MID-APRIL 1962:

34 Court Flats,
Wilton Place, Dublin

Dear Bill,

I came in to Harriet the other night, wailing 'I want Bill Maxwell', and she said 'You mean you think you've done something good.'

I didn't mean that at all, but an hour with that hard pencil of yours making notes would leave me with a very nice opening chapter for the new volume, so if you find yourself inspired, do please scribble as the notion comes to you.*

Harriet got a note from Elizabeth, saying that after all it might be better if I didn't meet her young man, but two nights later he blew in on a party of priests and set us all by the ears. We were trying to find out our grounds of difference but when Betty's young man attacked me for insisting on attending Protestant funerals, the six priests turned on him and rent him.

Poor child!

Love to Emmy,
MICHAEL

---

* O'Connor enclosed an untitled version of the first chapter of *My Father's Son*, which was called "Rising in the World" when published.

WILLIAM MAXWELL TO FRANK O'CONNOR, MAY 9, 1962:

Dear Michael:

I got as far as page 8, making notes of a detailed sort, and then realized that this was not the way to say what I have to say, because what I have to say ends with a question mark, not a period.* Supposing, which I cannot help doing, that this were to be published in the New Yorker, the first thing Shawn would insist upon is that it be made to read in such a way that it would be clear to somebody who hadn't read volume 1. It doesn't read that way, of course. Do you want it to, is the question. I have meant to look up Yeats' autobiographies, to see what he does with this situation. Probably ignores it. I don't need to look up Sir Osbert Sitwell's volumes, because restatement is hard work, and no Sitwell ever gave himself up to that kind of discipline. Inartistic restatement, such as you sometimes find at the beginning of Parts 2, 3, 4, 5, 6, and 7 of a New Yorker profile, isn't, of course, what I mean. It should come, the necessary information, naturally and inevitably, and as if the author too had never heard of part 1. To show you what I mean, on page 1 these questions arise: what prison camp, why is the author able to call himself a gaolbird, is he serious or joking, what new government, where does he live (no mention of Cork on page 1) and what year was this? And Mr. Shawn would certainly insist that you explain the situation at home more fully than you have here. And I wished that you had given yourself more room, more rope, something, in describing that meeting with Lennox Robinson in the restaurant of the railway station. On the face of it, you seem to me to have been an odd couple. What do you suppose you said—the very first thing—on meeting him? (Did I dream that Heine, on meeting Goethe, remarked, to his everlasting humiliation, that the plums on the road from Jena to Weimar were very fine?) And what did Robinson say? And what did you both say after that. In short, could you *do* Robinson bargaining with a talented impecunious very young young man, between trains in the railway station in Cork, in a way—that is, with a fullness that would satisfy the heart of the novelist who is writing this letter?

There are many such scenes in volume 1, and I have a little the feeling that you are hurrying to get on to something more important, but what? (Yeats, no doubt.) But I feel that Yeats isn't going to go away, and in fact am not even worried about him. I am so certain, from talking to you over the years, that you will do beautifully by him. So, in the meantime, I want to know about Sligo. What was it like when you went there, what were those six months like? Who did you know there? What are the citizens of Sligo like? What does it look like. How did you pass the evenings, or did you study morning noon and night in the library, and what was the library like? The same goes for Wicklow. And shouldn't you, if possible, give some more concrete idea of the demoniacal element in Phibbs' poetry and personality? And try to imagine my feelings when I read "Russell, with whom I had become friendly . . ." and again no detail. I really must (unless it is none of my business) know how and where the friendship ripened. Consider, for instance, the loving care with which you did the ripening of your friendship with Corkery. I was particularly looking to Russell and you.† Are you saving him for later? And at what point did the sea begin to figure in your imagination to such an extent that you had to rent a cottage at Courtmacsherry? And what was C——— like? And all the time I have been writing this, I have in the back of my mind been asking myself if there wasn't some other way of doing volume 2 than the usual method of going on from where you left off. In certain ways, there *is* no going on from volume 1. Not only because it is a classic, but because there is nowhere higher to go in the realm that it deals with, and maybe the solution is to focus the second volume around a different thing—not just your life (though rising in the world is a spectacle that few can resist and I am not one of them) but your life as a writer. I can imagine, for example, a whole volume composed like a piece of music around the relationship with Yeats, in the course of which everything else is made clear, but never presented as part of the foreground. I wish you had sent me the whole boxfull of material. Anything I say now is pure guesswork, and I should think not the least help to you. What you have sent me, and I think I ought to hang onto it until I have heard from you, is beautifully done, of a high polish, but in some way gives me the feeling of closing in on itself instead of opening out into larger and larger matters, scenes and people to come. I would feel profoundly frustrated except for Harriet's letter this morning, saying that you are going to be here for at least two months in the fall. There will be time then for you to get it through my thick head what you are up to.

And fire the Moss carbon back, if you don't mind. I'm sorry I inflicted it on you, Proust isn't my man, and you may well be right in disliking it. I didn't mean for you to like it if you didn't like it, but only hoped you would for his sake, because I had.

And is it all right if I let somebody else—meaning Shawn—read the first chapter, with an eye to whether it is right for the New Yorker? While you have had your backs turned Brookie has shed two teeth, and Kate has taken up opera. "Is it true that Sembrich was a mezzo-soprano?" she asks, from the top of her double decker. "How could she sing Rosina and be a mezzo?" "I don't know," I say, torn between admiration and being appalled. At her age I hadn't mastered the pronunciation of Richard Wagner, and it took all my strength to remember to say V instead of W. The world is undoubtedly getting much cleverer.

Love to you both,
B.

––––––

* Maxwell's first letter, never sent, follows.
† Irish writers Lennox Robinson, Geoffrey Phibbs (later Geoffrey Taylor), Daniel Corkery, and George Russell (Æ) figure prominently in the autobiography.

WILLIAM MAXWELL TO FRANK O'CONNOR,
BEFORE MAY 9, 1962 (incomplete and never sent):

Dear Michael:
    I can't tell beans about that first chapter because I don't know
what it's a first chapter to. But this is what occurred to me along
the way. And mainly in the light of what I would be telling you if
you had submitted it to The New Yorker and we had got as far as
the galley stage.
    Page 1, line 1: What prison camp? The reader who read vol-
ume 1 will know, but what about the reader who didn't? That
goes for the new government and the local (local to where? no
mention of Cork on page 1) and what year was this?
    Page 2. Who is Daniel Corkery, the American reader of Vol 2,
who hasn't read Vol 1, is bound to ask.
    I don't suppose you could reconstruct your meeting (drama-
tize, dramatize, Henry James said) with Lennox Robinson in the
restaurant of a railway station? You would seem to me to have
been an interesting couple. What do you suppose you said—the
first thing—on meeting with him. And what do you suppose he
said? And what did you both say after that? Could you, in short *do*
Robinson bargaining with a talented impecunious young man,
between trains in the railway station in Cork? Instead of this sum-
mary and indirectly reported conversation? And could you, for,
again, the benefit of the reader who doesn't know vol 1, do yourself as you were at that period? And Mr. Shawn is certainly going
to want you to insert something about your mother's having
worked as a charwoman in the past, when there wasn't enough
money because your father was drinking, and what kind of houses
she worked in. I hear you scream with boredom at the thought of
repeating yourself, but that is something Henry James never bog-
gled at, and there are charms, there is an art in restatement which
New Yorker profiles aim at and never reach but I think you could.
Who did she get the loan of money from?
    Page 3: All I know about Sligo is that I seem to remember
that Yeats used to visit there as a child, and ride a pony that had

been with a circus and went round and round absentmindedly. There must be more than that to a place with such a wonderful name. And you have devoted six lines, no five, to six months of your life. To me this has all the earmarks of making a long story short, a thing that I cannot abide. For god's sake tell me about Sligo, and tell me about yourself, man! Who did you know there? And how did you pass the evenings, or did you study librarianship morning, noon, and night. What does Sligo look like? Did you study in a library? And who else was there? Are these people in your early stories?

And the same thing goes for Wicklow, about which I am equally curious because Maeve's mother came from there. And what does it mean to be the heir of a West of Ireland Big House? Should I see *Bowen's Court,* for instance, or was that not typical?* And where did you and Phibbs read each other's poetry? And did he publish his poetry later, and could you offer one of his demoniacal passages? and what kind of nothing would he fall into a childish rage about? And what did you earn five shillings at when you bicycled out into the mountains one night a week? And what about the mountains? Michael why this *hurry?*

Page 4, I wouldn't point out, but the checkers would that 250 pounds, in those days, wasn't (see middle of page 2) a thousand but twelve hundred fifty dollars. Were they again short changing you? And try to imagine my feelings when I read "Russell, with whom I had become friendly . . ." and again no detail. To begin with, you are talking about AE, and to continue, he was Diarmuid's father, and I must know how and where and when the friendship ripened.† Consider, for example, the love and care with which you described your friendship with Corkery. I'm sure Russell has been written about over and over, but surely he wasn't beyond being different with you than he was with anyone else, or else you weren't beyond taking or mistaking him in a way that was different and worth talking about. I was particularly looking forward to Russell. Are you saving him for later? (You see what I mean by not knowing what this is a first chapter to?) And the reader has no idea what Harrington's Square was like (the new reader, I mean) and so shouldn't you tell him? And in fact it can't have been the same for you as a young man that it was as a child. So isn't it worth having another go at? And while you are doing Harrington's Square, shouldn't you do your father and his family, to account for the roots?

Page 5—now about that joke, We writers ma'am—just how much had you written? Any of the stories that you still value? Any stories? What? In vol 1, the accomplishment was always in the mind, in the imagination, never in fact; had this begun to change yet? Were you still living in dreams and falling into the abyss between dream and actuality? And why (for the new reader, that is) did your father think you were going to be a liability? I like this paragraph as it is, but feel that if you let yourself go, the relations between you and your father at this period would have a good deal more narrative interest.

Page 6: Why can't you, at this late date, at least try to plumb the reasons that your father identified himself with the house? And how old would he have been at this time? And page 7, what would have happened if you had tried to keep a car in Harrington's Square? I can guess, but it wouldn't be as interesting by half as the reality your answer would provide. And why did you determine to rent a cottage by the sea? So far, I don't remember the sea figuring in your imagination, and it must have come to have a place of some importance, if you did this? I want to know about you and the sea. Is Courtmacsherry the place the cottage by the sea was? And what was it like? And what did you say, and what did your mother say, to the farmer whose daughter-in-law played that trick on him? It is a beautiful little scene that I feel you are holding back on because of having written a story about it.[‡] Oh, I guess she wasn't present. But still, you were, and if there isn't anything to add, I wish you'd start a new paragraph with "Father only listened . . ." because the scene shouldn't be seen through his eyes, but through yours, on whom it made such an impression. And shouldn't you explain, on page 6 about the military pensions? When and how he had soldiered, I mean. In writing this you seem to have had two unconscious assumptions, one that it was going to be as good as published in volume one—that there was no real break. And that the reader was Irish and so needn't have a great many things explained or described to him. The Irish are not readers, they're writers, to a man. You'd better go on writing for Americans. But all the time I have been composing these quibbles, I have been wondering about this approach to the second volume, whether it is the right way to begin. I don't suppose Sir Osbert Sitwell bothered to repeat or explain anything that he had already explained, and it is perhaps just a New Yorkerish thing. The problem, really, is that volume 1 is a classic, and you can't descend from it into ordinary light of day autobiography. So I find myself wondering if there isn't some more architectural way of doing it, such as beginning with your first meeting with Yeats and composing the whole volume around that relationship, with the counterpoint provided by your relations with your actual father and actual family. The first volume is dominated by the figure of your mother, and I somehow gathered that the second was dominated by Yeats. I like very much the rising in the world, but think it could be accommodated along the way, or else could be done with more loving detail, one or the other.

Page 8, I think you know, or can guess at, the basis of his insecurity, and should say what you think it was. And what was Cork itself like, that Russell had such a low opinion of it. Knowing it only from your stories and Corkery's novel, I have always loved it. I know there was no intellectual life there, but when were fiction writers ever dependent on intellectual life. There were people, weren't there? And what world would your mother have felt at home in? And I would dearly love (though perhaps you don't want to do it) an analysis of the difference between a young man's friendship, what he got, from men like Phibbs and Russell, compared with what he got from Hendrick and Corkery. In short, the advantages and drawbacks of parochialism and life in the capital[§]

---

* Elizabeth Bowen's 1942 memoir of her family's house.
[†] Maxwell knew Diarmuid Russell, the literary agent who represented Eudora Welty, among others.
[‡] "Michael's Wife."
[§] The letter breaks off here.

WILLIAM MAXWELL TO HARRIET O'CONNOR,
MAY 1962:

Dear Harriet,

Very melancholy occasion it is going to be, with no Himself.*
Looking on the bright side, I could point out that it is the longest
occasion of its kind anywhere in the world, and enough to break
the strongest bottom. Speech after long long speech. So.

Until I have had an answer to my last letter I will continue to
walk the floor with my hands behind me. Major undertakings discussed through the mail are so like trying to converse in Japanese,
and I feel as if I had accomplished nothing beyond exposing how
unperceptive I really am. Also I have been working on a story that
keeps dropping me through into the layer below, not the one
where stories take place, with action in the past continually sub-
stituted for action in the present, and he could show me the way
out and he isn't here, and that can't be managed through the mail
either.

I believe there is a box of Katiebrookie's best loved clothes on
the way to you. That can be managed through the mail, thank
God.

Love, and then some.

w.

It's too early to find out about sublet flats. The bulletin board
notices are all for summer sublets. But I'll be on the watch for you.

---

* The May 24 National Institute of Arts and Letters awards ceremony.

FRANK AND HARRIET O'CONNOR TO WILLIAM MAXWELL,
JUNE 1962:

34 Court Flats,
Wilton Place, Dublin.

Dear Bill,

Hold your horses! The second chapter should reach you next week some time, and you'll get some idea of where the damn book is going. That was the first chapter and should be called 'Father and Son.' The second is about Phibbs and Wicklow. Robinson has to be held up until much later.

You see, I'm not writing pieces for the paper. Later, if you think the material for a piece or pieces is there you have only to give me the wind of the word and I'll write it for you.

For weeks it has been a steady forty, except when it gets cold, so I haven't seen Elizabeth as I usually do in the Green, but last time I saw her she was dizzy with creative excitement and I suspect not eating. I envy her. I get that feeling from New York. Poor Harriet gets nothing but diseases. At the moment she is waiting for tests from one doctor of her uterus another of her gall bladder, and undergoing diathermy from a third person. I composed a limerick against her which she doesn't like, but I admire the professional competence of it—

> The neurotic American female
> Was always intended to *be* male;
> When things get too bad
> Remember her Dad
> And pack her up safely and re-mail.

At present she is searching for rhymes to 'Celt' and 'husband.' Hallie Óg entertains the other children in school by the hour with stories 'like what Daddy writes.' She hasn't yet learned the past imperfect.

Love to Emmy,
M

P.S. from Harriet: (I'm not really all that falling-to-pieces—it's just that doctors in this country are the only men who look at you when they talk to you—and I couldn't stand another second of the usual male conversation—which is always conducted with averted eyes—monkish training no doubt.)

Life in Ireland Dept: While baby sitting with 4 yr. old daughter of American who'd been here 3 months, I heard her go into the kitchen, give the washing machine a good kick and then say: 'Oh dear God.' 'Don't say that Katie' says I. 'What's wrong.'—Katie answered: 'But that's what my Mummy always says—and then she cries.'

WILLIAM MAXWELL TO FRANK O'CONNOR, JULY 2, 1962:

Dear Michael:

How long do I have to go on holding my horses. Here I stand, week after week, with my hand on the reins, waiting. And no signs of Phibbs and Wicklow. If I don't hear pretty soon I will think you have succumbed to the charms of being famous in your own country.

Anyway, I am glad to leave the New Yorker out of it for the time being. That way I can just read and think about it and save up my opinions for when I see where the book is really going.

I finished a story about my father—snatched from the jaws of failure by Emmy's comments on the previous version. I wanted to make him funny, which he was, but he wasn't always funny. At least not to me. So it was a kind of tightrope I had to walk, with late adolescence yawning under me at every step.*

It seems you cannot have my friendship without having to pay for it. What I have gone and done now is give a letter of introduction to somebody who is coming to Dublin.* John and Margot Wilkie and several of their grown children. I don't know which. But they are five, which is too many to do anything about, but if you will see them and give them some steers about Dublin I will be most beholden to you.

I like John, who is a business man, something of a philanthropist and oh rich enough to be a philanthropist. I adore Margot. If I wanted to send the two of you a present, she would be it, but it is always rash to hope that your dear friends will love each other, and in any case, as I said, there are five of them, which rather puts a ceiling on the possibilities of getting acquainted. Margot's father was the friend of de la Mare and I don't know what all poets. He knew everybody, wanted to be a writer, and took care of the family instead. I never knew him, but old men at the Century Club speak of him with tears in their eyes. I talked to her on the phone a few minutes ago, mostly about your autobiography, which she was passionately excited about. Emmy loves her too— the question I hear Harriet asking in the background.

E and the children left for Oregon last Thursday, and yesterday afternoon, Sunday, she called from a booth by the general store in Neskowin, Oregon.† Last night I slept for the first time. Until then I would wake up from I don't know what, feeling as if I spent the night outside on the grass. And the children's rooms—unspeakable. A teddy bear, a stuffed dog, black, and a stuffed cat, white, on Brookie's pillow. Day after day. Never moving. And in Kate's unnaturally orderly room, piles and piles of books that no head is ever bent over.

In the basement puppies. The dog is no comfort because she is as bad off as I am. She is so used to going from room to room to see what everybody is doing, and I am never doing anything. At least nothing that is of any interest to a Dog. So she bangs through the screen door and goes to see if by any chance they are at the neighbors'. What she doesn't know is that on the 10th of July *I*, boring as I am, will take off too, leaving her with the Davises or with the kennel, depending on how she and the puppies behave. We'll be back in Yorktown on August first, and I'll be back in the office on the sixth, hoping to find Phibbs and Wicklow waiting for me.

Love,

B

*Arriving tomorrow, as a matter of fact. Old Just-under-the-wire, that's what I am.

———

* "The Value of Money," first published in the June 4, 1964, *New Yorker.* Maxwell told David Stanton: "The most important living reader I have is my wife. When I think I have finished something I take it first to her, sometimes in a state of unjustified euphoria. She has good literary judgment and a good sense of when I am or am not doing my best work. Often she has said, when I was quite pleased with something, 'I think this is going to be one of your best ones,' and so sent me back to the typewriter."
† Emily's family came from Portland, Oregon.

FRANK O'CONNOR TO WILLIAM MAXWELL, JULY 1962:

34 Court Flats,
Wilton Place, Dublin

My Dear Bill,

Talk of all the god-damn coincidences. I send you my first chapter in which I refer to Geoffrey Phibbs and you ask why I don't develop Phibbs' character, and Phibbs' character has already been written about, and is now being dissected because too much interesting material has got in which does not refer to Phibbs at all; and then Mrs. White writes a piece on Gardens and quotes the work of Geoffrey Taylor whom she assumes to be Director of the Botanic Gardens at Kew, and my piece explains that, owing to a row with his father, Geoffrey Phibbs changed his name to Geoffrey Taylor and wrote some books on gardening of which I am not competent to judge.* Geoffrey has been consistently unlucky in references to him. He has appeared in the Oxford Book of Irish Verse as having been born in 1890, which is most improbable as there was only a year or two between us. He was one of my three or four literary heroes; there weren't many and you've met one. Poor Mrs. White will probably be deluged with letters because his

great friend in later years was John Betjeman, and those gardening essays were mostly written for the B.B.C., where he was well-
known.

Now I really must write something worth while about him.
It's not fair to be dead only five years, to be praised so nobly by
Mrs. White and have all the credit go to someone else.

Love,
MICHAEL

---

* In *My Father's Son,* O'Connor wrote, "Phibbs became the dearest and best of
my friends, and I have had many." Mrs. White's essay, on lawns, lawn mowers,
apple trees, and Taylor, "For the Recreation and Delight of the Inhabitants," appeared in *The New Yorker* on June 9 and was reprinted in *Onward and Upward in
the Garden.*

WILLIAM MAXWELL TO FRANK O'CONNOR, JULY 3, 1962:

Dear Michael:

Well it turns out that the Wilkies are going first to Cork and
the southern part of Ireland—looking for crosses, etc. (!)—and the
Aran Islands, and arriving in Dublin about eight or nine days
from now, so you can relax. Also, the people I give letters of introduction to never use them. I am not sure that this can be considered one of my failings. As for Phibbs, he clearly is crying out to
be the subject of a letter of Amplification and Correction. Mrs.
White will be delighted that you read her piece and to be
straightened out on the subject of Geoffrey Taylor, and all you
have to do is to tell everything you know or want to say about the
right and the wrong man, and that's it. As with the letter about
Casement, it should be addressed to the Editor, but I'd send it
with a note, if I were you, to Robert Henderson, telling him that
I put you up to it. The last sentence of my letter—that is, your letter to me—would do nicely to end it with: (in case you've forgotten what you wrote) "It's not fair to be dead only five years, to be

praised so nobly by Mrs. White and have all the credit go to someone else."

Emmy has moved my arrival in Oregon up a few days, showing I won't go into what. As of this minute, all is confusion. Love
to you both,

B

WILLIAM MAXWELL TO HARRIET O'CONNOR,
AFTER JULY 5, 1962:

Dear Love:

Isn't he exasperating!

Do you know what I think? I think he's *happy,* that's what I
think. And very cleverly concealing it from us.

If there is a way to get around him, I haven't discovered what
it is. Philosophy is indicated. And of course the weather here is
ravishing. The air like wine. Cool. Sunny.

And of course looking all that beautiful and distinguished in
the newspaper doesn't make him any easier to manage.*

And the real truth of the matter is *I* need *him.* I keep dropping
my fish hook, all properly baited, into the water and it bobs hope-
fully and I draw it up and there is nothing on it, not even the bait.
While that wise old novel swims round and round unhooked. All
because of a deficiency of proper conversation.

H-O is marvelous, but it is her feet—her shoes that do me in.
We have passed beyond that kind of shoe in our family, and I am
afraid will never see its like again. Puss-in-boots looks very much
at home in Ireland.

Tell him I am waiting for the next section. Or three stories.
One or the other.

Elizabeth says that Michael is reading her manuscript. I am
very glad, because I want to check my opinion against his. Also,
he is—Oh no, I won't say it. I won't give him the satisfaction.

XXXXXXXX and love,

B.

* O'Connor received an honorary doctorate from Trinity College on July 5, 1962. Harriet remembered, "He was as delighted as a child, particularly by the fact that they read his citation in Latin."

WILLIAM MAXWELL TO FRANK AND HARRIET O'CONNOR,
OCTOBER 1962:

Dear Michael and Harriet—

I never thanked you for all your kindnesses to Margot Wilkie and her family and she has thanked *me* three times. They adored you.

I have a photograph of Michael's portrait by AE looking up at me from under my plate glass desk cover, and Michael receiving his L.L.D. at Trinity College, and Michael beguiling a coon on somebody's front porch (How did I come by that snapshot? I don't *know*) but do I have Himself? And it's *October.*

Love,
W.

FRANK O'CONNOR TO WILLIAM MAXWELL,
AFTER NOVEMBER 25, 1962:

22 Court Flats,
Wilton Place.*

Dear Willie,

This is harder on you than it is on me. I know where I'm going, but you only see the floundering round. The next story on the schedule would only bewilder you more, so, instead, I'm sending you one that is vaguely sign-posted. Herself says I shouldn't because she thinks it's all wrongly written. I don't because I know there's nothing dull in it that won't drop out in one re-writing. If you see where it's bound for I'll rewrite it for you, but if you don't put it aside or in the waste paper basket because I'll be rewriting it anyhow for the new book.† The new book is Hamlet's father's ghost, knocking at various points under the floor while I chase round the stage trying to pretend I perceive it quite clearly. I don't, but I like to hear the knocking going on and try to encourage it.

We've been discussing the possibility of a summer in America. It depends on the Book, but if it progresses I shall probably ask you to look out for a small house somewhere not too far from you, so that I can proceed with your education.

Love,
MICHAEL

Yes, of course, rewrite anything you want. If it's any good it will be accepted without gratitude. If not———.

———

* They had moved from 34 Court Flats to the more spacious 22 Court Flats on November 25.
† While continuing his autobiography, O'Connor was also preparing *Collection Two*, his revision of *More Stories*, a collection he had found unsatisfying. The "vaguely sign-posted" story is "The School for Wives," published in *The New Yorker* after his death.

FRANK O'CONNOR TO WILLIAM MAXWELL,
LATE DECEMBER 1962:

22 Court Flats,
Wilton Place,
Dublin.

Dear Willie,

This is a New Year's card or a love letter or what have you just to prove that I haven't dropped dead or lost interest or anything else you like to impute to me. All the stories are old chestnuts which are no use for the paper, but they may amuse you who have heard them all, and if I can get next week end off, as I've taken this, I'll send you the second bundle of them.* They're all written out and ready, and only need a little editing to face your steady eye.

I'm looking forward to February and seeing you and the family again. By that time I may have the pretty little book of translations which I've done and had printed but which the Oxford Press has held up.† It should have reached you as a card, instead of the enclosed.

Love,

MICHAEL

———

* The "chestnuts" were recollections of Yeats that appeared in *My Father's Son.* Here, in two parts, they were "Yeats" and "The Death of Yeats."
† *The Little Monasteries.*

1963

_____

When O'Connor was at Stanford, Wallace Stegner had urged him to publish his thoughts about the short story and its greatest exponents, and the book that resulted is *The Lonely Voice: A Study of the Short Story*. O'Connor states that the short story "has never had a hero" but "has instead a submerged population group" whose identity is formed by "material squalor" and spiritual aridity. Thus, the short story depicts "outlawed figures wandering about the fringes of society" and is characterized by "an intense awareness of human loneliness."

In October, he began teaching at Trinity College; he offered a weekly writing seminar and, as a Special Lecturer in the Literature of Ireland, spoke weekly on the development of Irish literature from saga to the present.

FRANK AND HARRIET O'CONNOR TO WILLIAM MAXWELL, JANUARY 6, 1963:

22 Court Flats,
Wilton Place, Dublin.

                                                            January 6th.
Dear Willie,
    Second part of New Year's card as promised. Not so good but more interesting. Old horse started bucking and arguing that he

needed at least twenty thousand words even to canter in. I'll see that he gets it.

At present I am working on a 'Dublin Book of Irish Verse' from A.D. 600 on, a quite impractical job which I must see finished before I die.* I know I shall write better when I have rid myself of this compulsion. Even to see the first quarter of it in proof would give me the feeling that I could mitch and write stories.

Betty came to a party with her boy, and who should be here but an Englishman who was on the committee that gave him a prize. 'So sorry,' he said as he left. 'He shouldn't have got it, you know, but he was everybody's second best.'†

If you remember what that means.

This time next month I should be on my way to see you and Emmy. Meanwhile, my love.

MICHAEL

P.S. [from Harriet] Proof Reader has queried at least 20 small points, but the man is too tired and pleased at having written it to make another change.—So I must drive him to the G.P.O. (yes—scene of the troubles *etc.*) to mail it *NOW* (Sunday night.) We can quibble later.

We don't dare think about coming home—every time the phone rings I'm afraid it'll be something tempting him to change his mind. Keep *all* Gods propitiated please. The Christmas books are lovely—I'll write Emmy. See you *SOON*.

XXX

---

* Published posthumously as *A Golden Treasury of Irish Poetry*, A.D. 600–1200, edited and translated with an introduction by O'Connor and David Greene (1915–81), who was then Professor of Irish at Trinity College, Dublin.
† "Betty's boy," a distinguished writer, is better than everybody's second best: John McGahern (*The Barracks, The Dark, The Pornographer, The Leavetaking,* and others). He had received the Arts Council Macaulay Fellowship.

1963

WILLIAM MAXWELL TO FRANK O'CONNOR,
JANUARY–FEBRUARY 1963:

Dear Michael:

It isn't that the stories are chestnuts, because they aren't, but in form it isn't a New Yorker piece. I can't think that any literary magazine wouldn't jump at it. What shall I do with the manuscript: hold it till you arrive? Give it to Don? Wait for Part II? What I would like is to hold on to it until you come, because it might make talking about the autobiography easier. Assuming that you want to talk about it. I keep feeling that you are subject to the pull of the convention of autobiographical second volumes, which is to go right on as if they were a part of volume I, and all my training is against this, so what I keep thinking is that if only you focused the camera on yourself as you were at this period, you would also capture, in focus, whoever was standing beside you, which to a large extent would always be Yeats. Anyway, I want to ask you a lot of questions, because I don't understand how it came about—the change from the life of fantasy and obscurity to the life of public activity and the friendship of Yeats and A.E. and all the rest. I know in a general way that it just happened, but what I want is to read about it happening in something of the day to day way that your mother must have watched it happening. There are times when having an editor is like having a second wife. Who but a wife ever feels they know who you are and what you should do better than you do yourself? And then they have that annoying way of sometimes being right. Anyway, I see the relation between you and Yeats as narrative, with an emotional content that if you allowed yourself to express it would be about the same as the emotional content of the section of volume I that deals with your mother. WHY DID YOU LOVE HIM? I want to read about his greatness as if it were not a thing universally acknowledged but something that would never be known if you weren't writing about it. I regret not knowing E. M. Forster, but at least I have seen him. I want to see (and smell and touch and hear) Yeats. And my only chance of this is through the young man you used to be. Scold, scold, scold, how boring Protestants are.

W

WILLIAM MAXWELL TO FRANK O'CONNOR,
JANUARY–FEBRUARY 1963:

Dear Michael:

I just finished writing you a letter, when Tom Gorman handed me Part II.* It is what I have been waiting for. At last I see what it was like: a long, endlessly fascinating cat fight. And twenty damns to your Dublin Book of Irish Verse from A.D. 600 on. You are an elegant trifler who would do anything to keep from using the gift that distinguishes you from anybody else with two arms, two legs, two eyes, two ears, a nose, and a mouth. I AM WAIT-ING FOR YOU . . .

WILLIAM

———

* A secretary at the magazine.

WILLIAM MAXWELL TO FRANK O'CONNOR,
JANUARY–FEBRUARY 1963:

Dear Michael:

The book arrived today. I opened it, read one passage, about Napoleon, and rushed it into the hands of Miss Cullinan. This is her last week, before she returns to the place of her heart's attachment, and I want her to be stuffed with the best as she departs, so she will reflect credit on her associates. It is clearly a marvel. If it is as good as I think it is, I may have to share it with you. Six months at our house, six months at yours. Stone silent she is out there, lapping it up.

I'm happy that Harriet is coming, and that we can hook necks with her. But I think you ought to come too. I think you ought to come because I have such a clear idea of what volume II of the autobiography is like; must be like; and how do I know that you have grasped it as clearly as I have? I see it as a classic of the form. Just that. Seeming to do one thing and actually doing what has never been done before. No effort, all accomplishment. Characteristically yours and as impersonal as Sophocles. Are you quite sure you understand about all this?

Elizabeth is returning to Dublin with half a novel, and the other half in her head. What I have seen is very good.* You can write stories sitting at a desk job that is only busy by fits and starts, but to write novels you need to close the door. You can begin teaching her Gaelic anytime you've got a mind to.

Alfred is in Brazil, doing what, do you suppose? Eating and drinking, no doubt. And going to concerts.

I found, for Kate's Christmas, a facsimile of a Pollack's theater, at the Museum of the City of New York. Not hand colored, but she doesn't know about that. And we put it together when we were in the country, between Christmas and New Year's. *Aladdin.* I have never seen such a feverish child. Simultaneously we have the life of the Mozart family, the bear school, and the Widow Crow's boarding house, all going on at once, like concessions at a carnival. And belatedly she has learned to whistle. Brookie, who is as light on her feet as a bag of wet cement, delights me by doing ballet positions. I think how, if she is a ballet dancer when she grows up, the stage will shake. She also informed me yesterday evening that when she cried and I picked her up and comforted her it only made her cry much more. This is quite true, I have noticed it myself, but it also struck me as the opening wedge—that she should have realized it herself. Never mind, in a couple of nights she'll have a dream about a tiger and then we'll see a different tune being played on that bagpipe. Viz: knock, knock. Bad dreeam . . . at two A.M.

I have bought myself all the sonatas and all the quartets and quintets of Schubert, and all the quartets of Mozart, in somewhat the same spirit that I bought myself the collected works of Colette, except that you can't put her collected works on the record player, so there they sit, because I don't have the strength to cope with her vocabulary, after dinner. Before dinner I am not allowed to. And before lunch I don't allow myself to. There is no way out.

I am happy that you are going to have a room of your own, like Mrs. Woolf. I have one too; I drove the family out of the breakfast room. I have been on the exact point of going there and beginning something for four and a half months. Just as soon as life calms down and stops being life, you will see. How I miss you.

My love to you both,
B.

---

* This became *House of Gold.*

WILLIAM MAXWELL TO HARRIET O'CONNOR,
SPRING 1963:

Monday

Harriet my angel:

It is two things: the office has been running me ragged since last August and (2) I took—did I tell you—I took up the piano. I often think of Himself, and what would have happened if he had ever done this.* And usually I tell myself that of course he has done it, he has taken up everything, some time or other. But anyway, instead of writing letters to my friends or writing novels for Alfred Knopf, I sit ravished by the way Bach puts notes together, and Mozart is not a put-er at all but a singing bird, and Purcell is really writing for the clarinet. That sort of thing. After roughly six months I can do music box tunes is what it boils down to.

Now about this journalism.† Did you ever notice what happens when I put my foot down with your husband? Because I have. It is always the same thing. The foot keeps right on going, because there is no opposition, no argument, nothing but whole-hearted agreement, which leaves him free to go right on doing the thing I have put my foot down about. In short, he is—but who knows better than you do what he is. I am saddened by your move—not the move next door but to Ireland, but I can't pretend that I think it was right where you were, and I can't think where it would be. But I don't see why Michael doesn't want to do stories. The autobiography is another matter, thorny, full of problems and difficulties. He has to bring Yeats to life, and that means he has to kill him off when he is through with him, all very wearing, to say the least. But just a couple of stories now, or rather three, since they always come in threes, just a muscular flexing to make sure that he hasn't lost the knack?

About coming over. As of this minute, I don't know whether we can afford to go anywhere next summer, and won't know until taxes are figured out. We got taken by surprise this year, *horridly,* if you know what I mean. And have been being very frugal, and the more frugal we were the more money we spent, which is a fundamental law of economics, I expect. Maxwell's Law. All I can say is I would *like* to come. The Wilkies did indeed tell us how nice Ireland was, but parenthetically, in the midst of telling us how marvelous you and Michael were.

It is funny how one cries out one's love to children. Brookie is just as smug and unsurprised. They damn well ought to be surprised, the little rascals. It isn't automatic, and thrown in with a birth certificate. But never mind. Hugs and kisses to you and I didn't write SOON I wrote IMMEDIATELY. . . .

WILLIAM

------

* In "Meet Frank O'Connor," a 1951 interview conducted by Larry Morrow, he said of his childhood, "At that time I wasn't quite sure whether I wanted to be a writer, a painter or a musician, but soon after I decided on the writing because the raw materials cost less. If I'd had the money for a piano nobody would have been able to ban me now."

† The forty-three articles O'Connor wrote for the *Sunday Independent* from March 1962 to February 1966.

WILLIAM MAXWELL TO FRANK O'CONNOR,
EARLY APRIL 1963:

Dear Michael:

Some money. I am happy to think you are about to have Óg
back again. It must be like six months of no sunshine.

Love,
W

(Written en route from the Grand Jury to the income tax file.
When is a writer supposed to write?)

WILLIAM MAXWELL TO HARRIET O'CONNOR,
BEFORE APRIL 8, 1963:

Harriet dear:

I get back from delivering a lecture in Urbana and find a book
on my desk, "The Lonely Voice" and open it at random and read
"Now a man can be a very great novelist, as I believe Trollope was,
and yet be a very inferior writer . . ." and almost burst into tears.
It has been so long!

Yes, it's true, we had things worked out for a moment so
that we would have arrived in Dublin just after you had left for
America. You have read *Evangeline?* What happened is that Emmy
started asking around among mothers who had taken their
children to Europe and that answer was shockingly consistent:
"DON'T" So we aren't. On the other hand, I now no longer entirely believe that you are coming here. At least not this summer.
I mean I will believe it when I get a letter from you with an American postage stamp on it. (Incidentally, a lady told me at a dinner
party two nights ago that the schools in Brooklyn Heights are
very good.) But I am sorry about your mother's illness.*

We are in Yorktown Heights, for the Easter vacation, and five
inches of snow silently covered the ground during last night. But

it will be gone when I get home. There has been an enormous amount of work at the office, and Rachel MacKenzie had a massive coronary, and is still in the hospital, though perhaps going home this week, for a probably fairly long convalescence. What with one thing and another, the magazine has been lively, though I am not. I miss you both, terribly. It is just as well you went while my back was turned, because I would never in the world have allowed it. I am learning the third section of a sonata by Clementi, and I must be making progress because I can now tell that the piano in the country is frightfully out of tune. And I have discovered the journal of Delacroix. And the speech was about The Impulse toward Autobiographical Fiction, and I based the whole thing on the memory of the sound of your husband's voice, proclaiming that I was an egotist.

Love, and thank him for the book, until I can pull myself together and thank him my ownself.

B

———

* Harriet's mother was suffering from cervical cancer but did not die until August 1972.

WILLIAM MAXWELL TO FRANK O'CONNOR, APRIL 8, 1963:

Dear Michael:

You are giving me an absolutely glorious time. I read a chapter, and then I go to the bookshelf and get down the books and read the stories, usually for the first time, and therefore with amazement. With what seems to me now rather extraordinary shrewdness, I saw, in my early twenties, that I was not within a million light years of being able to duplicate this kind of writing. So, having taken one frightened look, I turned my back on all of them—K. Mansfield, Hemingway, Lawrence, etc. and concentrated on something much easier, the writing of novels. But as an act of piety I acquired the books and kept them on the shelf, and those I didn't acquire you presented me with. So now I am having this blazing experience. Your book is a beauty, but then you knew that already.

Love,
BILL

WILLIAM MAXWELL TO FRANK O'CONNOR, JUNE 3, 1963:

Dear Michael:

It isn't me that would be selling your published works but my executor, God forbid. I am thinking of making arrangements to have "The Little Monasteries" buried with me, to frustrate this, but also because it is so beautiful. In every way. I don't know which I like the best. I like them all: The Seasons, the Ex-Poet, the Angry Poet, and the Thirsty Poet, Advice to Lovers, the Dead Lover, and On the Death of His Wife, and so on, with a heavy underline for I am stretched on Your Grave, and "Ice would not be anywhere / Wild white winter would not be. . . ." I found myself marveling that there could be a whole period of poetry of the highest excellence that I knew nothing about, and then realized, when you get right down to it, that school of poetry is *you.* Because, as my friend Fitzgerald says, a poem is an aesthetic object and you can't translate it, you can only do another poem from it. Which, finally, makes me wring my hands. The number of things you can think of to do, the number of talents you can come up with, to keep from writing stories, exceeds all comprehension. And it is always something you do so well that there is no getting at you. You're a very good poet, more's the pity, is what I mean. And a very good critic. And for all I know, a very good lecturer— why not. But where are those stories that always used to come in threes?

I think that breakfast with Harriet and Fitzgerald was a kind of turning point in the children's lives. They didn't know you could be gay at breakfast, and have all sorts of unusual food, like I forget what. Strawberries, maybe. Anyway, they refer to it. Emmy and I have risen in their estimation, as a result of it. But it also had a sad side. For we can't get over the feeling that the friend that is just right, who knows everything so you don't have to say it, and is most delightful to be with, blew in, blew out, and God knows when we'll see her again, and meanwhile if we can't have Harriet we don't want any friends. (Oh yes, and the Protecting Tree. I especially admired that one also.) So that's the way we've left it.*

The Saturday that we were expecting to have Harriet and Hallie-Óg with us in Yorktown Heights, Kate came down with the mumps, and to my horror looked like the older generation of my father's family, who were rather fond of fried food and lots of it. Before we had any children I used to worry for fear they would look like the Maxwells, and it just goes to show that sooner or later, every fear comes true, if only for a few days. It's enough to put the fear of God into one, provided that it isn't there already. Then Brookie developed a temperature of a hundred and four, by way of reacting to a measles shot. So you see how exquisite Harriet's timing was?

Liadain dropped by today with the Moss ms and though I missed her, I talked to her on the phone, and she said there was no bad news about your health, so I take it that I can relax. Believing as I do in ghosts I have the feeling that your mother won't let any of these things come off. Just when it begins to look bad, she goes to the Central Committee, and they can't resist her because she is an orphan, and the first thing you know you are back on your feet again. Or else it's the whiskey.

All the rain in the world is falling, by way of advance publicity for Kate, who is going to be Noah in a pantomime Wednesday morning. One more river to cross. She goes around the house leaning on a stick and practicing looking 600 years old.

Thank you for the treasure from the 7th to the 12th centuries, and love,

w.

------

* The breakfast took place late in May 1963. "The Protecting Tree" is a poem in *The Little Monasteries.*

WILLIAM MAXWELL TO FRANK O'CONNOR, JULY 10, 1963:

Tuesday

Dear Michael:

My common sense tells me you are just going about your life, since Harriet got home, but I am a born worrier, and so I keep listening, with an imaginary hair-ball (see Huckleberry Finn) held to my ear, and what I hear is *silence.* The first rhetoric teacher I had in college, and in fact the only one, impressed on us that it was a good idea not to put a silence into a description in order to have it broken only by something, but this silence can only be broken by word from you saying that you are—that your insides are—in good form. Providing of course that they are. And no need to lie about it in any case.

We have had a housefull of company, arriving last Friday and leaving today. I dealt with the problem—and since I am a guest and not a host it of course is a problem—by drinking coffee to stay awake and taking mild doses of a stomach medicine that has phenobarbital in it, to go to sleep. Even so, by yesterday morning I felt like a walking (but cheerful) corpse. One of my oldest friends called up and wanted to have lunch, and I wanted to go to the apartment and practise scales, but I told myself either you are friends or you aren't, so I didn't go to the apartment but had two vodka martinis instead, with lemon twist, and they seem to have put a permanent smile on my face. Do you think I should take up drinking? I'm not sure I have the stomach for it, but who does? And went to the apartment today. It is covered with a fine layer of dust. As if we had all died somewhere on our travels, and left everything tied up in litigation. The painter has been there, and working with the windows open.

Emmy had a very charming note from H's mother about the

clothes. It is now July tenth, and on July 31st we will be standing waiting for the ferry to Fire Island, in the town of Bay Shore, which I—or maybe it is Sayville—haven't seen for twenty years. Two bicycles and enough luggage to last us—which is to say to last Lord Byron—for five weeks. Every last one of my writers has stopped writing. Which makes me wonder if it isn't an ideal time for you to write those three stories in a row that you once persuaded me you did regularly.

It appears that there may be a national railroad strike, beginning tonight at midnight, I suppose. Which means that I may be living in town next week, with a house full of commuting friends. Write me when you feel like it.

Love to you both,
w.

FRANK O'CONNOR TO WILLIAM MAXWELL,
AUGUST 6, 1963:

22 Court Flats,
Wilton Place, Dublin

August 6th.

My Dear Bill,

You write as though it were not my one ambition to write a couple of good stories for the paper before I die. This hurts me. At the moment I am trying to make my peace with God by sending off the revised version of 'More Stories' to Macmillan. We have just concluded a furious scene in which Harriet protested that the priest must NOT kiss the girl and I argued feebly that he would kiss her anyway. Naturally, in the final text the priest does not kiss the girl.* That disposes of the first 160 pages: what will happen after is another matter. In the Introduction I have quoted Bill Shawn as asking 'But CAN you remember the subject of a short story?' I don't think he'll mind, because I admit it's the bloodiest question I've been asked and I still don't know the answer. . . .

Anyway, the book is finished, thank God—326 pages of it— and I'm straight with Him. Now, to get straight with you. But don't worry if you get some awful rubbish to begin with. It won't mean that I've lost my talent, if any; only my sense of direction. The first, and most difficult, volume of the anthology of Irish poetry is with the printers. That means I'm straight with this distracted country.

Don't ever let your in-laws get hold of your children for more than one month. It's hell; almost as bad as lying awake and saying to yourself 'By God, I could really rock the N.Y. with that if only I could finish the book.' I have already one ulcer and one gallstone.

Give Emmy my love. Anything more would be treachery to my poor daughter who is being seduced with sunlight, beaches and swimming pools.

Love,
MICHAEL

------

* In "The Frying-Pan," as published in *More Stories,* Father Fogarty kisses the woman he loves, lonely Una Whitton, the wife of a parishioner. In *Collection Two* he does not. Harriet said, "As a good Protestant, I couldn't imagine that a priest would ever kiss a married woman. Hence my protest."

WILLIAM MAXWELL TO FRANK O'CONNOR,
AUGUST 1963:

Point O'Woods
Fire Island, N.Y.

Dear Michael:
    Why can't one remember the subject of a short story? I didn't know it wasn't possible. At any rate, I have no trouble remembering the subject of Guests of the Nation, or Chekhov's The Grasshopper, (If you knew how I dislike that Olga Ivanovna . . .)

or Tolstoi's tale of the three old men who couldn't remember The Lord's Prayer, and so on. Maybe I don't understand the question.

I think we are about to be washed away. After blowing all morning, it has suddenly started to pour, at a forty-five degree angle, from the direction of the sea. A little while before, Brookie and I went out for a walk. I was drawn by curiosity to know who it was brave enough to go swimming when the flag was up in front of the life guard's chair. (Boys is the answer, boys out of a painting by Winslow Homer. Wet as seals they were, and just as happy, though they didn't bark.) The air was enough to make me stand up straight. Brookie bent over, gathering lady bugs. The beach was strewn with them. I suppose the wind drove them to the protection of the sand. At nine wishes a lady bug, she came home wished out.

Do I imagine or is it that you once said you couldn't bear Seamus MacManus (E is reading a book of his tales, and I would hate her to praise somebody you couldn't bear)? [. . .]

You don't have to get straight with me. I don't know why I badger you so much. It is a silly habit I fell into, a sort of game, because you went to California to lecture. It is very queer about writing, and especially queer about the sense of direction. I have been trying to do some more of those fables, to round out the book, and what happens? I sit down at the typewriter, just the way I used to, and empty my mind, and write down a sentence at a time, as it comes into my empty head, and is it a story, it is not. Psychology, autobiography, didacticism, all the things I never had to worry about before. Myself, myself, is the trouble. Horning in on the act. But why now, and why not before? Good god what a lot of rain.

Do you know there are only a handful of grandparents in all of America. In a body, they resigned, refused the vocation and signed away all the pleasures, and said they didn't care for babysitting. It just happened that you got one of the handful of really gifted grandparents. Seducers they have always been. These are not exceptional in that, and I am sure that, not having married into them, I would find them charming. But I don't think the pleasure of sunlight, beaches, and swimming pools will weigh much with Hallie-Óg compared with the pleasure of defying her Da, and seeing the sparks fly. I have seen you together, and I say you are safe from anything Satan or the U.S.A. has to offer. But I don't suppose you could write me a story on this *subject?* It would be most interesting from her point of view: What Maisie had offered to her, in exchange for love.

Of course the priest kissed the girl, but you can always correct it in the next revision. Do you know Shawn has become cleverer and cleverer about fiction. I see him time and again take a bolder and more receptive stand than the other editors. Though I loved Ross, I doubt very much if he had much regard for me, and I continually ask myself what I ever did to deserve Shawn. In a curious way, it is beyond love. Nobody, I am sure, has ever taken his measure. He is like the old man in the house of logs that the King of Ireland's son found when he couldn't get over the crystal mountains. Not a wizard, but a match for them.

Ulcers and gallstones come, said he relapsing into didacticism, from worry about writing, about really rocking the N.Y. with that one. You are your mother's child, and a saint, though I dare say hell to live with, and when it comes it will come of itself, and without regard for The New Yorker or anything else. It will come, as it always has, and if necessary the old man who lives hard by the Heart of Darkness will produce three swans to escort you by the light of their whiteness. So stop worrying. A year and a day from now, it will all be accomplished. And owing to you, to the short story book, I have been reading Chekhov aloud to Emmy while she does needlepoint.

Kate has just announced that she is a desperate criminal. The storm has all but blown itself out. The waves at one point were within a hundred feet of the house, the water poured in under the window sills, and the bed I napped on was rocked as by an earthquake. The wind is still hooting around the top of the house, but it is quieter on the ground. I hope you are taking good care of yourself. It was really very gifted of you to get two things at once the treatment of each which was exactly contrary to the treatment of the other. If you had been meant to be hanged, you would have been during the Trouble, and I don't see any of these second rate illnesses carrying you away. What I do see is that in the end, somehow, you will outdo the old man, outdo Yeats, and naturally it will be wearing. But worth it.

Love,
w.

WILLIAM MAXWELL TO FRANK O'CONNOR,
OCTOBER 29, 1963:

October 29

Dear Michael:

It could just be that I am crazy. I was under the impression I had answered your last letter, and H's, and was wondering why I didn't hear from *you*. They have locked people up for much less. Harriet says in her letter you have roughed out three stories, and I pay the greatest attention to that word "three." If there are three stories, it means you mean business. As for the Trinity lectures, now that I have passed my fifty-fifth birthday, I am become so indulgent with my friends that I grant, for the first time, that they have a right to lead their own lives and that it is even possible that they know better than I do what they should be doing. Lectures on what?* Also I won't pretend that the fruit of that lecturing inclination of yours hasn't given me a great deal of pleasure. If you'd just do me the kindness to sit down and finish those three stories, biff, bing, bang, and send them off to me, I'd take it as most handsome of you. All this time I have been stewing about your health and thinking that it was keeping you from writing. Which only goes to show that the better you know somebody the more you misunderstand them. I am not reconciled to not seeing you and coming to lunch and all that, but it is only one of a number of things I am not reconciled to—for example, the presidential election of 1952, and what has happened to poker chips.

Today Emmy is finishing her children's book lead, which means that we are now about to come out into the light at the end of the tunnel in the forest.[†] Only to pop into another tunnel, Christmas. You will be happy to know that I have progressed with my piano playing. So my teacher informs me, and he is a truthful man. I haven't yet reached the stage where it would give a nice ear, or even an ordinary ear, pleasure to listen to me, but I am in the thick of it, I am where the music is, instead of playing records on a machine. I have done two more fables, and about ten that misfired before I realized that three things were required (1) that they shouldn't read like the usual fable (2) that they shouldn't be autobiographical (3) that they shouldn't be didactic. Self-induced daemonic possession of a quiet sort is the thing that is called for. I am now about to turn back to them, leaving Emmy to deal with Christmas, which I find not as absorbing as it once was. Oh yes, I nearly forgot. I bought a bicycle, and go riding before breakfast as far as 111th street, with Daisy. Sometimes Emmy takes Kate's bike in the afternoon and we ride together. It is very eccentric, but in New York you can be as eccentric as you like. It is a Rudge, with three gears, and a beauty. I dream about it.

This letter is really to Harriet too, whose letter provoked it, so I will answer her questions about the family. E has put on a little weight, from not smoking, and it becomes her. Brookie has a new doll, which comes with plaster casts for both arm and leg, measle spots that can be put on and taken off, and crutches. She loves it as she loved no doll since Baby-Baby, who disappeared from her stroller many years ago, between our house and the Schwartzes'. Kate has a romantic, stimulating teacher, and is ablaze with discoveries: Marie Antoinette, Marco Polo, the works. They are both even more enormous than when you saw them last spring. And both taking piano lessons. Brookie can ride a bicycle once she is in orbit, but can't stop and start. Kate is reading Lamb's Tales from Shakespeare and also the old man himself. Which reminds me, my old Dowden three volume set, cheap, with poor paper, is coming apart under her handling, and was never any good anyway, and I want to get a nice beautiful set, with each play in a volume, and large readable type, and I don't know which one you, Michael, will approve of, and I wouldn't dream of buying an edition you didn't approve of. So will you kindly tell me what I am to get?

The weather was summery for a while, and then it suddenly got tropical. Exhausted air. The thermometer up around eighty, the air hazy, and not like autumn at all. Last night it turned cold, thank God. But meanwhile, the whole country would go up in flames if you lit a match to it, it has been so long since there was any rain. It is time to cover the roses, but against what? Not the cold, surely. It's seventy.

The South of France for Christmas, is it? It's a good thing I am as fond of you as I am is all I can say.

Love,
W.

———

* O'Connor's lectures were described by Philip Edwards in "Frank O'Connor at Trinity," an essay in Maurice Sheehy, ed., *Michael/Frank.*
† From 1957 to 1965, Emily Maxwell wrote a year-end review of children's books for *The New Yorker.*

WILLIAM MAXWELL TO FRANK AND HARRIET O'CONNOR, DECEMBER 1963:

Dear Michael and Harriet:

What with too much to say to everybody, and the piano, and a full heart, and a weekend in Illinois, and this and that, I have fallen behind. The question is, will Christmas wait for me to catch up with it, and the answer is no, it won't. And then I think of the Christmas story you wrote for me, Michael, and something very close to serenity descends.* But it doesn't last. I don't suppose you would be in Paris during the last two weeks in June?

Love in gross quantities, but of the most discriminating sort, and from us all,

WILLIE

* "The One Day of the Year."

WILLIAM MAXWELL TO DON CONGDON,
DECEMBER 10, 1963:

Dec. 10, 1963

Dear Don:

Here is a renewal of Frank O'Connor's first-reading agreement, which we hope very much that he will want to sign. I have a feeling that he is about to blossom like a night-blooming I don't know what. These silences—with a real artist—always in the end lead to something even more remarkable.

Cordially,
BILL MAXWELL

DON CONGDON TO WILLIAM MAXWELL,
DECEMBER 16, 1963:

December 16, 1963

Mr. William Maxwell
The New Yorker
25 West 43rd Street,
New York 36, N.Y.

Dear Bill,

I'm returning, herewith, the Michael O'Donovan check, made out to us, in accordance with our telephone conversation. I have also forwarded the first reading agreement to his British agent, A. D. Peters, for them to send him.

Sincerely,
DON CONGDON

1963

WILLIAM MAXWELL TO FRANK O'CONNOR
(written on the preceding letter):

Except that there wasn't any telephone conversation. Am I right in thinking that Matson is no longer your American agent and we can make the check for two hunderd dollars, as people say in Lincoln, Illinois, out to Michael O'Donovan?

I am at a stand still. Fatigue, I guess. From trying to learn to play the piano while being already overextended. I have collapsed in front of the door of the Two-part Inventions of Bach. Christmas, like a fog, all around me. I get a good night's sleep and wake up bouncing and by two thirty in the afternoon it is all seeped away. I expect you know Elizabeth is coming home. I shouldn't think New York would be easy after Dublin. I miss you both,

B.

FRANK O'CONNOR TO WILLIAM MAXWELL,
DECEMBER 27, 1963:

22 Court Flats,
Wilton Place, Dublin.

December 27th.

My Dear Willie,

Yes, Matson boosted his commission to fifteen per cent, which is too much for poor saps like me.* I enclose the agreement which includes and implies that the undersigned is going to get six stories into the paper in the coming year. I am tired of being a gowned lecturer and discussing deep matters of scholarship with my nice kids. For the remaining years I want to be a writer again, even a bad one. Also, I want to get to America again for a respectable holiday, and see my friends. Two New Year's resolutions—see if I don't keep them!

I have a grievance against Elizabeth, who left without saying good bye, taking messages or anything. I am trying to induce Hallie to come to the South of France for ten days, and she is studying temperatures, records of recent accidents to planes and trains and the effects of high altitudes on elderly alcoholics.

You'll get some time the revised 'More Stories' which Macmillan are gently drowsing over while the author wonders if the revision has gone far enough.

Love to Emmy and the family,
MICHAEL

------

* Don Congdon told me that the commission was shared by O'Connor's European and American agents.

1964

O'Connor began to collect and rewrite his Trinity lectures as a history of Irish literature; they were published posthumously as *A Short History of Irish Literature: A Backward Look.*

Collection Two (1964), the British version of the 1954 *More Stories,* was the last he assembled before his death. The opening of his introduction is revealing:

> Eleven years ago *The Stories of Frank O'Connor* was published. By the time it was finished I had to see a specialist who took a poor view of my condition, but the book itself was a success. More important, it was a book which I could, and still can, take for granted.
>
> This was my downfall, because I agreed to publish a successor. I worked at *More Stories* during emotional and financial troubles, and I have never been able to take it for granted. All I could do was to refuse to allow it to be published in England until I could tackle it as I felt it should be tackled. Off and on, this has taken the best part of ten years.

"A Life of Your Own," "The School for Wives," "The Corkerys," "The Cheat," "A Mother's Warning," and "An Act of Charity" were intended for *The New Yorker;* only "The School for Wives," "The Corkerys," and "An Act of Charity" appeared there, all posthumously.

WILLIAM MAXWELL TO FRANK O'CONNOR,
JANUARY 8, 1964:

                                                                Jan 8
Dear Michael:
    Here is the check that parted company with the contract
somewhere along the line. Made out to you, this time.
    In H's last letter the word I have been waiting for turned up.
Three stories, she said. So now I know it is a matter of time, and
that they exist, and all will be well, and all manner of etc. But
thank God, just the same.
    I had a bug before Christmas, and didn't know it. Herpes
Angina virus, or some such name. Limpness, and then a mild sore
throat that persisted so long I went to the doctor and found that
there is an epidemic of limpness here. I thought it was merely the
failure of the Christmas spirit, at my age only to be expected,
though hard on Emmy. I came to the office but didn't do any
work. But that didn't bother me, since my employer is a saint.
What alarmed me was that suddenly I didn't feel like practicing
the piano. And I would find myself laden down with packages and
suitcases from the apartment, in a snowstorm and not a taxi to be
had. Time after time this happened. And each time I would say
out loud, "I give up,"—to the Management, you understand. And
a taxi would draw up beside me and that would be that. Giving up
and being taken care of by Providence I finally arrived in Yorktown Heights, where there was beautiful white snow on the
ground and no need to go anywhere, not even outdoors. I sum-
moned the energy to set up the tree, and the children trimmed it.
I'm myself again now. Proofs flow out of my outbasket like meat
from a sausage grinder. Tomorrow I intend to do some *writing.*
    Elizabeth turned up, and agreed to fill in during part of Feb-
ruary and March, while my present secretary goes off on her honeymoon. I chided her for sneaking off without saying goodby to
you. She admitted to that, but not to lack of affection, which in
any case I didn't chide her with, because she has reason enough
to be fond of you and I know is. Do you know anybody who

isn't? Privately I suspect that it was that she was avoiding the pressure of unasked for explanations. (Also, she is still a child and children have to be made to say goodby.) Never did anybody hate explaining the way that girl does. I have no idea, for example, why she came home. I was encouraging her to write stories instead of taking a permanent job, so she can come and go between New York and Dublin, which I somehow see as the only possible thing for her.

I think also that for your remaining years you should be a writer. I would not agree to the "again", knowing perfectly well that you have been writing something or there would have been no living with you.

Love to you both
W

WILLIAM MAXWELL TO HARRIET O'CONNOR,
FEBRUARY 3, 1964:

Feb 3

Harriet Love:

Do prod Michael again about what edition of Shakespeare to buy. Kate is ruining her beautiful eyes on my old three-volume Dowden edition. Macbeth and A Midsummer Night's Dream are her favorites, but that doesn't stop her from plowing through those early, and I would think all but unintelligible to her, comedies. She asked a number of questions while she was reading "Measure for Measure" that I begged off answering. She's always so polite when you do that—as if it was always only a matter of a day or two before she found out from someone else, in any case.

Do you remember the story of Clever Hans?

Our new Mother's Help, to the life.

Your devoted,
B.

WILLIAM MAXWELL TO HARRIET O'CONNOR,
FEBRUARY 1964:

Harriet my love:

Emmy has Óg's picture tucked into the frame of her dressing table mirror. We both were staggered by her beauty. As for her refusal to read Shakespeare, she shows great sense. He was not writing for children, any more than he was writing for the people who compose footnotes. I have ordered all the Ardens available, and wish they had allowed a decent white space between the text and the notes, but it doesn't seem to trouble Kate, who, I am happy to say, does not read the footnotes. I tried reading them and not the text but it was clearly Never Never Land. I wish you could see Brookie pouring real tea out of the tea-pot into the teacups. It's enough to make you believe in the fairies.

I don't care (I do really) whether the New Yorker can use the new chapters or not, I am longing to read them, and happy that they are about to be mailed in this direction. I looked in my file to see what I did have, and found "Rising in the World" (17 pages) "The Death of Yeats" (15 pages) and "Yeats" (14 pages). Looking back I seem to have bedeviled him with suggestions about what kind of book it ought to be. It will be so nice to see what kind of book it turned out to be. (How patient he is! Never a snarl out of him, when it would have been so easy to point out that no man has yet written another man's book for him.)

The letter you wrote me telling me that Michael said yes he would read the fables you wrote in your head alone. This is always happening to me, so you don't need to explain. (Only you did, angelically.) The ones I felt reasonably sure of, I submitted to the New Yorker, and so far they have bought six and turned down two. Now that I have Himself's permission, I will be gathering together a few of the doubtful ones, to see what he thinks.

Apart from a light cold, which I have just shaken, I am in good health, thank God. And Elizabeth is at her old place, while my present secretary is off on her honeymoon. She, Elizabeth, was on television yesterday afternoon, a program about Dublin, which

I missed, alas, and which Maeve says was excellent. Brendan is going to arrange for a special showing, only he won't get around to it, probably. Elizabeth says Michael's picture is in the paper about once a week, which gave me great satisfaction.

Kate is going through the stage of making up plays. It is almost all she talks about. And yesterday afternoon Brookie had a friend over, and Kate wasn't home, and *they* gave plays, without any words and, to my surprise, without any action, either. They appeared from behind a screen, wrestled over a tommyhawk (dressed as a bat and Pocahontas) and went on wrestling, and would be wrestling still if the little girl's nurse hadn't come and taken her home. But in Kate's plays, Brookie is superb. As Cinderella crying her heart out because she couldn't go to the ball . . . as almost anything. But oh the excitement. Hansel and Gretel lost in a forest of pampas grass, and eating supper out of a Lowestoft ashtray. Which Emmy, biding her time, rescues tactfully. And the death of Old Marm . . .

If Óg fell in love with the Maitre d'hotel, according to Maxwell's Law, the Maitre d'hotel is night after night dreaming of Óg. Don't be urging her to learn to read. Once they can, you never have their entire attention again. I often think what Daisy must think of us—four people in four chairs reading four books. K's hair is long and B's short, which changes their personalities. Somewhat. And what K has on her mind you know. And what B has weighing on her heart you don't know. As a rule. I assume this will not change. Emmy is ice skating in Central Park and I am practicing the piano. I escaped out the side door from Bach into some childish Mozart. They're as different as love and duty.

We miss you and talk about you and hope you will drop out of the sky as you did before.

Love,

B.

WILLIAM MAXWELL TO HARRIET O'CONNOR,
APRIL 29, 1964:

April 29

Harriet m'luv:

I expect I forced that letter out of you, you had been so much
on my mind. I have called Cyrilly, and am sending the manuscripts over to her this afternoon. She was very pleased that you
wanted her to act for Michael, and said she would write you.*

Emmy doesn't know yet but she will be enchanted when I tell
her that you are bringing Hallie-Óg for a visit in June. We will be
in Yorktown Heights, which is all the better for a visit from you.
Every once in a while I come upon evidence, in the children's
photograph books, that we once had Himself there, and am
amazed. So far off his orbit! Though it has come hard, and slowly,
I think I am now reconciled to letting himself lead his own life
(especially since that is what he is bound to do anyway) and in this
I have had you for a model. I doubt if he could have been any hap-
pier than lecturing at Trinity about Yeats, and another book, on
the history of Irish literature, would, I cannot deny it, make me
happy. But I wish to God he wouldn't flirt with illness the way he
does. Yours was a respectable ailment, but his showed a certain
creative fancy that . . . well, never mind, never mind. Six stories
did you say? In addition to those three? Very good. I'll inform the
bookkeeping department and tell them to get the check writing
machine oiled, in preparation.

We are going to Oregon in July, so your visit is perfectly
timed. There is talk about Europe next summer. There has been
talk of this kind for years, so I don't lean heavily on it. Kate is now
of a mind for travel. I am old and feeble, but can be led anywhere.
I think there is reason to hope, but not to start making hotel reservations.

In my life I have never been so busy as I have since the first of
the year. And since I would not give up the piano, I have sunk
deeply into confusion and incompetence but managed somehow,
so long as we had no social engagements. The last two weeks my
soul has been sorely tried by dinner parties, of the formal variety,

the opera, visiting firemen (France) and visiting—I won't go on. Whole days have passed during which I hardly was able to sit down and do a single chromatic scale. The end is in sight but not here. And just when I was beginning to make progress, with that delightful, though second (or maybe third or fourth) rate Kuhnau. I have conquered, tell Michael, the trick of sesquialtera, just when I thought I never would.[†] Elizabeth is gone back to her typewriter, but is returning to the office for a fill-in job for two months this summer. This subject I will save till I see you, except to say, in passing, that there is, in Sheridan's *The Duenna,* a song entitled "Oh what a plague is an obstinate daughter . . ."

From afar, I look at the pile of fables, finished, unfinished, etc. And think when, oh when . . . But shortly I will send you some, just to cut down the size of the Atlantic ocean.

Take care of your beloved selves, no more interesting illnesses, please.

And love,
B.

———

* Cyrilly Abels had begun to act unofficially as O'Connor's American agent as early as 1962 and eventually replaced Congdon.
† A sesquialtera is a triplet figure played over a rhythm of two beats rather than the usual one beat.

WILLIAM MAXWELL TO HARRIET O'CONNOR,
JULY 1964:

Wednesday
Dear Harriet:
We start home tomorrow, and I decided I'd better write you now, because when I see you (if you haven't already flown across the Ocean) I will deny it absolutely, but *I see what you mean about the West.* I don't think it is necessary to tell Michael. It might shake his faith in me as an editor. We have had a simply lovely

time riding and swimming and eating and sleeping, in surroundings of great natural nobility. I haven't been able to relate any of this to reading and writing, and so I don't suppose I am really changing my mind. It was the dry brightness in the air, the smell of the huge pines, the cold nights and the unusual amount of outdoor exercise that seemed to drive everybody to a positive pitch of happiness. After two weeks in mountain country, we drove to the seashore for twenty-four hours and the Pacific Ocean put on the kind of display that you can only do for visitors who aren't staying too long—a brand-new sand spit for the children to wade on, seashells, a long sunset, fog, and more sunshine, and quiet waves incessantly making lace. Today E is paying and receiving calls from family friends, the open suitcases have nothing in them, the plane leaves at 11:15 tomorrow morning. . . .

love

B

FRANK O'CONNOR TO WILLIAM MAXWELL,
SEPTEMBER 5, 1964:

22 Court Flats,
Wilton Place,
Dublin.

September 5.

Dear Bill,

The next six months are yours entirely as witness the story enclosed.* It's full of aches and rheumatics, which could have been eased by a walk uptown, but you are a lazy man who won't come and live uptown where I can consult you.

I've told Cyrilly that I won't allow any intervention between you and me, but when you have business to do with me, either in sending stories back or otherwise, let her have the benefit. She needs it, and nobody deserves it more.

Bless you for looking after Hal, who came back so cocky that I haven't yet reduced her to Irish wifely obedience. But, as you know, I am a stern Biblical character.

Love to Emmy and the kids,

MICHAEL

————

* "A Life of Your Own," rejected by *The New Yorker,* published in *The Saturday Evening Post,* February 13, 1965. When Cyrilly Abels read it, she wrote O'Connor on October 7, 1964, "I love this story, because although it's sad that she has to give up, she gives me heart because that kind of woman exists. I love *her* is what I'm trying to say and you make her so clear to me I love the story."

WILLIAM MAXWELL TO FRANK O'CONNOR,
SEPTEMBER 9, 1964:

Dear Michael:

If only it was a matter of coming uptown. I *think* you want the story to be about both the girl and the housebreaker, and to link them in that final moment, and to give something of the housebreaker through her. But it doesn't work. She's unreal, and her problems are vague and unconvincing, or else they just don't ship over the water. I wish (especially in the light of your thesis in the book about the short story) that you had grasped hold of the other end of the stick, instead. When the final moment comes and she calls out of the window, this reader longed to be in the bushes, sweating with the poor sweating pervert, if he is a pervert. The last two paragraphs of the story read like an outline of the author's intentions—what the reader is meant to feel. But I didn't feel any of these things. I only wanted to know about the housebreaker.

Instead of mailing the story to Cyrilly, I am sitting on it, hoping for a letter from you which will produce one of those moments that in the funny papers are conveyed by a light bulb.

I mailed you a set (having two) of Nabokov's translation of Eugene Onegin, mostly for the commentaries, which I thought might amuse and entertain you. I don't think much of the poem itself, as it comes through in English. (A young girl I know who has been studying Russian recited three stanzas of the original, and *it* sounded as lyrical as Keats.) I itched to uninvert the inversions and turn it into simple self-respecting prose, since the poetic aspects are obviously beyond translation.

The summer has gone by like a bullet. It seems only yesterday afternoon that Harriet and Óg were riding out to Yorktown with me on the train. Nothing to show for it, either. Óg's face stays with me, however. It is the kind of face that sinks whole navies.

Love to you both,

B.

WILLIAM MAXWELL TO FRANK O'CONNOR,
SEPTEMBER 15, 1964:

Dear Michael:

What pleasure to hear your voice. And of course you are right about the story, and I am too.* But what an obliging girl, to stay on the wrong side of the line, in real life instead of on paper where she belongs.

Love,

B

———

* "A Life of Your Own."

WILLIAM MAXWELL TO FRANK O'CONNOR,
OCTOBER 10, 1964:

Dear Michael:

Our annual pirouette. God willing, it will turn out to be the Year of the Flood.*

Alfreda Urquhart said, four times in a row the other night, "You mean you haven't read *Jane Eyre!*" in such a way as to leave me no choice but to go out and buy the damn thing.† Though I hate Victorian novels (they are always abusing children, and this one is no exception) I am afraid that I am hooked. If only the people weren't quite so real.

Tell H. that Brookie was counting (along with thirty-nine other little girls in the third grade) on being the Virgin Mary in the Christmas play and they gave it to Danuta. There's a Christmas story. Such big wet tears, shed in silence. They asked Brookie what she would *like* to be besides Mary, and she said an angel, and it turned out there wasn't room on the stage for another angel, so she said she'd like to be a little girl gathering flowers. So that's what she is, and as far as the fond eye can see, a quite cheerful little g g f's.

Love,
W.

---

* "Our annual pirouette" was *The New Yorker*'s first-reading agreement, and "the Year of the Flood" was Maxwell's wish for a deluge of new stories.
† A long-standing friend of the Maxwells, daughter of the British publisher Constant Huntington. Until her 1963 divorce, she was married to Brian (now Sir Brian) Urquhart, Undersecretary General for Special Political Affairs of the United Nations and assistant to Ralph Bunche.

WILLIAM MAXWELL TO HARRIET O'CONNOR,
NOVEMBER 2, 1964:

Harriet dear:

Such pleasure to have a letter from you. To think that we should have to live on letters! Not that I didn't appreciate you when I had you.

I keep waiting for the sound of those two other shoes dropping. Someday when I am not listening, there they will be, no doubt. And I will have a chance to redeem my obtuse performance with You Know What.*

Does Michael ever haunt second hand book shops? Are there any to haunt? There virtually aren't any here, any more. And I have been trying to complete my Chekhov. Will youse keep your eyes open for Vol IV (The Party, etc.); V (The Wife, etc.); VII (The Bishop, etc.); X (The Horse Stealers); and XII (The Cook's Wedding, etc.)? Also, if you should see a copy of a book that Virginia Woolf wrote the preface for, of the photographs of Margaret Cameron, called something like "Famous Men and Fair Women of the Victorian Era"? This project, if you were successful, will run into thousands of pounds, and so I not only expect to reimburse you, but will come over and get the books, because it would take a year out of your life wrapping and mailing them. We did *seriously* talk about coming next spring, and then the intolerable landlord sprang a plan for turning the building into a cooperative on us, and it is so heavily loaded in his favor that if it succeeds, we may have to move, in which case the movers will get the money that would have taken us to Dublin. There you are, that's life, though it is not literature.

I spent two weeks reading an intolerable life of Rupert Brooke, who, handsome as Apollo, nevertheless was a most unhappy man. What held me was the fact that my college days in Illinois were so saturated with his particular kind of romanticism (it may even have come more or less directly from him, I don't know now) that I was at the same time embarrassed for him and for myself. He went to Tahiti, and I, God knows, tried to but it was the depression by that time and I only got as far as Martinique. My poems were if anything *worse* than his. And I didn't look like Apollo (luckily for me). I believe it is a fact that writers find their way to good models through the bad ones. And he wasn't all that bad, perhaps; it is in good part that the world went off in a different direction, taking writing with it.

Unless every newspaper man in the United States is out of his mind, Goldwater is not going to be elected tomorrow. No one seems worried any more. My poor father-in-law will feel bad, because he views things from the fiscal point of view alone, and likes to balance the national budget. And isn't, of course, a Bircher. Just an old fashioned Republican.

I am on the last two or three fables, before I leave that project, and so you can expect a couple shortly, for a careful looking at. E has just finished the children's book review, and suddenly there is time for all sorts of things. The children both picked up coughs trick-or-treating in insufficient clothing—No, Brookie got hers lying on the ground in a highly disobedient fashion the next day. She was a lion (by Renoir) and Kate was a king (out of the dress-up box) and they both came back depressingly loaded down with candy. Last year their cruel mother threw it out. And may again.

There is a very good translation of the Journal of Jules Renard (about one quarter of the whole thing) by Louise Bogan and somebody else.[†] It's a beautiful book. Ask Himself if he would like to own it. If so, say the word.

Brookie has taught herself to knit on two pencils. *And* purl.

Love,

B.

---

* Maxwell's rejection of "A Life of Your Own."
† *The Journal of Jules Renard,* translated by Bogan and Elizabeth Roget (New York: George Braziller, 1964).

FRANK O'CONNOR TO WILLIAM MAXWELL,
CHRISTMAS 1964:

22 Court Flats,
Wilton Place,
Dublin.

Dear Bill,

My usual Christmas card to show I still think of you, though this year it is more impossible than ever.* Read it carefully, and then pass it on to Cyrilly who may find it a home.†

I have advertised for those damn Chekhov's, both here and in England, and apparently nobody wants to part with his copies. I don't blame them. However, if you read The Wreath in the new collection and remember that you disapproved, and blush, everything will be forgiven you.‡

Love to the family. I gather from hysterical scenes in what passes for the nursery that my daughter is sending your daughter A QUARTER. Of course, I never interfere. I contemplate and sigh for lost innocence.

Love,

MICHAEL

———

* Liadain remembered that her father "wasn't crazy about holidays . . . because they broke the routine. He always claimed that what he wanted for Christmas was a ham sandwich, a glass of beer, and to be left in peace to work."

† O'Connor enclosed "The Cheat," published in *The Saturday Evening Post* (May 8, 1965) after being turned down by *The New Yorker.*

‡ "The Wreath" appeared in *Collection Two* and *A Set of Variations*. On January 5, 1954, Gus Lobrano had written Congdon, "I'm sorry to have to report that the vote went against this one. Seems to us that the characters aren't fully developed, particularly Jackson's, and that Fogarty's musings in the final paragraph are hardly justified. But we're grateful to have had a chance to consider the story."

1965 ~ 1966

The changing texture of O'Connor's late work is exemplified by "The Cheat," his dark story of marriage, religion, and betrayal. Dick Gordon, an atheist born Catholic, marries a Protestant and must endure the community's repressive expectations. When he discovers his wife has begun taking instruction to become Catholic without telling him, he is heartbroken. If O'Connor's earlier fiction suggested that emotional dilemmas were remediable, his late stories are less optimistic. Even for the most earnest, forgiving characters, wounds do not heal. Fortunately, the last letter O'Connor received in this correspondence was Maxwell's wholehearted acceptance of "The Corkerys," a more cheerful story. Their relationship was no less close in this period, and Maxwell called the O'Connors frequently, concerned about his friend's health.

O'Connor was hampered by major illnesses, including a gallbladder operation in February, but he did not limit his activities, and spoke at Yeats's grave on June 12, the hundredth anniversary of his birth. In 1966, he gave two lectures on Irish storytelling at Trinity—his last, in late January. On March 10, he suffered a fatal heart attack.

His posthumous publications (1966–67) in *The New Yorker* were "The School for Wives," "The Corkerys," "An Act of Charity," and "Bring in the Whiskey Now, Mary." *My Father's Son,* edited by Maurice Sheehy, was published by Knopf in 1969, as were collections of late stories, *Collection Three* (in Britain) and *A Set of Variations* (in America). Maxwell's *The Old Man at the Rail-*

road Crossing and Other Tales, a collection of fables, was published in 1966.

WILLIAM MAXWELL TO FRANK O'CONNOR,
JANUARY 6, 1965:

Dear Michael:

It is the same as with the last story. The characters do not have the breath of life in them, and so it isn't a story.* I have been writing to you all afternoon, my wastepaper basket is full of letters to you, but there is no point in saying any more than this, unless you were to agree that there is a possibility that I am right.

I reread "The Wreath" and didn't, of course, blush. Editors don't, I think. Not because they are infallible or think they are but because they are a species of medium. With closed eyes and open mouth, looking like the village idiot, they wait for judgment to come from somewhere outside. And they stand by what comes. But I am most happy to have the book. There's enough in it, and more than enough, to get you into Heaven without that story, which may be everything you feel it is.

We ate our Christmas dinner in eighteenth century Dublin. In theory place mats are informal, but these have just the opposite effect. They made our country cottage seem like Wilton or Blenheim or something palladian and vast and grand. They are being reserved for state occasions. Your return, for example. If it weren't for the wicked landlord of One Gracie Square, we should have been turning up in Dublin this June, instead of reading the Unfurnished Apartments, five rooms and over, columns in the Sunday Times. I keep hoping he will drop dead the way wicked people so often do, and the heirs on bended knee will implore us to go on renting. I told you, didn't I, that I walked through a turnstile of the subway with Kate's cello in my hand. It is (I hope) a high watermark of foolishness. Forty years too late, I am reading Jane Eyre. Though I like Mr. Rochester, and the descriptions of nature.

But how I would have loved the insane wife in the attic at fifteen! Sixteen, I mean. The years are beginning to count for no more than a feather. And was it the Industrial Revolution that gave the English their appetite for melodrama?

I know that your good nature is boundless, but what will restore me to the good graces of Harriet? Nothing. Or perhaps Time That Heals All Wounds . . . You are as dogmatic as Ruskin, Matthew Arnold's sister said to him, and he answered Ruskin was dogmatic and wrong.

Love,
W.

――――

* *The New Yorker*'s rejection of "A Life of Your Own" and "The Cheat" was especially disappointing to Harriet, who had telephoned Maxwell, without her husband's knowledge, to say that these were his first stories in some time, and that she hoped the two friends could revise them together so that Michael's confidence would not be undermined.

As these letters show, having to turn down a story of O'Connor's pained Maxwell greatly, and Emily Maxwell recalled, "When Bill retired from *The New Yorker* because of a new automatic retirement policy on January 1, 1976, he didn't easily reconcile himself to giving up his close association with his writers. Although he was eventually grateful for the additional time for his own writing, at first there seemed to be only one compensation. He said to me, 'Thank God I will never have to reject another manuscript!' "

WILLIAM MAXWELL TO FRANK O'CONNOR,
JANUARY 25, 1965:

Jan 25

Dear Michael:

You will have trouble believing this, but there are times— when you aren't here—when you are here nothing comes between us whatever—when the thought that you are—as you are, God knows—a master of the short story so addles my brain that I forget something absolutely vital, which is that you would rather rewrite and rework a story than eat. Much rather. And that the form a story arrives in is not necessarily the form it is going to be forever. Anyway, when this seeped down through layers and layers of grief at not being able to take that story the way it was, I grabbed the phone and called Cyrilly, and said had the Post bought it yet, and she said no, she hadn't heard from them, but she assumed that they would because she thought it was marvelous, and you too, and every word you said was marvelous, and that (said I to myself) is the kind of friend to have, not the picky kind, but anyway, I said *if* they don't will you let me look at it some more.* I want to think about it. So she said she would. But probably the lousy . . . never mind. No way to speak of a competitor. But if it should come back, you don't mind, do you, if I study it a little and try to convey how it might be expanded into a story that would work for The New Yorker?

Love,

B.

---

* Cyrilly Abels had written O'Connor about "The Cheat," "I dropped everything to read it . . . a *wonderful* story. Someone I know . . . called just as I was almost at the end and could tell from my voice I was crying. I had to say I was reading your story."

WILLIAM MAXWELL TO FRANK O'CONNOR,
LATE FEBRUARY 1965:

Sunday morning

Dear Michael:

I hope, with all my heart, that those invasions of your privacy being removed, as they must be by now, each day you are feeling more recognizable to yourself. As for those terrible nights when nothing but poetry worked, something must come of them.* From that level, I mean, where it seems likely you never were before. I blew myself to a set of Conrad, who must be coming back into fashion, for he is getting hard to get in his entirety, though there are hit or miss paperbacks, and read, for the first time since I was fifteen, "The End of the Tether". It is a mistake, of course, to think that the young don't understand literary masterpieces that have no counterpart in their experience. I understood it, but I don't remember being in the least upset by it. Any more than I was upset by "Jude the Obscure". This time I couldn't sleep and lost all power of small conversation for two days. I have never read Conrad's letters, but I gather that he was not a happy man. It seems clear enough that he knew what happiness was. But as for the other things—loss, the gradual withdrawal of all the props of life, the unequal struggle that love puts up against disaster—there is no one like him. I would like to have been able to leave some flowers—violets and apple blossom—in a paper basket, on the handle of his front door on May Day. Did you have that custom in Ireland when you were a little boy? We did in Illinois. Looking back on it now, it seems straight out of the Golden Bough. The violets came from Old Mrs. Harts's back yard. We had some but never enough, and I could go to her back door and knock politely and receive permission to pick them. I don't think she ever went out of her house except perhaps to the cemetery and to church. We never saw each other at any other time, and there can't have been very many little boys roaming the streets in search of violets, but I don't think she gave me any more thought than I gave her. In so small a place it is enough that somebody wants something. They didn't, so far as I know, in those days, go into the question of whether it was right for them to want it. Except sex, of course. But that had not yet entered my mind. Violets was what I was after.

We are out of orbit. Brookie had a cold and we decided to stay in town. Emmy went shopping on Second Avenue and came home with the information that there were a great many people in love in New York; you only saw them on the weekend. Brookie turned her bookcase into a doll's house, so successfully that I have put away the plans I was about to make her one from. And Kate went to see Olivier in Richard III, and came home so informed about the Wars of the Roses that it would do your scholarly heart good to hear her.[†] The princes were illegitimate, it seems, and therefore Richard had nothing to gain by doing them in. And probably it was Henry VII. As for Warwick and Clarence . . . on and on. History is mother's milk to her. Or will be until she gets to college and some imbecile with a Ph.D. reduces it to charts and economic tensions.

I've been meaning to ask you—did you ever get the galleys of your last story?[‡] There is no hurry about returning them, but it occurred to me that they might have gone astray instead of, as I have been assuming, simply been put aside until you were feeling up to doing them.

I sat on a committee with Padraic Colum last week. He struck me as a rather vain old man. Is that too harsh a judgment?

By the end of this week very likely you will be home, a tyrannical convalescent. If it were only Brooklyn now, I would whip under the river and pay you a visit. The ocean is too much for me to whip under, but in my mind I am there.

My love to you both,
WILLIE

------

* Due to intense pain, O'Connor was hospitalized and underwent gallbladder surgery in mid-February. Even after the operation, his pain was unabated. Unable to sleep, he tried to distract himself by reciting lines from Shakespeare about sleeplessness.

[†] This was the 1956 film version.

[‡] Either "The School for Wives" or "The Corkerys."

WILLIAM MAXWELL TO FRANK O'CONNOR, MARCH 1965:

Dear Michael:

On the top floor of the Public Library, in room 318, in a maze of glass cases, are forty-five manuscripts of novels, mostly in longhand, and beginning with "Evelina". The ink of that has turned brown, the brown of Rembrandt's drawings, and perhaps always was brown. The handwriting is quite legible, and there are no margins at all, the sheets rather small, half the size of this, and for some reason it is perfectly clear that it was written in the latter half of the 18th century. Scott and Cooper. (Is it in Lockhart, the story of the man who was staying at an inn, and saw a lighted window with the shade drawn to within six inches of the sill, and a hand moving across a sheet of paper, and the paper dropping to the floor and the hand moving across another sheet of paper, and another—Scott writing the Waverley novels, without a pause, far into the night?) Hawthorne. Thackeray—tiny, erect, cut into the paper. The Posthumous Papers of the Pickwick Club. Miss MacKenzie. Wilkie Collins—What an untidy man he must have been, the smudgiest manuscript I ever saw, and very black. Mark Twain, in pencil, with lots of space between the lines. And Ouida, as ornamental as wallpaper, and as confident. Hardy, Stevenson, and George Moore. Shaw. The opening page—the absolutely wonderful opening page of Dorian Gray, the writing so happy—as if he had just that day or just that week discovered that it was not only possible but easy to get by with murder. And Conrad's unhappy corrections of a typescript he had dictated and was so dissatisfied with that hardly a word remained: The Rover. Somerville and Ross. The Hound of the Baskervilles. The Little Minister, which is written in the most constrained unhappy hand of all. The Red Badge of Courage. Max Beerbohm. And then this: "The plan of this book is roughly that it shall consist of three parts: One, Mrs. Ramsay (?) sitting at the window: while Mr. Ramsay walks up and down in the dusk: the idea being that there shall be curves of conversation or reflection or description or in fact anything, modulated by his appearance or disappearance at the window: gradually it shall grow later; the child shall go to bed; the engaged couple shall appear. But this is all to be fitted up as richly and variously as possible. My aim being to find a unit for the sentence which shall be less emphatic and intense than in [Mr. W?] An everyday sentence for carrying on the narrative easily.* The theme of the first part shall *really* contribute to Mr. R's character: at least Mrs. R's character shall be displayed, but finally in conjunction with his, so that one gets an impression of their relationship. To precipitate feeling, there should be a time of waiting, of expectation. The child waiting to go to the lighthouse: the woman awaiting the return of the couple.

(2) The framing of time. I am not sure how this is to be given: an [illegible] experiment giving the sense of 10 years passing.[†]

(3) This is the voyage to the Lighthouse. Several characters can be brought in: the young atheist: the old gentleman: the lovers: Episodes can be written on women's beauty; on truth; but there should be [*grubby* or *greater or less knobbly than thou* is so help me God what it looked like] in Mrs. D; making a more harmonious whole.[‡] There need be no specification of date.

Whether this will be long or short I do not know. The dominating expression is to be Mrs. R's character."[§]

Mrs. D is Mrs. Dalloway, of course, and who [Mr. W] is I don't know. Or it might be *Mrs.* W. She makes Mrs. and Mr. exactly alike, and it must have confused her husband no end, when he was away from home and got a letter from her. But perhaps they were not often separated. The entry was made on August 6, 1925, and the novel was not started till the following January, and took fourteen months. Probably when I get home tonight I will find it in her diary, but to come upon it in this way was so much better. This is the voice of the novelist talking to himself. In the midst of miracles, the future lying all clear around him, modesty struggling with pride, the work all to come, and farther away still the nagging doubts that will slow the whole thing down and spoil his pleasure after the accomplishment is in hand. Next to it is a pile of manuscript, open at a page so continuously corrected that it is totally unreadable. I doubt if even she could have read it. She perhaps looked at it and remembered what she meant to write. But there it is, anyway. She did it. Mrs. R woke in the night and called, the scarf unwound itself from the sheep's skull or pig's skull on the wall, and the little boy got to the Lighthouse, only without the person he meant to go there with, and so it was—so it was a literary masterpiece. Though I know I shouldn't, I believe in the life everlasting, and the communion of saints, provided the saints are writers.

Your friend who loves you,
W.

---

* This was the second page of the handwritten draft of *To the Lighthouse*. The brackets are Maxwell's. Susan Dick transcribes "Mr. W" as "Mrs. D."
† Dick: "The passing of time. I am not sure how this is to be given: an interesting experiment, ~~showi~~ giving the sense of 10 years passing."
‡ Dick: ". . . but these should be greater & less knobbly than those in Mrs. D. . . ."
§ Dick: "The dominating impression is to be of Mrs. R's character."

WILLIAM MAXWELL TO FRANK O'CONNOR,
MARCH 9, 1965:

Dear Michael:

Don't let the sawbones get this; rush out and spend it on books. Or you can let them have the ten per cent.

Mary Lavin came to our house to dinner last Thursday night.* She was enchanting. And also unwell. On the boat coming over she got an abscess in her throat, and didn't know what it was, and was, I suspect, afraid to find out. But anyway, the morning of the day she came to dinner Rachel MacKenzie carried her off to her doctor, who diagnosed it as that—she had had ferocious headaches as well as the swelling—and said she was getting over it all right. She was in no way dimmed, and carried the whole evening on her capable shoulders, but afterwards I was sorry I hadn't followed my usual inclination, which is to get the Love Object off to myself and talk, instead of being a host, which God never intended me to be, to a room full of people. She was going off somewhere for a week, and then coming back through town for five days, and I think then going home.

I spend every spare moment on my hands and knees. Not praying, but measuring with folding rulers and tape measures. The new apartment is just enough smaller than the present one so that it is touch and go fitting things in. And shortly the house in the country is going to be bursting at the attic seams with material possessions, removed from the city. Just as we should be rolling up our sleeves in preparation for the move, Emmy has to fly out to Oregon for her parents' golden wedding anniversary. I think though that by the first week in May we ought to be in a state of sufficient chaos.

Are you beginning to get your strength back?

Love,

BILL

———

* The renowned Irish short-story writer and novelist (b. 1912), about whom O'Connor wrote in *The Lonely Voice:* "She fascinates me more than any other of the Irish writers of my generation because more than any of them her work reveals the fact that she has not said all she has to say."

WILLIAM MAXWELL TO HARRIET O'CONNOR,
MID-APRIL 1965:

Tuesday

Dearest Harriet:

Yes of course, only answer some questions first. Houses in the country usually rent for the summer—i.e. July and August, but when exactly would you like us to rent such a place as you describe for? And how much do you want to pay? How many bedrooms? The houses I know about don't have air conditioning, or a pool (one has a pool, which is at the mercy of the heavens, and this is a drought year) but I expect they have screens. Anyway, we'll get in touch with a real estate agent, when we have heard from you. You are welcome to the apartment in town, which Emmy thinks will be hotter than One Gracie Square, because the back is folded in among other buildings, and if worst comes to worst and we pass in mid ocean, you are welcome to our house in Yorktown (only what would you be doing there if we weren't there?) but in any case we ought to know shortly. People almost buy the apartment and then don't, and it is that that will determine whether we stay home or go to Europe or spend August in Fire Island or whatever. If we stay in Yorktown, I come to the office Monday, Tuesday, and Wednesday, as of old. I might be able to find a sublet in the city with air conditioning, by putting a note on the office bulletin board, and of course every door you duck into here is air conditioned, so you might think about that too. I wish we were more definite. I expect you do too. It is that kind of a year. Emmy is taking off for Oregon for a weekend, day after tomorrow, to celebrate her parents' fiftieth anniversary, right in the middle of moving, or getting ready to move. The actual upheaval is scheduled for the twenty-ninth of this month. What else? Oh yes, a box is on its way to Óg, of mostly dress-up costumes.

Love,

B

You understand I don't *really* intend to play hide and go seek with you? Somewhere, somehow, we'll be together.

WILLIAM MAXWELL TO HARRIET O'CONNOR,
APRIL 26, 1965:

Harriet dearest:

This is just right. The apartment is at 544 E. 86th Street, which is just around the corner from East End Avenue and the little park, and the esplanade, for Michael to walk up and down. With Miles's* air conditioner you ought to be comfortable there. It is cooler than midtown, in any case. And you can't sublet it from us because (a) no subletting in the lease and (b) we love you too much to be taking money from you. What I suggest is that I come for lunch every day the whole time you are there. And Emmy when she can. And the rest of the time you whisk onto the train at Grand Central and we meet you at Harmon, and there we are under the apple trees, talking about writing. Simple? July? So we won't get ourselves tied up somewhere else and mess up these happy arrangements?

Providence has arranged it that Emmy's father is celebrating his eightieth birthday next spring, and I don't intend to miss this celebration, having failed to attend my own father's, with disastrous results to my stomach, and Emmy of course will have to be there, which means we can come to Europe in June of 1966 *without fail.*

We move on Thursday. Brookie produced a cough that sounds like whooping cough but isn't, and only keeps us up at night. Emmy has a cold and takes Ornade to keep going, and looks like somebody in a Redon picture. The house looks like as I think I told you as if we were undergoing a shipwreck.* By Friday morning I will be hard at work putting up coathooks in the closets of the new place, which is really quite nice, all things considered.

So far as I can make out Elizabeth isn't unhappy. Just going through some kind of change, and she is no one to hand out details, as you know. Tell Michael I love him. You know I love you.

W.

*I act as if nobody had ever moved before!

———

* Myles O'Donovan, O'Connor's eldest child, then twenty-five.

WILLIAM MAXWELL TO HARRIET O'CONNOR, MAY 1965:

Dearest Harriet:

I'm so sorry. It doesn't matter about the apartment. It will be there if you come. And I will see that Miles has a key—two keys, because the front elevator sometimes balks, and you might need to use the back entrance. I persist in thinking you will come, while understanding Michael's reluctance to travel in a cloud of uncertainty. Don't cardiograms indicate anything? Obviously they don't, or you wouldn't be in a condition of uncertainty. But I don't have Miles' address. At least I don't know that I do. My desk is becoming like a scene out of Dickens and anything *could* be there.

It grieves me that you have been so worried, and it also grieves me that we may not get that month of visiting that I have so counted on. Also, the new apartment is getting better, and I want you *in* it. The night before your letter came, I brought three boxes of books in from the country, for Michael to come upon, among the ones already there. And the next morning Emmy opened one eye and said When did you last hear from Harriet? And I went to the office and there you were. What good mediums we would make.

From the neck down, Kate looks just like Ariel. From the neck up, you have braces on the teeth, which is something Ariel knew nothing about, and the uncertain look of someone who is ten and a quarter years old. Brookie has just passed out of a bad period into a good period. Like a weathervane, only the old man (dry) and the old woman (rain) are the same person. Emmy is having trouble with her back, which makes her impatient, because she has always prided herself on being the one member of the family who wasn't having trouble with her back. The roses are in bloom in the country. Very nice, though I'm sure nothing like Ireland. The study is put in order, and the washing machine has broken down. Yin and Yang, always at it.

My love to you both,
B.

Is your New Yorker coming to the right place?

WILLIAM MAXWELL TO FRANK O'CONNOR,
JULY 12, 1965:

Dear Michael,

God was good and luck was with me and nobody sent me a sixty page story to read for opinion this morning, or put his/her head in the door and said "Are you busy?" So here the galleys are. I grieved all the time I was going over them that we should be deprived of sitting down together, to correct the corrections, and expound, in such flights of fancy as were granted to us. But never mind. You will write another story, soon, and we can sit down to that.

This one is awfully good, don't you think?*

Miles, who I swear is too tender for this world, called up and offered not to go to Annapolis if breaking the lunch date with me would inconvenience me in any way. Whatever did you do to him to make him so scrupulous? The answer, alas, I know, is nothing; his mother did it by being unscrupulous. Anyway I told him to call me when he got back.

Elizabeth's story I thought was her best, and rather Jamesian, and to have portrayed the young man as a heel wouldn't have served her purpose.† Which doesn't mean that she doesn't, somewhere in her heart, know this. Though one wouldn't deduce it from her conversation. Thank God she didn't marry him. Though I don't suppose it was any of His doing.

What else? Brookie didn't go to Oregon, or rather, isn't going—for it was to have been the first of August. She showed signs of not being old enough. And from one or two things it occurred to us that she probably had not faced the fact that we weren't going to be there to kiss her goodnight and tuck her in, and having considered the possibility of staying, at great expense and some discomfort, in the neighborhood (our old place couldn't take us, at this late date), and having realized that this still wouldn't make it possible for us to kiss her goodnight, we decided that there are times when parents have to decide for children, even though it means a bitter disappointment. This idea our parents

would not have taken such a long time and so much joint intro-
spection to arrive at, but never mind. Things were simpler in
those days. Or different, anyway. If she was disappointed, she has
concealed it very well, and Emmy now thinks she was trying to
tell us, in the indirect fashion of children, that she *was* afraid of
going. So we have rented Maeve Brennan's house in East Hamp-
ton, for August 7–Sept. 7, and will have a look at the end of Long
Island, where we have never been. The Ocean is the Ocean, no
matter how thickly the shores are lined with people in the Social
Register. It ought to be all right. Anyway, we made up our minds,
which wasn't for a long time possible. I was afraid we had lost the
faculty of doing anything but stringing interlocking considera-
tions on an endless necklace of inaction. E's back is better, tell H.
And now if your spasms will oblige by being a thing of the past,
we can look forward to a visit in September or October. Meanwhile, you can think of me reading vol 2 of Osbert Sitwell's autobiography and practicing the Mozart C Major sonata.

Love to you both,
w.

P.S. I forgot. Saturday I built a tree house for the children, and
was as pleased as if I had written something.

---

* The galleys may have been "The School for Wives."
† Cullinan's "A Swim," published in the June 5 *New Yorker* and reprinted in *The
Time of Adam.*

WILLIAM MAXWELL TO FRANK O'CONNOR,
DECEMBER 9, 1965:

Michael O'Donovan
22 Court Flats
Wilton Pl, Dublin 2

Dec. 9, 1965

Dear Michael:

I just had to tear out of my typewriter a sheet beginning dear Harriet, because, necessary though she is and attached as we both are to this intermediary, she didn't write those stories, *you* did. By a roundabout fashion I have had news of you. Through Roger Angell, who had a letter from Pritchett, who lunched with you, and says you have been ill and are much better.* And a few nights ago, Emmy and I went to Brooklyn Heights, to have dinner, on Willow Street (112) with a young writer from the middle west named L. Woiwode, and his even younger wife.† Waves of missing you both as I went through those streets for the first time since your departure. If I had known what it was going to be like and for how long I would never have let you do it.

Tomorrow Padraic Colum is speaking at the luncheon of the National Institute on his great friendship with W. B. Yeats, and I feel the least I can do to express my skepticism is not go to hear him. So I'm not. Not that Yeats wasn't a friendly man, or that Colum wasn't there. But you know. When I want to hear about Yeats, I prefer to hear about him from you. Simple oldfashioned loyalty.

I wish you'd tell me why I am more interested in writing short stories than in writing a novel. Change of life? Change of me?

How are you really?

Love,

w

---

* Sir V. S. Pritchett (b. 1900), noted British essayist, literary critic, short-story writer, and novelist.

† Larry Woiwode (b. 1941) met Maxwell in 1964. He has said that his short fiction, published as *The Neumiller Stories* (1989), owes much to Maxwell, and he dedicated the novel *Born Brothers* (1988) to Maxwell.

WILLIAM MAXWELL TO FRANK O'CONNOR,
JANUARY 31, 1966:

Monday

Dear Michael:

Well it's only me talking, and I won't know until early next week whether I am talking through my hat—but I thought it was fine.* The people had all crossed the ocean nicely and were full of the breath of life, as of the first of February. Making me a happy man.

Since the landlord has immobilized us, I think it is a perfectly beautiful idea—for you to spend the summer on the Baptist Church Road or thereabouts. There are two that I know about that are always for rent—The Ice House, which has a pond, and I think two bedrooms,—it belongs to a painter and photographer, and is set in the woods, against a rock cliff, and so cooler than the other places. And the first house I lived in, which is a 1840 saltbox that got ruined by injudicious remodeling, but is still rather charming. Might be mosquitoes. I will look into it. People like to rent in our neighborhood and usually can't, so it ought to be possible to find you something. Just a question of what is most agreeable. Then we could talk. About writing. About the mystery of material. Where it comes from and why, when you haven't got it, you think it's you when it isn't. How I wish I could hear a novel knocking under the floor and have that to encourage.

The book of fables is, roughly, done. A matter of which to combine for their initial appearance in the magazine. And what order to run them in a book. And one last revision. I didn't send them to you in the end because finally, rewriting and rewriting and rewriting, I was able to make up my own mind about them, and it is better to save your friends for those awful times when you can't possibly, as with The Château. If you hadn't carted that heap of paper away and read it, it would still be a heap of paper. And it is not true that gratitude is not a very strong emotion.

After lunch: I am so happy with all those people—particularly the Dean and his dislike of the Bishop. I think the girl's father and mother might be looked at a little more, for the pleasure that there is in distinguishing between shades of what is ordinary. And I wished too that you had done the houses of the two families— but then as you know I have a thing about houses, I long to know what people in fiction surround themselves with. Small town up- bringing, partly and part that when I was a small boy every house was so different, and such an expression of the character of the peo- ple who lived in it.

What a pleasure it is not to be sending this manuscript to Cyrilly. I am assuming that Mr. Shawn will be of my opinion, but in this case it is a safe assumption, I feel sure. Love to you both,

w —

———

* "The Corkerys," published in *The New Yorker* on April 30, 1966.

POSTSCRIPTS

After O'Connor died suddenly at only sixty-three, Harriet and William Maxwell devoted themselves to keeping his memory alive and making his work available to readers. What follow are excerpts from their later correspondence, beginning with two April 1966 letters from Maxwell to Cyrilly Abels about O'Connor's *A Short History of Irish Literature: A Backward Look.*

WILLIAM MAXWELL TO CYRILLY ABELS:

[before April 18, 1966]

Dear Cyrilly,

I couldn't find a section that would lift out of this and fit into any New Yorker category, standing by itself. It is a marvelous book, and I think would stand in the empty place that evoked it forever. It is also heartbreaking. Harriet was clearly surprised that I found anything mysterious in Michael's nature, but I do find mysteries nevertheless—how, for example, the man who produced that quotation from the Autobiography of Father Peter O'Leary to wind up Chapter 11 could at the same time be so utterly without indignation. At me, I mean, and all descendants of Anglo-Saxon Protestants.* In a way that is so sweet it is almost baffling, people are people to him, even in this often indignant book. But the poems! And the radiant intelligence! And the grand view of things!

Thank God he was permitted to finish it.

Affectionately,

B.

———

* In his autobiography, O'Leary illustrated the horrors of the Great Famine by narrating the deaths of Paddy and Kate Buckley and their two children (from hunger and disease), a story that ended: "Next day a neighbour came to the hut. He saw the two of them dead and his wife's feet clasped in Paddy's bosom as though he were trying to warm them. It would seem that he felt the death agony come on Kate and her legs grow cold, so he put them inside his own shirt to take the chill from them."

April 27, 1966

Dear Cyrilly,

The reason for our eccentric behaviour is that after the manuscript of Michael's book had started for your office Mr. Shawn dropped in on me and we had a conversation about it, which led to a further conversation on his part and a raising of my hopes, but in the end he decided that there wasn't any section (I was hoping that the two chapters on Yeats would do it) that he could use as an essay on the book page. The requirements are peculiar—that it should not depend on the reader's previous interest in, say, W. B. Yeats. Anyway, he handed it all back to me, saying that he thought it was a very good book indeed, which God knows it is, say I, having read it twice. But I wish we had been able to take something.

Yours, ever,

BILL

WILLIAM MAXWELL TO HARRIET O'CONNOR:

Harriet m'luv:
  Do you know, there are two pieces missing from that book: F O'C as poet and angelic idiot by Geoffrey Phibbs, and F O'C as a pupil that got to be too good for me by Daniel Corkery.* No, three: The Patience of F O'C with his friends, by F O'C.

Your loving
B.

———

* "That book" was *Michael/Frank: Studies on Frank O'Connor*, ed. Maurice Sheehy (1969), a collection of essays, probably not yet finished at this time.

Harriet dear:
  Here's the clean proof, and also a xerox of the unfinished new version. What I wish, this morning, is that we could publish all of them, one after another, with his name at the end. Love in job lots to you, and to Hallie (since she doesn't any more want to be Hallie Óg) and to Mary, and to Uncle Dan and Uncle Maurice.

B.

  P.S. And to M. Lingus, too, why not.*

———

* "Uncle Dan" was Daniel Binchy. "Uncle Maurice" was Maurice Sheehy (1928–91), O'Connor's close friend during his last years. In 1969, he became Harriet's second husband. "M. Lingus" was Maxwell's name for the imaginary proprietor of the Irish airline.

Harriet M'luv:

Emily complained bitterly about how quiet the house was after you left. We both dearly loved having you. Not to mention the feelings of Miss Kate and Miss Emily Brooke. The books were mailed in three packages, the Boutet de Monvel being too long to go in the box with the others, and Wolfe Tone was sent first class registered. If somebody sends me first class registered when I have been dead as long as he has, I shall certainly know it, and turn over in my grave with pleasure. . . .

B.

Harriet M'luv:

I couldn't find one (and of course I am not the only editor to read them and we are in agreement) story that seemed really finished. The structure is there, but in every case something essential is lacking or just roughed in. The one I regret the most is "The Call", which just doesn't come up to what Michael's trying to say until he reaches the end, and then it's too late. "A Mysterious Case" could have been a very funny story, but again it is just the bare bones. As your loving friend I have to tell you that I think it would do his memory no service to publish them, but that doesn't mean you have to accept what I say. Do you want Cyrilly to see them?*

Love,
B.

––––––

* Readers can form their own opinions about "The Call," in *The Cornet Player Who Betrayed Ireland;* "A Mysterious Case" remains unpublished.

Harriet dear:

I've run down that story. It is in Knopf 1952 volume (The Stories of Frank O'Connor) under the title of "First Love," and it was completely rewritten, and changed from a first-person story to a third-person. The odd thing is that "Crossroads" was published in the New Yorker in 1952, so he probably rewrote it even before it appeared in the magazine. What that man wasn't capable of!

I finished editing the new story this morning. I took four days at it, with versions spread out in every direction in front of me, and the scissors and paste (but I didn't cut up his manuscripts, only xerox copies), and I hope you will like the result, but if you don't, I will have another go at it. Or you can, if you prefer. I don't fool myself in to believing that it is what he would have done if he had done the job himself, but on the other hand, whatever version he made of it would, in all chances, have been tinkered with at a later date, so it is possible to consider this an interim version. Anyway, it seemed to me to come out a good story. I am having it set up in type, and probably will not be able to mail it to you but will give it to you when you come. I figured that if you read it in manuscript form, it would seem just version number 5, and you could see more plainly in type what it reads like. But don't let this exert any pressure on you. Just because it is in type means nothing whatever.

Kate just came home from the field day in Randall's Island, having sprained her ankle in the high jumping. It doesn't seem to have kept her from carrying on like a cricket. We're taking two little girls to the country for the weekend. Much late giggling, and all that. The apple blossoms should be out. I keep thinking of the roses blooming when I am not here to prune and feed them. What will they think?

Love,
w

Harriet M'luv:

Sunday morning in the country. So bright you can't look at the snow-covered ground outside. Like living inside a diamond. Sunday Times all over the kitchen floor being read by Kate and Emmy who lean drunkenly from their chairs. Brookie went horseback riding yesterday in the freezing cold of an unheated riding academy and is stiff as a board today. Daisy can't wait to get back to the city. I have been looking at, reading, and thinking about Michael's volumes of Chekhov. So lived with—turned down corners, turned down sides of the page, coffee stains, whiskey stains, and perhaps tears. It is almost as if you had given me his bathrobe and slippers. I know I don't deserve to have them, but I will try to deserve to have them.

Your loving

B.

Wednesday [February 7, 1967]

Dear Harriet:

Here is the preliminary editing of the Russell piece.* It is made up of two chapters from which I cut here and there as seemed sensible, and an introduction lifted from various other places. The introduction is needed to explain the circumstances of Michael's life, because one cannot assume that all New Yorker readers have read the pieces that made up the first volume of his autobiography, and understand, also, how he came to be seeing Russell about a petition *against* Yeats. At first I used much more of what he had written about Phibbs, but then I had finally to ask myself if this was a piece about Russell or a piece about Phibbs. The whole truth about Phibbs being untouchable, it has to be a piece about Russell, which, of course, is what Shawn agreed to buy in the first place (to keep the train on the track). Anyway, here it is. I won't set it up in type until I have had your approval.

About the priest story.† I showed it to Rachel MacKenzie, in whom I have great confidence, and asked her to tell me what it was about, and she did, right down the line, all correctly. She also said that the surface of the last galley was a little wavering, which is also correct, and maybe can be fixed. I await all Uncle Maurice's suggestions with interest. I don't really feel doubtful about the story—or about any story, much, that the New Yorker thinks is good enough to print, because they do, within their separate categories, keep to a (I think) dependable standard of excellence. You have to, and will, of course, allow for my being prejudiced in this opinion. You also, I'm sure, will think of those other stories of Michael's that the New Yorker didn't accept, that he felt we should have. And finally, you know, I think, that anything that is within range of being possible for us that Michael wrote I want us to take; the opinion was unanimously against those stories and there was nothing I could do. It was unanimously in favor of the story about the priest. As to whether publishing it will harm Michael's reputation—which is what is bothering Uncle Maurice—that is a decision only you can make. And whatever you decide, the New Yorker will abide by.

Love,

B.

———

* "Bring in the Whiskey Now, Mary."
† At this point untitled, the story of a priest's suicide was eventually called "An Act of Charity."

Monday, May 15, [1967]

Dearest Harriet:

Mary Kate went off to Cyrilly.* Michael's stories are being gathered up to be mailed to you. I'm glad there are enough to make a new collection. Emmy says either May 24 or May 25 is all right for spending the night at our house. If you can, tell us which, though, because the days are closing in. Bring in the Whiskey is not scheduled, and I don't have any say in the scheduling, but I shouldn't think they would wait forever to run it. I don't at all feel that we tampered with An Act of Charity. Quite the other way round, that, on our knees, so to speak, *humbly*, we got it the way Michael would have wanted it to be, and it wasn't that way to begin with. I don't feel any nervous need to go and look to see if this is really true, I just know it is. We worked it out together, in a way that neither could have done alone. But it wasn't changing or adding, it was figuring out the text.

Love to the three of you,
BILL

———

* *The Saint and Mary Kate*, O'Connor's 1932 novel.

Harriet m'luv:

Two manuscripts that turned up in the New Yorker files and that the office thought you might like to have. From the address on the folder, I think they must go back to Gus's time. So moving, the handwriting and the folder. Like finding one of his shoes.

Was it you who told me or can I tell you that they are covering the Paris cobblestones with asphalt so they can't be used as weapons. Don't go see the movie of War and Peace, whatever you do. I came away thinking Tolstoi was about of the same stature as Morris L. West.*

We are half in town, half in the country. Sixes and sevens. Love in gross lots,

B.

———

* The Russian version (1968).

Dearest Harriet (otherwise known as Harriet M'luv)

Going through a dusty box of letters I came on three marvelous ones from Michael. It made me so happy to find them and I can't wait to show them to you. I can't wait for you to arrive, either.

love,
BILL

———

In September 1967, a *New Yorker* reader, Elizabeth Corcoran, unaware that O'Connor had died, wrote to the magazine:

> Gentlemen:
>   Would you please forward my love and appreciation to Frank O'Connor (Michael O'Donovan) for "Bring in the Whiskey Now, Mary" and also for several other wonderful, wonderful things he has written.
>   I'm middle-aged and find the brave new world pretty confusing, but Frank O'Connor I understand.

Maxwell sent the note to Harriet with his comment: "This, I believe, is immortality. Or the only kind of immortality that is worth having."

MICHAEL AND HARRIET

BY EMILY MAXWELL

Harriet has long wanted to see these letters in print. After Michael died, she began to collect his letters and managed to get her hands on more than five hundred of them, including his letters to Bill, which we had saved and sent on to her. Michael almost never dated his letters (Bill, of course, didn't either) and she thought it important to do this. Her letters to us for the past five years have been peppered with questions: What was the date of my parents' fiftieth wedding anniversary? In what year did our daughter Kate have her tonsils out? And so on. It is always more interesting to read both sides of any given correspondence, and she felt that the letters that passed back and forth between Michael and Bill were worth publishing. She showed them to Michael Steinman, who is a professor of English at Nassau Community College. He had published a book-length study, *Frank O'Connor at Work,* of—to use his other name—O'Connor's manuscripts, and in particular of his habit of revising and sometimes completely rewriting a story after it had appeared in a magazine, or a collection of his stories. Michael Steinman was as enthusiastic about the letters as Harriet was. He was able to track down a good number that she hadn't known about, and he took up the work of dating and annotating where she left off.

While Michael and Harriet were living in Brooklyn, I was living in northern Westchester County, absorbed in taking care of our two small children, so I saw much less of Michael than I would have liked. He was an enchanting and irresistible man, with his deep musical voice, and his humor, and his large nature and tremendous enthusiasm for life. In 1959, when we moved to the city (though we kept the house in the country and lived there during the summer months), Michael and Harriet were already gone, living in Dublin, and they never again settled in New York. What an unspeakable loss! We became even closer to Harriet after Michael's death. We travelled together, celebrated together, laughed and mourned together, and have never been out of reach, if only by overseas telephone, for over thirty years. Twice in recent years I found myself in the hospital, and, miraculously, there she was, running errands, coming to Bill's rescue, and making me get well. She now lives outside Dublin, in a house looking out on the Irish Sea, but comes to America frequently.

EM AND BILL

BY HARRIET O'DONOVAN SHEEHY

Em and Bill Maxwell have been close friends for so long I find it hard to imagine that there was a time when I didn't know them. And I certainly can't even be sure when or where I met them. I remember meeting Bill first and I suspect it was when he came to our flat in Brooklyn Heights with the proofs of a story Michael had written that was scheduled for publication in *The New Yorker.* As a rule Michael went to the *New Yorker* office, but this time he suggested that Bill come home with him for a change. This was in the 1950s and Bill came often after that. I remember bottles of wine and books and flowers. Once, as he gave me some freesias, he said sadly, "I hate the rough way florists treat flowers, throwing them down and smothering them with paper. You'd think they hated them." He always brought a handful of sharpened pencils which he spread out on the table with the proofs, and after Michael pocketed a few of them, Bill made a point of bringing too many and leaving them behind. (There was almost nothing in the world Michael coveted more than somebody else's pen or pencil and I often found several sharp pencils and a little metal sharpener in his pajama pockets.)

I have an absolutely clear memory of the voices of the two men at the table working on the proofs. Such a pleasure it was to listen to them—Bill's voice quiet, soft, almost hesitant—Michael's deep, strong, more insistent—but the ease and admiration between them creating a harmonious atmosphere. Michael never failed to marvel at Bill's skill as an editor—the way changing a word here or rearranging a phrase there would make the meaning which Michael had intended clear. I never heard a cross word. Michael might say, "Well, blast you anyway, Mr. Maxwell," but he said it as to a magician who had not only pulled the rabbit out of the hat but then put the hat back on the rabbit. They would work away amiably, then fold up the proofs, Michael would pocket the pencils, and they'd smile and say, "Another masterpiece," or "If we do say so ourselves . . ." or even "Poor Chekhov." After that I'd give them lunch and we'd sit around in dreamy contentment talking, talking and watching lights go on in Manhattan across the river.

I knew Bill quite well before I met Em and I was rather dreading meeting her. I liked him so very much; suppose I didn't like her? When we finally met at the American Academy of Arts I was struck by the beauty of her eyes and the expression in them. In those days she wore her hair long and pinned up on top of her head and the memory of her delicate features and thin cool hand is with me. She seemed so self-possessed and beautiful, but she had a warm and disarming manner, and when we got home that night I said, "I think I like Em a lot already," and with that amused fond smile with which he greeted my more obvious remarks Michael replied, "And why wouldn't you?" However, it took me a while to stop being in awe of her. (Somehow, though I thought Bill was perfect and compared every other writer to him, I was never in awe of him, perhaps because his relationship with Michael was so easy.) Two very different events dissolved the awe and cemented the friendship. One day, when I was coming up in the elevator to their apartment, the elevator man said, "I've been wanting to ask you. Are you Mrs. Maxwell's sister?" "No, why do you ask?" "You look and act a lot like her," he replied. That made me very happy and when I told her she said, "But I feel as if you *are* my sister." Another evening, while the men sat in the living room discussing Conrad, I went out to the kitchen, where Em was concocting an elaborate dessert. A dollop of this, a spoonful of that, layer after layer. When it was nearly finished, she tasted it, made a face, and poured the whole thing down the kitchen sink. And without even giving me a chance to taste it!

Looking through datebooks of the 1950s, I find that the Maxwells came to dinner with us, we went to plays with them, and I know that at least once we drove to Yorktown Heights, because there's a snapshot of Michael watching Kate, Brookie, and Hallie Óg playing on a slide. Some of Hallie Óg's favorite books, *James in the Rain, Mr. Dog, Goodnight Moon,* have "Katie-Brookie" on the title page and I remember boxes of dress-up clothes and special party dresses that were too small for Brookie but perfect for Hallie Óg. What did we send in return? Perhaps an Irish doll or books about fairies.

So many happy memories. The day we had lunch in the Italian restaurant in Greenwich Village (incongruously named Chez Vous). We talked and talked and laughed and ate and sipped wine and suddenly it was five o'clock and the owner and his wife started cutting out the ravioli for dinner and insisted that we stay on because we were so happy it made them happy too.

The visit to Yorktown Heights which Hallie Óg and I made in the early 1960s about which I wrote to Michael: "Bill met us at 4:30 and we took the train to Yorktown Heights. On arrival we went swimming—in a pond—which broke the ice between the kids. We had a lovely evening—leisurely and good talk and turned in around 11. I woke, at 7, to hear Brookie reading out loud to Óg: 'Consider the lilies of the field—how they reap not, neither do they spin . . .' followed by a murmured conversation in which Óg and Brookie exchanged information about God. I drifted off and woke later to hear Brookie saying, 'So Jesus spoke in a loud voice and said "Rise Lazarus".' Such a lovely visit . . ."

After Michael died, Hallie Óg and I went back to Annapolis to live. This was when my mother, a Southerner who set great store by manners (the real kind, which spring from respect for other people's feelings), got to know the Maxwells through phone calls and letters. One day she looked at me thoughtfully and said, "If the Maxwells are such good friends of yours then you must understand more about what I mean by 'good manners' than you pretend." I told Em and Bill, and it became a standing joke between us that to preserve her illusions my mother must at all costs be kept from meeting them. It was around this time, too, that after staying with the Maxwells I went on to pay another visit which was a disaster. I couldn't go into details on the phone, but something in my voice prompted Bill to say, "Come home, come home." He met me at the door, threw his arms around me, and said, "To go so far and not be welcomed," and I felt that Michael was there beside me.

Perhaps the greatest solace I got after Michael's death was the way Bill included me in the editing of the stories which *The New Yorker* had bought but not yet published. The way we found a title for the story about a priest's suicide sums it up. Titles were important to Michael and he had obviously had trouble with this one because several possibilities had been typed in and then crossed out. One evening I found myself saying aloud, "Oh, Michael, what in the world shall we call that bloody story?" and into my head popped "An Act of Charity." It felt absolutely right and though it was late at night I immediately called Bill to tell him. "That's perfect. Michael would approve," he said. To feel that I knew what Michael would have wanted was deeply comforting. A circle had been completed.

FRANK O'CONNOR

AND *THE NEW YORKER*

BY WILLIAM MAXWELL

A poet friend whose literary judgment I greatly respected [Louise Bogan] told me to read a book of short stories called *Crab Apple Jelly,* by an Irish writer named Frank O'Connor, and I did. Shortly afterward I met him—by accident, I think—in the office of the man who at that time was his editor at *The New Yorker.* His voice was the thing I noticed above everything else. As a rule when I am being introduced to a man or woman who interests me, I am so intent on searching the eyes I don't even hear what they are saying, let alone the quality of the voice. Michael's I heard with astonishment. I am grateful that it is there on the records he made and gave me, but I don't need to go to the record player to find out what his voice sounded like. I hear it whenever I think of him. And it is that as much as anything that keeps me from being able to accept the fact that he is dead.

His voice, his face, his innocent nature, his knowledge of the world—these come to mind not in any order of importance; they are just part of the way I remember him. I was aware of them all during that first meeting. Also of something else: he seemed to be talking to me and looking at me as if he liked me. On sight. Nothing that I learned about him later has ever suggested that he was cautious in getting to know people or about the people he got to know, though he was, I have been told, sometimes concerned about what might happen to the people who got to know him.

His clothes; those rough Harris tweed coats. The smell of his pipe tobacco. His smile. His kindness. There is a snapshot of him that I keep under the glass top of my desk—taken in Vermont, on the front porch of a white clapboard house. He is addressing a raccoon. Their size being very different, Michael is bending from the hips in what looks rather like a formal bow, and from the way the fingers of his right hand are arranged he is either offering the raccoon a morsel of food or making an important literary distinction. The raccoon is balancing on his hind legs, his nose lifted as high as it will go, his gaze earnestly directed not at the food (if it is food) but at Michael's face. He is, obviously, head over heels in love. No human being has ever bothered to understand him before, and the understanding of other raccoons is not the thing he has needed all his life. What is also clear from the snapshot is that the affection is reciprocated. Without this blaze of understanding, which he had hardly dared hope for and perhaps no longer expected to find, that raccoon might well have perished. The conversation is not in words but direct from the heart, one creature to another.

His voice, his face. The horn-rimmed glasses. The eyes, that, when I try to recall them exactly, give me trouble; their color varies all the way from hazel to a brown so dark that it seems black, and this cannot have been possible. It can only be an effect of distance. The thick gray hair and the gray mustache. The fiery black eyebrows. The color of his skin, and the habitual lines of his face, in his forehead, at the corners of the eyes particularly, and bracketing his mouth. Though he was not free from worry, it didn't show. The lines expressed only animation, the mind excited by and delighting in perceptiveness. To say that someone's voice is like a musical instrument, or like a bell, is not in the least accurate; you are describing the effect and not the thing itself. But Michael's voice did have, did suggest, the quality of reverberation and, compared to the flat and toneless way that Americans speak, it was musical. The Irish accent (unlike the English) often strikes Americans as enchanting, but I have never met an Irishman whose voice reminded me of Michael's. Speech being learned by imitation, no doubt his took its quality from the voices he heard in earliest childhood. How he used it was something else again—one of the innumerable gifts he appears to have been born with, like the ability to teach himself a language, and that most people do not have.

Though it is quite true, as one hears said, that we are the sum of all that has happened to us, the converse is quite true: before anything whatever has happened to us we are something, and we continue to be that something all the rest of our lives. If you don't believe me, look at the photograph in *An Only Child* which bears the caption 'Minnie O'Donovan and the author aged four months'. If that baby suddenly began to explain just how the Casement diaries have been tampered with, or said 'Even from its beginnings, the short story has functioned in a quite different way from the novel', I wouldn't turn a hair. It is so unmistakably himself, half buried in lace and a white bunting, and squirming with discomfort at having to sit for the photographer. As for the woman, she died before I ever knew Michael, but I was present during the period in which he was engaged in bringing her back to life.

He came to my office frequently during those months when he was writing and *The New Yorker* was publishing a large part of the first volume of his autobiography. The moment of his arrival I can re-enact at will. The shape in the doorway, the smile of delighted greeting, the big wool tam-o'-shanter—the only tam-o'-shanter in the whole city of New York—the voice speaking my name, and the envelope in his hand, containing manuscript. We sat at a table, with the manuscript spread out in front of us or with galleys embroidered with queries from the proofreader, and talked. His conversation was so easy, so broad-ranging, so without vanity or suspicion. And he was so quick to sense what can and what cannot be talked about. When we had wandered far enough afield, we would come back to the work at hand. Directing his attention to this or that place on the page, was all there that the situation had in it, I would ask. Was this word right? Was that sentence what he really meant? Did he need to say that? Wasn't it implied? And weren't there too many adverbs describing how the characters said what they said? And so on. Finicky laboring away at the surface of the writing. And he embraced this new game (or perhaps it was not new; he may have run across the disease of perfectionism before this) with the enthusiasm and receptivity of a big friendly sheep dog. It was not, of course, where his heart lay at all. Probably he was just being polite, though it may have interested him; all sorts of things did. But left to himself, he would not have been putting his mind to these matters. In the course of an interview published in the *Paris Review* in the fall of 1957, he was asked the question 'How do you start a story?' and answered,

> 'Get black on white', used to be Maupassant's advice—that's what I always do. I don't give a hoot what the writing's like; I write any sort of rubbish which will cover the main outlines of the story, then I can begin to see it. When I write, when I draft a story, I never think of writing nice sentences. . . . I just write roughly what happened, and then I'm able to see what the construction looks like. It's the design of the story which to me is most important, the thing that tells you there's a bad gap in the narrative here and you really ought to fill that up in some way or another. I'm always looking at the design of a story, not the treatment.

You cannot say that the man who wrote 'The engine shrieked; the porter slammed the door with a curse; somewhere another door opened and shut, and the row of watchers, frozen into effigies of farewell, now dark now bright, began to glide gently past the window, and the stale, smoky air was charged with the breath of open fields' was indifferent to which word he used, or to the shape of his sentences. Or that he wasn't, indeed, a poet. But in the main it is true—style wasn't his besetting preoccupation. He had it, and he used it, like any other tool of his trade. It was the design he worked at—the design and one other thing. In that same interview he says:

> . . . if you're the sort of person that meets a girl in the street and instantly notices the color of her eyes and of her hair and the sort of dress she's wearing, then you're not in the least like me. I just notice a feeling from people. I no-

tice particularly the cadence of their voices, the sort of
phrases they'll use, and that's what I'm all the time trying
to hear in my head, how people word things—because
everybody speaks in an entirely different language, that's
really what it amounts to. I have terribly sensitive hearing
and I'm terribly aware of voices. If I remember somebody,
for instance, that I was very fond of, I don't remember
what he or she looked like, but I can absolutely take off
the voice. I'm a good mimic; I've a bit of the actor in me,
I suppose, that's really what it amounts to.* I cannot pass
a story as finished unless I can act it myself—unless I
know how everybody in it spoke. . . . If I use the right
phrase and the reader hears the phrase in his head, he sees
the individual. . . .

It used to amuse and interest him that when we were considering an early draft of a story together, I would ask what the furniture looked like, or what the inside of the house looked like.
'Oh, Lord,' he would exclaim, 'don't ask me that!' And he
couldn't, in fact, tell me. He was not interested in interior decora-
tion. If he was writing a story, he would place a house in its street,
and that street in its surroundings, and then he would do the front
garden, and then, having delivered the reader at the front door he
went blind at the very moment the door was opened, because now
there were people, and the people were talking, and it was a matter of getting the voices right.

A sudden doubt about the correctness of what I have been saying sent me to the bookcase, and I re-read 'The Man of the World',
a story in which an interior figures importantly:

At that moment a faint light became visible in the great
expanse of black wall: a faint yellow starlight that was just

---

* Emily Maxwell said, "In 'Interior Voices,' televised in 1962, Michael reads
three stories, acting all the parts with passion, and there can be no doubt that he
was in fact a magnificent actor."

sufficient to silhouette the window frame below us. Suddenly the whole room lit up. The man I had seen in the street stood by the doorway, his hand still on the switch. I could see it all plainly now—an ordinary small, suburban bedroom with flowery wallpaper, a colored picture of the Sacred Heart over the double bed with the big brass knobs, a wardrobe, and a dressing table.

So he could do it when he needed to. And in a way that was masterly. But linger over the details he did not. That's all the description there is. From there on, the focus is entirely on the characters.

Fiction can and often does deal seriously with ideas, but it is not really fiction at all unless the ideas are embodied in believable characters. Evelina, Lord Belmont's daughter, Pip and Joe and Miss Havisham and Estella and the convict. The reader must be able to identify himself with the characters and care what happens to them or the book falls from his hands of its own weight. It is conceivable that in order for a writer to be able to deal with human beings in an imaginative way he must at some time have been deeply and wholly committed to *a* character—someone large enough and important enough to come between him and the light of common day. Which brings us back to the photograph on page 87 of *An Only Child:* Minnie O'Donovan in a dress of striped silk, with a silk scarf pinned to her throat, and one of those boat-shaped hats women wore at the turn of the century, trimmed with an ostrich feather. The thin face, the brave, purposeful, beautiful eyes, the sensitive mouth. The orphan who was driven to the brink of suicide by misfortune and unkindness, the figure that all through his childhood came between Michael and whatever was unbearable. The air he breathed. The climate of love. If you have tears to shed, read the page that faces that picture and you will shed them.

Stature has to come from somewhere, just like the color of eyes and hair, the shape of hands, mouth and nose, the timbre of the voice. His, one can only suppose, came from her. Because of her the relationship one entered into when one became his friend was totally without smallness. He did not say, 'There is nothing I would not do for you,' he merely bided his time and eventually demonstrated that this was so. And for all the essential innocence of his nature, he did not, I think, become friends with people he could not in some way admire. ('There is only one man in each town one can learn from, and he's always moving. I told you many times about Binchy . . . Now he's got a professorship in Harvard.') Even those friendships that did not last out the lives of the two people involved—for example, his friendship with Daniel Corkery—had about them a kind of afterglow, a light and warmth that time had no effect on. He put Corkery's best novel into my hands and insisted that I read it. He made me forever aware of Corkery's gifts as a writer, as a teacher. Sometimes I even catch myself thinking that Corkery was *my* friend.

An only child, Michael behaved as if he were the oldest of a large family of boys and girls. With patience and good humor he put up with a great many things that were not to his liking. Not bullying, though. The size of the bully was something he measured accurately, but with one part of his mind only, the detached part, that had no control over his actions. Now I *am* in for it, he remarked to himself and rushed into the fray, to defend the weak, the timid, the defenseless. The defamed dead. The misunderstood. Though he made fun of himself as the defender of the weak, I never saw anyone push him around.

He did not go in for being an important writer, though he was one; or an important anything. Writing was what mattered to him. The fascination of it. The difficulties. The happiness of getting it down right. The whole area in which artists, in their absorption and singlemindedness, are like solitary children playing with building blocks or crayons or clay. In his case it was black on white. He was an original and I think a first-rate literary critic. What he could praise honestly he praised. And he did not require you to praise him. '. . . this isn't even supposed to be a story but a piece of pure lyricism in which the characters are regarded merely as voices in a bit of instrumental music. It's one of the odd things I do for my own satisfaction, without expecting anybody in the world to like it except myself.' Very often he spoke as if the idea or the experience out of which the story came about had itself some-how done the writing, while he stood by and watched. Cuts, transpositions of sentences, rewording of phrases, all tinkering of this kind he accepted enthusiastically; so much so that sometimes, having made a suggestion, one then had to turn around and pro-tect him from a too quick and unconsidered acceptance of it. When we were finished he would carry me off to look at a ne-glected church or to pay a visit to some bookstore. Or, as if we were schoolboys, I must go home with him. If I could have stopped him from going back to Ireland I would have.

When I had his friendship I tried to make the most of it. When he went back to Ireland I tried to go on being his editor, but the Atlantic Ocean came between us. Letters are not the same as sitting down at the table with manuscript and galleys spread out in front of you and saying whatever comes into your mind. Stories he felt were entirely successful I could not like. And he was ill. 'Bill doesn't love me any more,' he said to Harriet.

When I think of him I hear his voice, I see his extraordinary face, I remember the affectionate and amused expression in his eyes, the kingly turn of the head, the beautiful smile. In speaking of him I cannot bring myself to use the past tense.

WORKS CITED

―――――――――――

FRANK O'CONNOR IN *The New Yorker*, 1945–67

"Achilles' Heel." 1 November 1958: 41–46.
"An Act of Charity." 6 May 1967: 48–51.
"The American Wife." 25 March 1961: 42–46.
"The Babes in the Wood." 8 March 1947: 31–36.
"A Bachelor's Story." 30 July 1955: 25–30.
"Bring in the Whiskey Now, Mary." 12 August 1967: 40+.
"Child, I Know You're Going to Miss Me." 6 December 1958: 8+.
"Christmas Morning." 21 December 1946: 26–29.
"The Corkerys." 30 April 1966: 45–51.
"Crossroads." 23 February 1952: 29–32.
"Darcy in the Land of Youth." 15 January 1949: 27–31.
"Daydreams." 23 March 1957: 28–32.
"Dept. of Correction and Amplification." 17 May 1958: 102–3.
"The Drunkard." 3 July 1948: 24–27.
"The Duke's Children." 16 June 1956: 28–32.
"Expectation of Life." 13 August 1955: 20–25.
"The Face of Evil." 3 April 1954: 24–28.
"Fish for Friday." 18 June 1955: 23–29.
"Francis." 13 November 1954: 36–40.
"Go Where Glory Waits Thee." 26 March 1960: 40+.
"A Great Man." 10 May 1958: 34–38.
"The Idealist." 18 February 1950: 24–27.
"I Know Where I'm Going." 14 February 1959: 31–36.
"Lost Fatherlands." 8 May 1954: 26–32.
"The Man of the House." 3 December 1949: 32–36.
"The Man of the World." 28 July 1956: 19–22.
"Masculine Principle." 24 June 1950: 20–25.

"Masculine Protest." 28 June 1952: 22–25.

"The Mass Island." 10 January 1959: 26–31.

"A Minority." 28 September 1957: 36–39.

"Music When Soft Voices Die." 11 January 1958: 27–30.

"My Da." 25 October 1947: 30–34.

"News for the Church." 22 September 1945: 24–27.

"The One Day of the Year." 19 December 1959: 31–33.

"An Out-and-Out Free Gift." 26 October 1957: 38–42.

"The Pariah." 8 September 1956: 28–32.

"The Party." 14 December 1957: 44–48.

"The Pretender." 2 December 1950: 40–43.

"Requiem." 29 June 1957: 31–34.

"The Rivals" ["Judas"]. 26 October 1946: 31–34.

"A Salesman's Romance." 3 March 1956: 29–32.

"The School for Wives." 5 November 1966: 59–66.

"A Sense of Responsibility." 2 August 1952: 24–30.

"A Set of Variations on a Borrowed Theme." 30 April 1960: 46–52.

"The Study of History." 9 March 1957: 32–36.

"Sue." 27 September 1958: 34–38.

"The Teacher's Mass." 30 April 1955: 30–33.

"A Torrent Damned." 13 September 1952: 40–44.

"Unapproved Route." 27 September 1952: 24–28.

"Vanity." 18 July 1953: 24–28.

"The Weeping Children." 21 January 1961: 38–44.

OTHER WORKS BY FRANK O'CONNOR

"At the Heart of the Martyr's Myth, a Haunting Mystery." Review of *The Accusing Ghost of Roger Casement* by Alfred Noyes. *New York Times Book Review* 17 November 1957: 1+.

"Awkward but Alive." *The Spectator* 31 July 1964: 159. (Review of Patrick Kavanagh's *Collected Poems*.)

"The Casement Diaries." Letter. *The Spectator* 28 August 1959: 276.

Classic Irish Short Stories. Selected and introduced by Frank O'Connor. New York: Oxford University Press, 1992. (Originally published in 1957 as *Modern Irish Short Stories*.)

The Collar: Stories of Irish Priests. Selected and introduced by Harriet O'Donovan Sheehy. Belfast, Northern Ireland: Blackstaff, 1993.

Collection Three. London: Macmillan, 1969.

Collection Two. London: Macmillan, 1964.

The Common Chord. New York: Knopf, 1948.

The Cornet Player Who Betrayed Ireland. Selected and introduced by Harriet O'Donovan Sheehy. Dublin: Poolbeg, 1981.

"Discovery and Rediscovery Within the Covers of a Book." (Originally titled "The Modesty of Literature.") *New York Times Book Review* 15 January 1961: 3.

Domestic Relations. New York: Knopf, 1957.

"The Future of Irish Literature." *Horizon* 5:25 (January 1942): 55–63.

A Golden Treasury of Irish Poetry A.D. 600–1200. Edited and translated with an introduction by Frank O'Connor and David Greene. London: Macmillan, 1967. Rpt. Kerry, Ireland: Brandon, 1990.

Kings, Lords, & Commons. New York: Knopf, 1959.

The Little Monasteries. Dublin: Dolmen Press, 1963, rpt. 1976.

The Lonely Voice: A Study of the Short Story. Cleveland: World, 1962.

The Mirror in the Roadway. New York: Knopf, 1956.

More Stories by Frank O'Connor. New York: Knopf, 1954.

My Father's Son. New York: Knopf, 1969.

An Only Child. New York: Knopf, 1961.

"Orpheus in Exile." Harriet Sheehy Collection. Unpublished typescripts held by the University of Florida Libraries, Gainesville, Florida.

The Road to Stratford. London: Methuen, 1948.

The Saint and Mary Kate. London: Macmillan, 1932.

A Set of Variations. New York: Knopf, 1969.

Shakespeare's Progress. Rev. and enl. ed. of *The Road to Stratford.* Cleveland: World, 1960.

A Short History of Irish Literature: A Backward Look. New York: Capricorn, 1968.

"Some Important Fall Authors Speak for Themselves: Frank O'Connor." *New York Herald-Tribune Book Review* 12 October 1952: 18.

Stories by Frank O'Connor. New York: Vintage, 1956.

The Stories of Frank O'Connor. New York: Knopf, 1952.

"The Writer and the Welfare State." Rpt. in *A Frank O'Connor Reader.* Edited by Michael Steinman. Syracuse, N.Y.: Syracuse University Press, 1994. Pp. 283–91.

WORKS BY WILLIAM MAXWELL

All the Days and Nights: The Collected Stories. New York: Knopf, 1994.

Ancestors: A Family History. New York: Knopf, 1971. Rpt. Boston: Nonpareil Books, 1985.

Billie Dyer and Other Stories. New York: Knopf, 1992.

Bright Center of Heaven. New York: Harper & Brothers, 1934.

The Château. New York: Knopf, 1961.

The Folded Leaf. New York: Harper & Brothers, 1945. Rev. ed. New York: Vintage, 1959.

"Frank O'Connor and *The New Yorker.*" In *Michael/Frank: Studies on Frank O'Connor.* Edited by Maurice Sheehy. New York: Knopf, 1969. Pp. 140–47.

The Letters of Sylvia Townsend Warner. Edited by William Maxwell. New York: Viking, 1982.

The Old Man at the Railroad Crossing and Other Tales. New York: Knopf, 1966. Rpt. Boston: Nonpareil Books, 1987.

The Outermost Dream: Essays and Reviews. New York: Knopf, 1989. (This contains, on pp. 140–49, "The Duke's Child," his essay on James Matthews's biography of O'Connor, *Voices.*)

Over by the River and Other Stories. New York: Knopf, 1977.

So Long, See You Tomorrow. New York: Knopf, 1980.

"Stevenson Revealed." Review of *The Letters of Robert Louis Stevenson,* vols. I–II. *New Yorker* 26 December 1994–2 January 1995: 134–43.

They Came Like Swallows. New York: Harper & Brothers, 1937. Rev. ed. Boston: Nonpareil Books, 1988.

"Three Fables Written to Please a Lady." *STORY* 42:2 (Spring 1994): 25–33.

Time Will Darken It. New York: Harper & Brothers, 1948. Rev. ed. New York: Vintage, 1962.

SECONDARY SOURCES

"Author to Lecture at Harvard." *Irish Times* 4 February 1952: 7.

Bayley, Isabel, ed. *Letters of Katherine Anne Porter.* New York: Atlantic Monthly Press, 1990.

Cowley, Malcolm, ed. *Writers at Work: The Paris Review Interviews.* New York: Viking, 1959. Pp. 161–82. (O'Connor's 1957 interview, conducted by Anthony Whittier.)

Dahlin, Robert. "*PW* Interviews William Maxwell." *Publishers Weekly* 10 December 1979: 8–9.

Deevy, Patricia. "Harriet's Husbands." *Sunday Independent* 5 June 1994: 4L.

Flanagan, Thomas. "Angry Son of Ireland." Review of of *Voices: A Life of Frank O'Connor* by James Matthews. *The New Republic* 25 April 1983: 32–34.

————. "Remembering Michael: A Talk with Thomas Flanagan." *Twentieth Century Literature* 36:3 (Fall 1990): 259–68.

Frank, Elizabeth. *Louise Bogan: A Portrait.* New York: Knopf, 1985.

Gill, Brendan. *Here at "The New Yorker."* New York: Random House, 1975.

Ginsberg, Harvey. "A Modest, Scrupulous, Happy Man." *New York Times Book Review* 22 January 1995: 3+.

Longley, Michael. "Frank O'Connor: An Interview." *Twentieth Century Literature* 36:3 (Fall 1990): 269–74.

Matthews, James. *Voices: A Life of Frank O'Connor.* New York: Atheneum, 1983.

Maxwell, William. Interview by Leonard Lopate. "New York and Company." WNYC-AM, New York. 8 March 1995.

————. Interview by Charlie Rose. Public Broadcasting System, New York. 1 March 1995.

McGee, Harry. "The Keeper of the Flame." *The Sunday Press* 17 April 1994: 31.

Morrow, Larry. "Meet Frank O'Connor." *The Bell* March 1951. Rpt. in *A Frank O'Connor Reader* (pp. 305–9).

O'Connor, Harriet. "Listening to Frank O'Connor." *The Nation* 28 August 1967: 150–51.

O'Donovan, Liadain. "Michael O'Donovan, Frank O'Connor & Me." *Frisco* December 1981: 31.

Plimpton, George, ed. *Writers at Work: The Paris Review Interviews, Seventh Series.* New York: Penguin, 1988: 39–70. (Maxwell's 1981 interview, conducted by John Seabrook and Plimpton.)

Ross, Jean W. *"CA* Interviews the Author [William Maxwell]." *Contemporary Authors* vol. 93–96. Detroit: Gale, 1980. Pp. 347–48.

Sheehy, Harriet. "The Perils of Biography: A Talk with Harriet Sheehy." *Twentieth Century Literature* 36:3 (Fall 1990): 243–58.

Sheehy, Maurice, ed. *Michael/Frank: Studies on Frank O'Connor.* New York: Knopf, 1969.

Solomon, Eric. "Frank O'Connor as Teacher." *Twentieth Century Literature* 36:3 (Fall 1990): 239–41.

Stanton, David. "An Interview with William Maxwell." *Poets & Writers Magazine* 22:3 (May–June 1994): 36–47.

Steinman, Michael. *Frank O'Connor at Work.* Syracuse, N.Y.: Syracuse University Press, 1990.

"William Maxwell." *Current Biography 1949.* New York: H. W. Wilson, 1950. Pp. 415–16.

Woolf, Virginia. *To the Lighthouse: The Original Holograph Draft.* Transcribed and edited by Susan Dick. Toronto: University of Toronto Press, 1982.

INDEX

A NOTE ABOUT THE AUTHORS

Frank O'Connor (pseudonym of Michael O'Donovan) was born in Cork, Ireland, in 1903. He was the author of forty-one books. His first collection, *Guests of the Nation*, established him from the start as a master of the short story. He taught creative writing at Harvard, Northwestern, and Stanford. In 1962, O'Connor was awarded an honorary doctorate from Trinity College in Dublin. He died in 1966.

William Maxwell was born in 1908, in Lincoln, Illinois. For forty years he was a fiction editor at *The New Yorker*. In 1995, he was awarded the Gold Medal for Fiction and the Chicago *Tribune*'s Heartland Award for his most recent short-story collection, *All the Days and Nights*, and the Lifetime Achievement Award from the American Academy of Arts and Letters. He lives with his wife in New York City.

Michael Steinman was born in New York City in 1952. He is an Associate Professor of English at Nassau Community College and has written three previous books. He and his wife live in Melville, New York.

A NOTE ON THE TYPE

The text of this book was set in Garamond No. 3, a modern rendering of the type first cut by Claude Garamond (c. 1480–1561). Garamond was a pupil of Geoffroy Tory and is believed to have based his letters on the Venetian models, although he introduced a number of important differences, and it is to him we owe the letter that we know as "old style." He gave to his letters a certain elegance and a feeling of movement that won for their creator an immediate reputation and the patronage of Francis I of France.

Composed by North Market Street Graphics,
Lancaster, Pennsylvania

Printed and bound by Berryville Graphics,
Berryville, Virginia

Typography and binding design
by Dorothy S. Baker

Dear Bill

Dear Michael:

    I just finished writing you a letter,
It is what I have been waiting for. At las
endlessly fascinating cat fight. And twen
Verse from A.D. 600 on. You are an elegant
keep from using the gift that distingu'
two legs, two eyes, two ears, a nose,

chael:

    I'm working away at that piece now,
nd you know it would be duck soup if
nly you weren't such a good writer.
I get it all neatly lined up and look
around for you, and lo, you've got out
for a cup of coffee. I put it back the
way you had it and you come back in
wiping a smile off your lips. It is
very _instructive_.

    I sent Don Congdon another check,
saying to myself this will make himself
morbid again or I don't know Arkansas.
$2500, roughly. Adjustment for the whole
year of the cost of living adjustment.
There is no news because I have too much
to say...Love to H and Queen Mab and you,
B.

VA 1 9TH 527P= NEWYORK NY VIA

MICHAEL ODONOVAN 34 COURT FLATS W

NO I WONT GET A FELLOWSHIP IN ROM

BACK= W++